MANAGEMENT OF INDUSTRIAL PARTICULATES:

Corporate, Government, Citizen Action

MANAGEMENT OF INDUSTRIAL PARTICULATES:

Corporate, Government, Citizen Action

JOSEPH M. HEIKOFF

Professor of Public Administration
Graduate School of Public Affairs
State University of New York at Albany

ann arbor science PUBLISHERS INC.
POST OFFICE BOX 1425 • ANN ARBOR, MICHIGAN 48106

P.O. Box 1425, Ann Arbor, Michigan 48106

Library of Congress Catalog Card No. 74-83855
ISBN 0-250-40069-3

Manufactured in the United States of America

PREFACE

Public concern with environmental conservation follows popular recognition that air and water, like land and forests, are not inexhaustible resources. Only in recent decades have we suddenly been confronted with pollution so pervasive that we can no longer use and enjoy rivers and lakes as we once did. Even the fish taken by commercial fishermen or sportsmen may be contaminated. We live in the air as fish live in the water, and in some urban areas our native element is perhaps as murky and dangerous to us as dying rivers and lakes are to them.

The operation of our market economy has demonstrated that pollution cannot be controlled by the voluntary action of individual producers and consumers. Public action must follow up public concern for conserving the environment so that our communities may be habitable for us and for future generations. Governments, therefore, are assuming responsibility for managing environmental resources. But they are faced with many problems in carrying out these new responsibilities. Scientific knowledge and technologies are still being developed to reduce pollution to levels where air and water will suffer no further degradation and may be restored to former conditions of quality for life support and enjoyment.

An even greater obstacle to controlling pollution is the reluctance of producers and consumers to give up their traditional freedom to decide what they will make, sell, or buy for profit or satisfaction of use and ownership. Environmental management is faced, therefore, with both the uncertainty that goes with insufficient knowledge and the administrative difficulties that arise from institutional arrangements that are as yet inadequate for public decision making and effective action to reduce pollution to acceptable levels.

This inquiry into the administrative aspects of air pollution abatement has a primarily educational purpose. It is intended to show students of public administration how particular problems in steel and cement plants were mastered under the present structure of law and government organization and with available technology.

An alternative system of economic inducements created by residuals charges, a system as yet undeveloped in this country, is also discussed. This study is intended to supplement similar inquiries on other aspects of air pollution and on other forms of environmental degradation, illustrating for students in pursuit of environmental management careers the procedures presently followed by public agencies as well as the opportunities and needs for administrative innovation.

The case narratives are supplemented by extensive appendices that contain some of the relevant legal documents. The organization and operation of the Department of Environmental Conservation are established by state law. Negotiations between state officials and corporate managers involve extensive formulation of legally adopted environmental standards and formal documentation of violations and required corrective action. In order that students may become familiar with the form and terminology of some of these documents, the appendices contain copies of state air pollution rules, commissioner's orders, environmental analysis report forms, and tax relief application forms. Court involvement in pollution control is illustrated by copies of court decisions and judgments.

I am grateful to Commissioner Henry Diamond for opening doors in the Department of Environmental Conservation. Without his support, this study could not have been carried out. I owe a particular debt to Harry H. Hovey, Jr., P.E., Associate Director of the Division of Air Resources, for his guidance and technical information. Mr. John R. Allen, Director of Administration, also gave freely of his time and made available assistance from his staff. Others in the Department of Environmental Conservation who were tolerant of my demands on their time and knowledge are James S. Moran P.E., Thomas Allen P.E., Greg Sovas, and David O'Toole P.E.

Olin Harper LeCompte, Assistant Attorney General, provided an explanation of the role of his office in dealing with air pollution problems and copies of documents relevant to the case described in the text. For this assistance I am particularly grateful.

Information about the dust collection system and the financial problem it posed for Allegheny Ludlum was provided by Thomas J. Gorman, Vice President of Operations, and his assistant, Anthony Andolina. They also read the manuscript. Similar assistance was provided by Juergen Meusel, Technical Director, and Robert Van Slyke, Community Relations, of the Atlantic Cement Company.

In spite of the help and information so freely given by these public servants and industrial managers, these are necessarily incomplete case accounts. I have tried to be fair to all parties in putting these stories together and regret any errors, omissions and misinterpretations of fact or opinion they may contain.

This report would never have seen the light of day were it not for Ann Wright, Ada Bradley, and Helen Ecker of the secretarial staff of the Graduate School of Public Affairs, State University of New York at Albany.

Albany, New York
September 1974

To Helen

CONTENTS

PART I

RUSTY AIR: STEEL PLANT PARTICULATES

PART II

GRAY AIR: CEMENT DUST

APPENDIXES

PART I

RUSTY AIR:

STEEL PLANT PARTICULATES

Chapter 1

THE RUSTY AIR PROBLEM

The Allegheny Ludlum steel plant has been operating in the Albany Metropolitan Area since early in the century. It is located next to the City of Watervliet, a community on the west side of the Hudson River a few miles north of Albany. Until the 1960's not much public concern was expressed about pollution from this or any other source in the region. It may be assumed that pollution was not considered critical during the first half of the century—it was a necessary consequence of economic activity. Allegheny Ludlum's neighbors may have felt that jobs and the prosperity of the community depended on the plant's operation. Since pollution was thought to be inevitable they learned to live with it. Besides, there was no one to complain to, and it seemed as though nothing could be done about it anyway.

THE NEIGHBORS COMPLAIN

In 1958 there was finally someone to listen to complaints. In that year the Division of Air Resources was established in the State Department of Health. Citizen complaints were sporadic, however. People who were affected by the emissions from the steel plant were certainly aware of the problem and may have talked about it among themselves, but there was little individual or concerted citizen action.

Nevertheless, complaints that were received were taken seriously by the State Department of Health. As an example, here is the chain of events set off by a letter dated October 21, 1963 from Mrs. Michael Burns, a resident of the City of Watervliet, in which she complained about "the large volume of red smoke" that came from the nearby steel plant.[1] The letter was referred to the Bureau of Air Pollution Control Services in the Division of Air Resources. The Bureau, in turn, requested the Division of Industrial Hygiene in the New York State Department of Labor to make an inspection of the steel plant. The Albany Regional Office of the State Health Department and the

Albany County Health Department were also informed of the complaint and of the request for an inspection.[2]

The Division of Industrial Hygiene went right to work on its investigation and filed its report in December of 1963, two months after Mrs. Burns' complaint. Mrs. Burns and another resident in the neighborhood were interviewed, and information about plant operations causing the smoke emissions was obtained from the Safety Supervisor at

(Photo Walter Fogg)

Figure 1. Rusty air over Allegheny Ludlum.

Allegheny Ludlum. The report on the pollution problem was filed with the State Health Department's Air Pollution Control Board.[3]

After its own deliberations, the Air Pollution Control Board communicated in the following February with the Industrial Relations Manager of Allegheny Ludlum. The Board noted that in response to a complaint an investigation of the steel plant's operations was made by the engineering staff of the Division of Industrial Hygiene, Department of Labor. The investigation showed that iron oxide smoke was emitted from the electric-arc furnaces, and that there was no pollu-

(Photo Walter Fogg)

Figure 2. No more rusty air.

tion control. The Air Pollution Control Board urged the firm to install equipment to reduce the emissions and asked for a meeting to review the matter.[4]

Nothing much happened, however. Two years later, on September 9, 1966, a Mr. E. S. Webster wrote directly to the Air Pollution Control Board. Mr. Webster lived in Wynantskill, New York, across the Hudson River and several miles east of the Allegheny Ludlum plant. He wrote that the Board must be aware of the frequent billows of smoke coming from the steel plant in Watervliet. Depending on the wind direction, the smoke covered large residential areas. Mr. Webster enclosed a clipping from the Troy *Times Record* stating that the red dust particles were corrosive because they pitted painted surfaces, automobiles and aluminum siding.* He also enclosed a clipping from the *U.S. News and World Report* that showed equipment was available to control steel plant emissions.[5]

On April 30, 1969 a complaint was received from Philip R. Hans of Watervliet. He wrote that shutting down the steel plant was not the answer to the pollution problem and also noted that filtration systems were available.[6] Yet neither Webster nor Hans appreciated the problems that would be faced by Allegheny Ludlum management and engineers in deciding just how to deal with the technical difficulties of controlling the iron oxide dust and meeting the changing standards of the pollution control agencies. The company had experienced problems with the dust control installation in its Brackenridge, Pennsylvania plant and wanted to avoid these in Watervliet.

The letters noted here were only a few of the complaints received by state agencies. The Air Pollution Control Board based its replies to these letters on the new Air Pollution Control Law that had recently been enacted.[7] The State Health Department, in its replies to complaints, wrote that Part 187 of the Official Compilation of Codes, Rules and Regulations (10 NYCRR 187) had been adopted to deal with this form of pollution.** It required that industrial firms must abate such

---

* Iron oxide dust from Allegheny Ludlum did not cause this kind of damage because it was already oxidized. The Republic Steel blast furnace in Troy caused the problem by emitting *iron* particles. When these rusted, the oxidation process affected the paint.

** Part 187 was in Title 10 Public Health of the Official Compilation of Codes, Rules and Regulations of the State of New York. On May 1, 1972 rules relating to pollution control were recodified into Title 6 Environmental Conservation, where Part 187 is now Part 212. All citations to NYCRR are those in the documents on which this study is based.

pollution by a January 1, 1971 deadline.[8] Allegheny Ludlum did not make the deadline, but late in the year the equipment that was installed finally went on line. Suddenly the rusty air disappeared from the skies over Watervliet.

THE ALLEGHENY LUDLUM STEEL PLANT

The Department of Labor investigation made in December, 1963, in response to Mrs. Burns' complaint took note of the steel production process at Allegheny Ludlum. The plant produced stainless steel and various grades of tool steel. The four furnaces were operated on a cold charge basis. The kinds of scrap metals and fluxes used varied with the grade of steel to be produced. The cycles of furnace operation were: (1) charging with the raw materials; (2) melt-down into liquid metal; (3) refining—the removal of impurities by oxidizing them and combining them with the fluxes; (4) tapping—first to remove the slag formed by the combination of fluxes and impurities that floated to the top of the melt, then to pour off the refined liquid steel.

There were at least three heats per day in the electric-arc furnaces. During each heat, the furnaces were lanced with oxygen. A probe was put into the pot and oxygen was blown in for 25 minutes. This was the period during which pollution emissions were greatest.

The metallic oxide fume consisted mostly of iron oxide. About 150 pounds were emitted at each furnace during each oxygen blow. Oxide particles less than half a micron (0.5μ) in size remain suspended in the outer air over distances of several miles. The iron oxide fumes were exhausted from the furnace house by natural draft. Because there was no cleaning of particles from the air before it was discharged from the plant, deep brown plumes were observed coming from the roof during the oxygen blows.

Other operations at the Allegheny Ludlum plant were rolling, reheating, grinding, and pickling. There was also a steam-generating plant that burned gas. These processes and the generation of steam produced much less pollution than the electric-arc furnaces. Even after complaints started coming in to the State Health Department, pollution increased at Allegheny Ludlum. A 17-ton electric-arc furnace was installed in February, 1964, and the steel production rate was increased about 4% in all four furnaces. Later negotiations for the installation of pollution abatement equipment referred to 25-ton,

15-ton, and 12½-ton furnaces that had replaced the original 10-ton furnaces.

EFFECTS OF AIR POLLUTION FROM ALLEGHENY LUDLUM

Iron oxide particulates settled out of the contaminated air as heavy dust falls around the plant. The dirty air and the dirty surfaces on which the dust settled were obnoxious, but their injuriousness to human health was not certain. The larger particles in the dust are screened out in the nose and air passages and do not enter the lungs. The very small particles remain suspended in the air, but they may not reach the lungs in any great quantity. The suspended particles certainly add to the dust burden that the lungs have to deal with. Any suspended particulates may cause health problems, especially if other contaminants are present. Nevertheless, the effects of the pollution were mainly visual and distressing to those concerned with a clean environment.

The Department of Health agreed with this assessment of the consequences of iron oxide smoke pollution. Part 187 of the Rules and Regulations, which will be described in more detail later on, prescribes four environmental ratings that correspond to the seriousness of the effects of air contamination from a particular source on plant and animal life and on property. The environmental ratings are designated by the letters A, B, C, and D progressing from the most serious to the least serious effects. An environmental rating of "C" was accepted by the Health Department for Allegheny Ludlum. This rating "includes processes . . . where the discharge of a contaminant . . . would reasonably be expected to result in localized adverse effects of an aesthetic or nuisance nature."[9]

The technical problem faced by Allegheny Ludlum was not simple. Dust control equipment had been installed in the company's Brackenridge plant, but this early design was found unsatisfactory. It was designed to meet standards lower than New York state requirements. Decisions about an emission control system for the Watervliet plant involved a complex of factors including engineering design, costs, possible relocation of operations, and a financial crisis caused by competition from cheap imported steel. The need to solve these technical and financial problems caused the firm to fall behind its original pollution abatement schedule.

CONTAMINANTS THAT CAUSE POLLUTION

There are many kinds of substances that cause air pollution. They may be solids, liquids, or gases. They may be natural or man-made. Even in remote mountains, deserts, or sea coasts, the air is not "pure" in the sense of consisting entirely of some ideal proportions of oxygen, nitrogen, carbon dioxide, argon, helium, neon or other gases. Natural particles such as plant pollen may be said to "contaminate" the air. Also, large quantities of solid and liquid particles are thrown into the air over the oceans, particularly where there are breakers along the shore.

Man-made contaminants come from heating homes, offices, stores, and other buildings; from electric power generation; from industrial processes; and from autos, trucks, and buses. Man-made contaminants are unavoidable consequences of economic activity and civilized communal living. Pollution becomes a serious problem under conditions where the contaminating substances become so concentrated in the air that they cannot be diluted or converted by normal atmospheric processes. Excessively concentrated pollutants are injurious to human health, to plant and animal life, and to property. Some are poisonous, some corrosive; others just add to the burden of dirt in the environment.

State and federal governments now have official agencies and concerted action programs to reduce air pollution to levels where it can be accommodated by natural environmental processes. There are a series of steps in these governmental strategies to deal with air pollution:[10]

Pollution Criteria: developed to identify conditions and concentrations of contaminants in the air when they become injurious to life and health, and are therefore causing pollution.

Standards: quantified levels of concentration of contaminants above which there is legal consensus that harmful pollution occurs.

Source Inventory: to identify single point sources of contaminants, such as power plants or factories, and more general sources, such as motor vehicles; it is then possible to determine the amounts of the various contaminants that constitute the pollution burden.

Rules and Regulations: adopted as a legal expression of emission standards that public agencies are to enforce and that contamination sources are to achieve.

Surveillance: air monitoring, inspection teams, and field patrols to measure pollution levels in the ambient air and from point sources.

Enforcement: violators of the rules and regulations, where pollution is documented by surveillance and inspection, are contacted, warned and, if necessary, prosecuted by public agencies.

Criteria, standards, rules and regulations, and other aspects of control strategy are directed at the individual components of the air pollution problem, such as particulates; hydrocrabons; nitrogen, carbon, and sulfur oxides; metals such as lead, mercury, cadmium, and beryllium; and other harmful substances. The predominantly iron oxide emissions from the Allegheny Ludlum plant are classed as particulates, solid particles that fall as dust or are small enough to remain suspended in the air. They are basically objectionable as dirt rather than as poisons. Their concentration in the ambient air can be reduced to acceptable levels by relatively simple, although perhaps costly, technological systems installed at the emission sources.

Control strategy requires surveillance to monitor the quality of the ambient air and identify point sources and their kinds and quantities of emission. In large metropolitan areas it is not yet possible to demonstrate cause and effect relationships between emission control at point sources and the quality of the ambient air. There are many other variables that affect air quality, such as the numerous dispersed area sources, weather conditions, the season of the year, and even economic changes that affect industrial production levels. Nevertheless, public action to reduce pollution requires measurement of emissions at their sources. Reducing emissions must certainly improve air quality.

MEASUREMENT OF PARTICULATES

Emissions From the Steel Plant

The metallic oxide particulates emitted from the furnaces are classed according to size as settleable and suspended. Suspended particulates are less than about half a micron in diameter. A micron is 1-millionth of a meter or about 25 hundred thousandths (.00025) of an inch.

Particulate emissions from an industrial plant are measured by stack tests. These do not differentiate between settleable and suspended particulates. They produce only estimates of the total weight of emissions during a period of time. These estimates are expressed as pounds per hour or tons per day or year. These are average rates of contaminant emissions. The amount of particulates from an industrial plant may vary from day to day depending on the volume of production. Where the process is cyclical, as in steel production in which the furnaces are charged and lanced with oxygen several times a day, the rate of emissions will vary from hour to hour.

The rate of particulate emissions from the Allegheny Ludlum plant may be calculated from information about the weights of raw materials used and the tonnage of steel produced from the four furnaces over a representative period of time. Given the inputs and outputs and the details of the electric-arc furnace processes, empirically-derived conversion factors make possible reasonably accurate estimation of the weight of metallic oxides emitted from each furnace per heat, per day, and per year. Steel production and particulate emission rate do vary from time to time, as noted, but deviations from the average are not considered significant in relation to the sizeable tonnage of steel turned out by the plant.

The Division of Air Resources in the Department of Environmental Conservation estimated that during 1971, before the air cleaning equipment went on line, the electric-arc furnaces were emitting iron oxide particulates at the rate of about 443 tons per year, or about 1.2 tons per day.[11] According to the standards established for Part 187 of the Official Codes, Rules and Regulations (See Appendix A), allowable emissions from the Allegheny Ludlum plant should have been at the rate of no more than 86.6 tons per year. The vacuum air cleaning system installed at the steel plant was rated 99% efficient. It may be estimated, therefore, that the iron oxide emissions have been reduced from over 400 tons per year to only about 4 tons, which is something like 24 pounds per day.

THE AMBIENT AIR

The Official Compilation of Codes, Rules and Regulations of the State of New York has promulgated four sets of ambient air quality standards rather than just one. It is not reasonable to insist on the same standards for New York City or the heavily industrialized Niagara Frontier as for the peaks of the Adirondack Mountains. Each standard, therefore, refers to delineated regions of the state where ambient air quality is not to fall below the prescribed standards, which are lower for industrialized urban areas than for rural areas.

Nevertheless, even the lowest standards are aimed high enough to protect human health. Air quality standards are related to four general levels of air contamination associated with these corresponding types of land use and degrees of urbanization:[12]

> Level I—predominantly used for timber and agricultural crops, dairy farming, and recreation. Habitation is sparse and confined to small incorporated and unincorporated communities. Industry is not developed to any degree and basically uses the natural resources of the area (*e.g.*, pulping of wood or food processing).
>
> Level II—single and two-family residences, small farms, and limited commercial services and industrial development or small sparsely inhabited land areas near large metropolitan complexes.
>
> Level III—densely populated, primarily commercial, office buildings, department stores, and light industries in small and medium metropolitan complexes or suburban areas of limited commercial and industrial development near large metropolitan complexes.
>
> Level IV—densely populated, primarily commercial, office buildings, department stores, and light industries in large metropolitan complexes or limited areas of heavy industry such as chemical and allied products, primary ferrous and nonferrous metals, stone, clay, glass, petroleum, and coal, and their adjacent commercial and densely populated areas.

The air quality standards for areas of the state designated for each level are given in Table I. The NYCRR also designates for each county in the state the boundary of the areas to which the standards for each of the four pollution levels apply.

For Albany County, the boundaries are given in Title X, Chapter IV, Subchapter C, Part 504. Only the first three levels are permitted in Albany County, so even in the areas directly affected by the Allegheny Ludlum plant, the ambient air should meet the standards for particulates that are shown in the third column of Table I.

ATMOSPHERIC SAMPLING METHODS

Settleable and suspended particulates in the air are measured by different methods. Settleable particulates are large and heavy enough to fall out of the air as dust. They are therefore collected in what is appropriately called a dustfall jar. This is a standard-sized jar of one-

Table I
New York State Ambient Air Quality Standards[a]

	Level I	Level II	Level III	Level IV
Settleable Particulates ($mg/cm^2/mo$)[b]				
Sampling period—30 days				
50% of values less than	0.30	0.30	0.40	0.60
84% of values less than	0.45	0.45	0.60	0.90
Suspended Particulates ($\mu g/m^3$)[c]				
Sampling period—24 hours				
50% of values less than	45	55	65	75
84% of values less than	70	85	100	110

[a] Official Compilation of Codes, Rules and Regulations of the State of New York, Title 10 Public Health, Chapter IV Air Pollution Control, Subchapter B Air Quality Classifications and Standards, Section 501.1.
[b] Milligrams per square centimeter per month.
[c] Micrograms per cubic meter.

gallon capacity with a mouth opening four inches in diameter. The jar remains in place for one month at the sampling site, after which the particulate matter is weighed. The rate of particulate fallout is stated as milligrams per square centimeter (the total weight of particulates collected divided by the area of the mouth of the jar in square centimeters) per month. This may then be converted to the more familiar rate expressed as tons per square mile per month or per year.

It has already been noted that settleable particulates are objectionable from aesthetic, nuisance, and cleanliness considerations. More attention is paid by environmental systems administrators, therefore, to the particulates that are small enough to remain suspended in the air. Because these particulates can penetrate to the lungs, they are a more obvious health hazard.

Suspended particulates in the air are measured by more sensitive equipment called high volume samplers. The sampler consists of a wood or aluminum housing that contains a frame for an 8″ x 10″ glass fiber filter and a blower motor. The motor draws a measured volume of air, about 25,000 cubic meters, through the sampler during each 24-hour sampling period. The suspended particulates in the sampled air are deposited on the filter. The filter is weighed before and after the sample is taken to determine the weight of particulates collected. Once this weight and the air volume in the sample are known, the concentration of suspended particulates can be calculated to the nearest microgram per cubic meter.[13]

There are a number of sampling stations in each region. They are timed to operate simultaneously every six days so that at the end of each year samples have been collected in rotation for each day of the week Monday through Sunday, through all seasons.

A new system already in operation provides continuous monitoring of air quality. The field stations are large trailers equipped with sensitive instruments to continuously monitor eight different kinds of contaminants and ten different weather characteristics.[14] The trailers also contain equipment to read these instruments continuously, to average the readings, and to convert the information to electrical signals proper for telephone transmission. Every fifteen minutes the

(Photo N.Y. State Department of Environmental Conservation)

Figure 3. The high volume sampler with rotameter. Clean filter in place on supporting screen.

Environmental Conservation Department's central computer automatically calls each field station. The values for the eighteen air pollution parameters are phoned back to the computer and are recorded in various forms, including a printout of the data. The field station for this system in the Albany area is located on the Hudson River in the City of Rensselaer.

Suspended particulates (the soiling parameter) are measured by

(Photo N.Y. State Department of Environmental Conservation)

Figure 4. A new filter being installed on a high volume sampler.

passing the air sample taken into the trailer through a white tape. Because the air flows through the tape for a given amount of time at a prescribed rate, the darkened spot on the tape is proportional to the concentration of particulates in the air sample. A phototube senses the amount of darkness and translates this into electronic information on the number of micrograms per cubic meter of air. The soiling measurement is one of the major criteria in the High Air Pollution Alert and Warning System maintained by the Department of Environmental Conservation.

At each sampling station the equipment shows how much suspended or settleable particulates are present at that location. When these results are averaged appropriately they can be compared with the Ambient Air Quality Standards shown in Table I. If the sampled air contains more particulates than are permitted by the standards, then the Department of Environmental Conservation knows that emissions from point or dispersed sources in the area must be reduced.

REFERENCES

1. Letter dated October 21, 1963 in the files of the Division of Air Resources, Department of Environmental Conservation.
2. Memorandum dated October 28, 1963 in the DAR files.
3. Memorandum dated January 22, 1964 in the DAR files.
4. Letter dated February 17, 1964 in the DAR files.
5. Letter dated September 9, 1966 in the DAR files.
6. Letter dated September 17, 1966 in the DAR files.
7. Letter dated April 30, 1969 in the DAR files.
8. Letter dated May 7, 1969 in the DAR files.
9. Official Compilation of Codes, Rules and Regulations of the State of New York, Chapter IV Air Pollution Control, Part 187 Contaminant Emissions from Processes, and Exhaust and Ventilation Systems, Appendix 4, Table 1 (See Appendix A).
10. Department of Environmental Conservation, Division of Air Resources, "Air Pollution Control Program: A Strategy for the Seventies," December, 1971 (Processed).
11. Letter dated May 26, 1972 from Harry H. Hovey Jr., Associate Director, Division of Air Resources.
12. Official Compilation of Codes, Rules and Regulations of the State of New York, Title 10, Chapter IV, Subchapter B, Air Quality Classification and Standards, Section 501.

13. New York State Department of Environmental Conservation, Division of Air Resources. *Statistical Analyses: Suspended Particulates*, 1967/1968, Report No. BAQS 14.
14. Donald E. Gower, "The New York State Continuous Air Quality Monitoring System," Division of Air Quality Resources, January 27, 1969 (Processed).

Chapter 2

POLITICAL AND ADMINISTRATIVE FACTORS

Identifying the nature and source of a particular pollution problem is only the first step in dealing with it. Pursuing the pollution control strategy aims at law enforcement and ultimately abatement of the problem. This is not merely a technical process. Important political and economic factors are involved. Public concern about pollution must first become evident as the motivation for politicians to act. Public policies must be debated, laws passed, agencies established and funded, and operations initiated and managed.

Governmental interference in private activities is not undertaken lightly. It is done only after legislators are convinced that it is necessary and justified in the public interest. The New York State Environmental Conservation Law is therefore prefaced by legislative findings and declaration of purpose:

> The people of the state have no greater responsibility than to make every possible effort to maintain a healthy environment. . . . Continued economic, technological and social progress are of little benefit if secured at the price of polluted waters, contaminated skies, a waste of land and a ravaged national heritage.
>
> The state's continued urbanization must be adequately balanced by increased emphasis on its priceless scenic and natural endowments. Population growth, technological advances, and unwise resource utilization have too often caused a serious burden on the quality of our environment, posing a threat to the life-giving ecological balance upon which man and his world depend.[1]

DEPARTMENT OF ENVIRONMENTAL CONSERVATION

Until 1970 responsibility for dealing with the problems of environmental pollution were vested in the State Department of Health. Political recognition of the seriousness of these problems led the Rockefeller administration to propose a reorganization of state agencies to "unify and strengthen the State's environmental protection . . . programs by creating the State Department of Environmental Conservation."[2] The Governor recommended the reorganization measures in his 1970 Annual Message to the Legislature. In his Special Message on the Environment, he described how the proposed reorganization would strengthen the state's future efforts to deal with environmental challenges.

The Environmental Conservation law was signed by the Governor on April 22, 1970, establishing a state policy for the protection of the environment. New organizations created were the Department of Environmental Conservation, the State Environmental Board, and the Council of Environmental Advisors. The new law provided for the transfer of environmental functions from certain existing agencies to the new Department, consolidating these functions and offices:

> The functions, powers and duties of the Conservation Department and Water Resources Commission not related to parks and recreation. (Responsibility for management, care, custody and control of the forest preserve and recreation facilities therein would be vested in the Department of Environmental Conservation . . .);
>
> The air pollution control, water pollution control and solid waste disposal functions, powers and duties of the Department of Health, Air Pollution Control Board, and Pesticide Control Board;
>
> The Pesticide Control functions, powers and duties of the Department of Agriculture and Markets;
>
> The functions, powers and duties of the Natural Beauty Commission.[3]

The Conservation Department, the Water Resources Commission, the Air Pollution Control Board, the Pesticide Control Board, and the Natural Beauty Commission were abolished. The new Office of Parks and Recreation was established in the Executive Department to take over the state parks. It was not possible to create a new department for parks and recreation because the state constitution limits the number of departments. The Department of Health continues to have primary responsibility for the quality and control of public water supplies and a critical role in the public health aspects of environmental conservation.

State Environmental Board

The basic function of the State Environmental Board is interagency coordination. It serves as a forum for various state departments and agencies and public members to exchange views and ideas for the proper balancing of environmental considerations—political, administrative, economic and technical. The Commissioner of Environmental Conservation is Chairman of the State Environmental Board, and the Commissioner of Health is Vice Chairman. Other voting official members are the Commissioners of Agriculture and Markets, Commerce, Transportation, Parks and Recreation, and Local Government, the Chairman of the Public Service Commission, and the Industrial Commissioner. Six additional members, to make a total of 15, are appointed by the Governor. The law requires that each of the members so appointed

> . . . shall be by professional training or experience and attainment, qualified to analyze and interpret matters of environmental concern. Of such six members, one shall be representative of conservationists of the state and shall be familiar with matters pertaining to the utilization of the natural resources of the state, one shall be representative of industry and as such will be employed by a manufacturer or public utility, and four shall be from the field of public health, natural sciences, agriculture, urban studies or other disciplines relating to the environment, ecology or natural resource management.[4]

Council of Environmental Advisors

The State Environmental Board is an integral part of the Department of Environmental Conservation, but the Council of Environmental Advisors is located in the Executive Department. Its primary function is to advise the Governor, not the Commissioner of Environmental Conservation, on the formation of environmental policy. The Council consists of seven private citizens representative of a broad range of interests. They are designated by the Governor with the advice and consent of the Senate.

Regulatory Powers

It has already been noted that the legal basis for negotiation with Allegheny Ludlum to abate the emission of iron oxide was contained in Part 187 of Chapter IV, Table 10, of the Official Compilation of

Codes, Rules and Regulations of the State of New York. Power to formulate, adopt and change these rules as they relate to environmental pollution is vested in the Commissioner of Environmental Conservation and the State Environmental Board:

> The Department, by and through the Commissioner, shall be authorized to: (1) with the advice and approval of the Board adopt, amend, or repeal environmental standards, criteria, and those rules and regulations having the force and effect of standards and criteria to carry out the purposes and provisions of this Act.[5]

This is an important responsibility charged to the Department of Environmental Conservation by the state legislature. In addition to making explicit its findings and declaration of purpose in enacting the Environmental Conservation Law, it also specifically stated this Declaration of Policy:

> The quality of our environment is fundamental to our concern for the quality of life. It is hereby declared to be the policy of the State of New York to conserve, improve and protect its natural resources and environment and control water, land and air pollution, in order to enhance the health, safety and welfare of the people of the state and their overall economic and social well-being.[6]

Execution of this policy is delegated to the Department of Environmental Conservation. The legislature has left to the Department the details of defining and enforcing environmental standards. No further legislative action is required for the promulgation of rules and regulations that will have the force of law to abate pollution.

This is a considerable delegation of power. It is, therefore, hedged about with safeguards against arbitrary or hasty action. Rules having the effect of pollution control standards formulated by the office of the Commissioner must be studied and approved by the State Environmental Board. This provides opportunity for review of proposals by other state agencies and representatives of private, economic, scientific, and public interests. Before proposals are forwarded to the Board, the Commissioner must present them at public hearings. Notice must be given by public advertisement at least fifteen days before the date set for the hearing. Members of the Board may participate in the hearings. If the Board approves the Commissioner's proposal, it becomes effective thirty days after publication in the

Official Compilation of Codes, Rules and Regulations of the State of New York.[7]

PART 187 OF THE OFFICIAL CODES, RULES AND REGULATIONS

(Now Part 212 of Title 6 Environmental Conservation)

Part 187 contained rules and regulations for particulate emissions. Its title was Contaminant Emissions from Processes, and Exhaust and Ventilation Systems. This regulation was adopted by the Department of Health to become effective on Feb. 6, 1968 as part of Title 10 Public Health, Chapter IV Air Pollution Control of the Official Compilation of Codes, Rules and Regulations of the State of New York. It was adopted by the Department of Health under a grant of legal authority in the Public Health Law similar to that which was transferred to the Department of Environmental Conservation by the Environmental Conservation Law described in the previous sections. At that time the Air Pollution Control Board had the power to make air pollution control rules.

Another consequence of the reorganization of state government, in which responsibility for the environment was transferred from the Department of Health to the Department of Environmental Conservation, was the revision of the Official Compilation of Codes, Rules and Regulations of the State of New York. Rules now administered by Environmental Conservation were recodified from Title 10 Public Health to Title 6 Conservation. The rule that has been referred to here as Part 187 is now Part 212 of Title 6. Nevertheless, the rule will continue to be referred to here as Part 187 because this is the designation it had while the pollution problem at Allegheny Ludlum was being resolved.

The heart of this regulation is the prohibiting of the emission of particulate air contaminants in excess of the emission rates specified in its three tables. Industrial or other operations begun or modified after the effective date of this Part, February 6, 1968, were to conform to these standards immediately. Emission sources in existence before that date had until January 1, 1971, or a later date set by the Commissioner of Health, to install equipment or modify their operations to conform to these standards.

Part 187 is reproduced in Appendix A. The procedure for determining the acceptable particulate emission rates for any source begins with the assignment to it of an "environmental rating." There are four ratings and different sets of standards that correspond to each rating. The rationale for these differences is based on present technical and economic limitations on imposing the same standards for all kinds of emission sources in all circumstances. Given the present state of technology and community dependence on certain sources of employment and production, emission standards must be "reasonable." As the potential for pollution abatement improves, standards are likely to be raised.

Table 1 (Appendix A) of Part 187 describes the four environmental ratings, which reflect less serious hazards in the progression from A through D.

Rating A: processes where contaminant discharge would reasonably be expected to result in *serious adverse effects* of a health, economic, or aesthetic nature.

Rating B: where air contamination would reasonably be expected to result in only *moderate and essentially localized effects.*

Rating C: where air contamination would probably result in *localized adverse effects* of only a nuisance or aesthetic nature.

Rating D: where discharge of contaminants *will not result* in measurable effects on receptors nor add to the atmospheric burden of contaminants.

Table 2 (Appendix A) of Part 187 specifies the degree to which emissions must be reduced for all liquid and gaseous particulates from sources with any environmental rating and for solid particulates with A or D environmental ratings. To determine how much emission abatement is required, the emission rate potential of the source in pounds per hour of particulates must first be calculated. The percentage by which emissions must be reduced may then be read from the table. For example, a pollution source causing "serious adverse effects" (Rating A) must reduce emissions by 99 per cent. Emission sources with less serious effects on the environment may be permitted lesser percentages of abatement, depending on their emission rate potential.

The Allegheny Ludlum plant was given an environmental rating of C. Table 2 therefore does not apply to this particular source of contaminants. Table 3 (Appendix A) is the one that refers to solid particulate emissions from processes with this environmental rating. This set of standards relates the amount of emissions allowed to the amount of raw materials used in the process. These amounts are expressed as pounds per hour. In the case of Allegheny Ludlum, the maximum permitted weight of metallic oxides discharged into the air in pounds per hour is related to the weight of steel scrap, fluxes, and other materials charged into the electric-arc furnaces per hour. Because steel production is a cyclical process, the per hour figures are averaged to obtain weights of process materials and particulate emissions on a daily or yearly basis. It has already been noted that before the air cleaning equipment was installed, the steel plant was mitting 443 tons of particulates per year, while only 86.6 tons per year would have been permitted by these regulations.

It is obviously no simple matter to determine the air pollution effects of an industrial plant, electric utility, steam plant or other emitter of smoke and fumes or to apply the standards prescribed in Part 187. The burden of supplying the required information is placed on the operators of the emission source. Section 187.4 of Part 187 states:

> When required by the Commissioner, the person operating or maintaining emission sources in operation before the effective date of this Part shall submit a detailed report including emission data, pertinent environmental factors and a proposed environmental rating so as to show conformity with this Part of proposed corrective measures and schedule for compliance. . . . Persons beginning or modifying operations after the effective date of this Part are required to submit . . . plans and/or specifications [and] a report including the proposed rating to be used for design purposes.

The information required by Section 187.4 is presented by the operator of the emission source in the form of an Environmental Analysis Report. The official forms currently in use to guide the preparation of this report are reproduced in Appendix B. The blank forms number only six pages, but the final report prepared by a firm with operations on the scale of Allegheny Ludlum may be inches thick. The Environmental Analysis Report contains four sections:

1. *Plot Plan:* shows land uses surrounding the plant, location of emission sources, location of nearest off-property receptor for each emission point, nature of refuse and location of disposal sites.

2. *Explanation of Plant Process:* description of each plant process including flow diagrams of materials and operations; indication of emission sources by reference to plot plan.

3. *Industrial Emission Source Inventory:* for each emission source, information must be provided about the system producing the emission, the process weight or emission potential, air cleaning equipment and its efficiency, the characteristics and quantity of each contaminant emitted.

4. *Environmental Rating Proposal and Permissible Emissions:* After inventorying their own emissions, the plant operators propose an environmental rating based on the criteria given in Table 1 of Part 187. They must then calculate permissible emissions using Tables 2 and 3.

In preparing its Environmental Analysis Report, the firm documents its own compliance with or violation of the standards set forth in Part 187. If the report is acceptable to the Commissioner, the operators of the emission source are so notified. If the report is not acceptable, however, the Commissioner notifies the operators as to the reasons for this, indicates what an acceptable environmental rating would be, and offers a time schedule for bringing the operation into compliance with Part 187. If the firm questions the Commissioner's findings, it may petition him for a hearing within thirty days after receiving his notice.

This, briefly, is the legal basis on which the State Department of Health and later the Department of Environmental Conservation pursued their negotiations with Allegheny Ludlum to abate the heavy emissions of iron oxide that were polluting the air over a large part of the Albany metropolitan area. Not until February of 1968 did the Department of Health have Part 187 as a legal tool with which to combat this kind of air pollution. The Department of Environmental Conservation brought new initiatives and rigor to enforcement, but Part 187 cannot be wielded bluntly or carelessly.

New York State's antipollution legislation has not been thoroughly tested in the courts. The Department of Environmental Conservation is, therefore, not yet prepared to force legal confrontations with industrial corporations that may be causing environmental pollution. The courts may find flaws in the law; and in any case, the accused companies could drag the suits through the legal process for a long time.[8]

The Department of Environmental Conservation, therefore, prefers to rely on the force of public opinion to induce pollution abatement. This may, in fact, be an efficient way of dealing with the problems of pollution during the early years of a new state policy. Publicity about pollution educates the general public and makes industry aware of changes in the political climate that will be conducive to changes in the economic system. Profit maximization, once the justification and legitimation in the American business ethic for any corporate action, may no longer be sought at the expense of environmental pollution. In the language of the economist, pollution is a cost to society of private industrial production, a negative externality of the process. In order to eliminate the social cost and convert it to costs that are privately borne by producers and consumers, the pollution "externalities" must be "internalized" and reflected in the market price of the product. As this is a change from traditional American ways of doing business, understanding and acceptance of it will take time. Hence the importance of public information and education.

THE ALBANY COUNTY HEALTH DEPARTMENT

Local health departments play an important role in the administration of governmental environmental systems management in New York State. The Albany County Health Department was involved very early in the Allegheny Ludlum case through its Office of Environmental Health Services. This organization provides field services to the Department of Environmental Conservation, as it did to the State Department of Health before 1970. Where county or regional health organizations do not exist, as in some thinly-populated rural areas, the Department of Environmental Conservation regional offices must perform the necessary field services.

The Albany County Office of Environmental Services usually receives the first complaints about environmental pollution. It has already been noted that the County Health Department was dealing with complaints about Allegheny Ludlum in the early 1960's. The County Office logs in the complaints received and makes a field investigation. It sends the complaint log to the Department of Environmental Conservation Regional Office and may reply to the person who made the complaint.

When industrial firms prepare Environmental Analysis Reports describing their manufacturing and related processes as required by Part 187, the County first reviews the application for an environmental rating and makes the initial recommendation. If industrial sources of air pollution fail to cooperate with the Department of Environmental Conservation, thereby necessitating enforcement action, the County Health unit is also involved. It makes the field investigation and prepares documentation on the case for review and further action by the Department's Regional and Central offices. By carrying out these field services, the County Health Department is close to local environmental problems and provides primary contacts with both residents and pollution sources in the area.

The Albany County Board of Health has adopted its own code on air pollution that follows the state code very closely. It has been incorporated as Article 11 of the Albany County Sanitary Code. Nevertheless, the County Health Department does not attempt to prosecute violators under its own code. The Office of Environmental Services refers complaints to the Department of Environmental Conservation for legal action. This obviously avoids duplication of effort where the state and county organizations are in the same location.

Other counties, especially the large ones in heavily urbanized and industrialized metropolitan areas, have adopted their own codes in order to provide a legal basis for their own initiatives. This may take the form of higher standards than are required by the state code, or it may be manifested in local action on complaints to which the state Department has not yet fully responded. County codes, in these cases, give the local health agency some leverage in inducing the state to give higher priority to local pollution problems. This may be disadvantageous to DEC, however, as disruptive to its own enforcement schedule.

ALLEGHENY LUDLUM IN THE ALBANY AREA

Although Watervliet is usually referred to as the location of the Allegheny Ludlum steel plant, it is really just over the city line in the Town of Colonie. Operations in this area have had a long history of development. The plant was established in 1907 when the firm that was eventually to become the Ludlum Steel Company decided to relocate from New Jersey. The Albany area was selected "after it was discovered that steel interests in the Troy area were in financial control."[9] In 1910 the plant abandoned the crucible process for making steel and installed electric-arc furnaces. Since 1919 it has pioneered in the manufacture of stainless and other alloy steels that have been important to the development of automobile and jet aircraft engines, industrial machinery, and space vehicles.

The Ludlum Steel Company and the Allegheny Steel Company of Pittsburgh merged in 1938 to become the Allegheny Ludlum Steel Corporation.[10] Periodically thereafter the plant was expanded to accommodate new technological developments and market demand for its products. Some of the highlights of this growth were noted in newspaper accounts. In November 1951 the president of Allegheny Ludlum reviewed a seven-year expansion program that had cost $10 million. Improvements included a new stainless steel extrusion process, seamless tube production, new 10-ton and 20-ton electric-arc furnaces to make high temperature alloys for jet aircraft engines, a blooming mill, and expansion of the power station.[11] In February 1960 the firm announced plans to build the world's largest vacuum melting furnace.[12] Seven years later it revealed plans to spend $15-20 million to expand and modernize its complex of steel plants where 1300 workers were already employed.[13]

POLLUTION CONTROL NEGOTIATIONS

The early stages of the negotiations, beginning with complaints in 1963 about the dust fallout, have already been described. Four years later no progress has been made in reducing the iron oxide emissions. The Department of Health then began to apply real pressure on Allegheny Ludlum, but from 1967 to 1971 technical and financial problems caused the company to delay final design and construction of the dust control system.

In 1967 the State Department of Health communicated with Allegheny Ludlum's manager of operations about the pollution problem as a follow-up on investigations that had been made in response to complaints about the red smoke.[14] The Department of Health noted that the plant was in violation of Parts 175-180 of Title 10 of the Official Compilation of Codes, Rules and Regulations of the State of New York—especially Section 176.1, a rule for the prevention of new air pollution that had become effective in April 1962. Section 176.1 required that plans and specifications for installations that could reasonably be expected to contribute to air pollution must be submitted to the Commissioner of Health for approval. In this connection, an increase in the rate of production would be construed as a modification that would increase the amount of air contamination. Allegheny Ludlum's violation consisted in the installation in February 1964 of a 17-ton electric-arc furnace and an approximate increase of four per cent in the production rate in all four furnaces.

Allegheny Ludlum's response to this allegation was a letter from the head office in Pittsburgh stating, "we would like to be on record as not being aware that the 1964 relocation of this furnace . . . was in violation of any existing rules and regulations. We would also like to go on record as being willing to and intend to comply with the Department of Health requirements."[15] The firm therefore requested a six-month extension of time to prepare plans and specifications for gas cleaning equipment to be installed on the furnaces. This was the first of a series of such extension requests that would be made over the next few years.

At the end of the six-month period (December 1967) Allegheny Ludlum proposed a two-stage schedule for installing fume collection and cleaning facilities for its four furnaces. Stage I would deal with the 25- and 17-ton furnaces for stainless steel melting. Sixty-six weeks would be required for system design, equipment bids, submission of plans and specifications to the Department of Health, and delivery and installation of the equipment. Stage II would require an additional 66 weeks for the 25- and 15-ton furnaces used for tool steel melting.

The total time of 132 weeks would see elimination of the iron oxide pollution problem by July 1970. Allegheny Ludlum declared that this approach would permit immediate progress in complying with Department of Health requirements, while allowing time to study areas of uncertainty and permit spreading of capital expenditures. The company already had experience with fume collection on furnaces producing stainless steel. For the furnaces producing tool steel further investigation was required of systems that would not adversely affect furnace practice or steel chemistry. Had this scheduled been adhered to, Allegheny Ludlum would have been in compliance by July 1970, well ahead of the January 1, 1971 deadline set by Part 187.

Unfortunately, Allegheny Ludlum had to confront the realities of steel market fluctuations, financial stringencies, technological change, and the uncertainties of future state pollution control regulations. The company had experienced the limitations, and on one occasion the failure, of its bag house at the Brackenridge plant. It had to decide how best to invest scarce capital resources in pollution control, and the choices included alternatives in location for various operations and in the design of the system. If it was decided that present melting and manufacturing operations would be continued at Watervliet, then the dust control system should be designed for long life and maximum efficiency.

The State Department of Health agreed to the two-stage 132-week schedule, but Allegheny Ludlum requested a change in July 1968.[16] Engineering studies indicated that it would be more advantageous to simultaneously install fume control equipment on all four furnaces. This would delay starting the control of emissions on two furnaces, as proposed in the original schedule, but it would reduce the total scheduled time.

More than a year later, in September 1969, Allegheny Ludlum proposed still a third emission abatement schedule.[17] It included five steps:

1. Submit plans and specifications to Department of Health: November 17, 1969.
2. Submit appropriation request to Allegheny Ludlum Board of Directors: January 5, 1970.
3. Award contract: April 1, 1970.
4. Start construction: October 5, 1970.
5. Complete construction and put emission control equipment on line: July 1, 1971.

Yet in December, only three months after submitting this schedule, the firm asked for another one-year extension for awarding the construction contract.[18] This would defer project completion until mid-1972 or later, more than a year and a half after the January 1, 1971 deadline required by Part 187. Allegheny Ludlum wanted this extension to gain time for detailed market research and economic studies of its manufacturing operations. These studies could lead to three alternative courses of action:

1. Move some steel melting operations to the Allegheny Ludlum plant at Dunkirk, New York, and reduce or eliminate operations at Watervliet.
2. Move melting operations to Brackenridge, Pennsylvania, with the same consequences for the Watervliet plant.
3. Spend $1.5 million for air pollution control at Watervliet

and expand steel melting operations to justify this investment.

This request for a one-year extension was made at a meeting with Health Commissioner Dr. Hollis Ingraham on December 1, 1969. In a letter to Commissioner Ingraham following up on this meeting, Allegheny Ludlum declared that the problem was not simply whether or not to spend the $1.5 million required for air pollution control, but rather where the money would be most advantageouly spent—in Watervliet or Brackenridge. On the basis of current information, the company would have preferred to shut down the melting operation at Watervliet. But rather than make a hurried decision, the one-year extension on awarding the construction contract would allow time to consider such economic variables as power rates, freight rates, equipment utilization, capital investment and future sales. It was estimated that nine months would be required to write the computer programs for the study and three months to run simulations of various operating conditions so that a choice could be made.[19]

The meeting was arranged by Assemblyman Fred Field, who was also an industrial engineering supervisor at Allegheny Ludlum.[20] In a newspaper interview he defended his action on the basis of his concern for the economic benefit of the district he served. Assemblyman Field said he "was aware of the possibility that some criticism might be leveled at my action in this case . . . but the continuation of the melting operation at Watervliet was certainly beneficial to the economic climate of the 103rd Assembly District."[21] About 175-200 jobs were at stake, and Assemblyman Field was not just doing a political favor for his firm. He had arranged a similar meeting six months earlier to save jobs at Republic Steel in Troy. Because he had no personal interest in this company, no political or press notice was taken on that occasion. The problem was serious, however, for Republic Steel did shut down permanently and abandoned its Troy blast furnace. Assistant Health Commissioner Alexander Rihm opposed the extension, however, because he thought that pollution control would not really force Allegheny Ludlum to shut down its Watervliet operations.

The final result of these negotiations was the granting of a six-month extension rather than the one year requested. According to the revised schedule, construction would begin on April 1, 1971 and be completed by January 1, 1972, one year after the Part 187 deadline.[22]

The delay also made it possible for the company to study a new melting technique for stainless steel, which might produce heavier future emissions that would have to be controlled.[23]

By this time the Department of Environmental Conservation had been established. Environmental Conservation Commissioner Henry Diamond assumed responsibility for the Allegheny Ludlum and other pollution cases from Health Commissioner Ingraham. The new department was not content with informal agreements, even in writing. It therefore instituted a new policy that any abatement schedule that extended beyond July 1, 1971 must be formalized in a Commissioner's Order on Consent. Allegheny Ludlum was therefore asked to stipulate to the dates in the latest schedule, which were incorporated in the formal Order.[24] In fact, however, Allegheny Ludlum beat its own negotiated schedule and put the new vacuum cleaning bag house on line in November 1971.

THE COMMISSIONER'S ORDER ON CONSENT

Because Allegheny Ludlum was ahead of its own schedule, the Commissioner's Order was never formally executed. The draft order is reproduced in Appendix C, however, as an example of the type of legal document that may be the end product of negotiations between Environmental Conservation and an industrial firm whose plant is emitting air pollutants.

It has already been noted that the Department prefers to rely on the pressure of public opinion rather than lawsuits to induce industrial firms to abate pollution. Adherence to the abatement schedule incorporated into a Commissioner's Order is the alternative to a hearing, with its attendant publicity. The draft order notes that Allegheny Ludlum had waived a public hearing and accepted the terms and conditions stated therein. These included installing a melt shop fume control system to meet the standards of the environmental rating assigned under Part 187, periodic submission of progress reports, and testing of the system. An appendix to the draft order set the construction and testing schedule to which Allegheny Ludlum would be bound.

The alternative to accepting the stipulation in a Commissioner's Order, for an industrial firm that believes it is operating according to its legal rights, is to have a public hearing. The Department of Environmental Conservation serves the Notice of Hearing and Complaint in the form reproduced in Appendix C. The notice specifies the complaint, in this case the alleged violation of Part 212 of Title 6 of the Official Compilation of Codes, Rules and Regulations (formerly Part 187 of Title 10), and sets the date and place of the hearing. The notice closes with this offer: "You may waive your right to a public hearing at any time prior to the hearing and agree to the issuance of the proposed order by fully executing the waiver and consent set forth thereunder."

The alternative of avoiding unfavorable publicity is thus held out to the firm until the last minute. It is advised of the conditions it would be required to meet in a draft order similar to the one prepared for Allegheny Ludlum. A recent revision of the form is reproduced in Appendix C. An important new provision is that to insure compliance with the conditions and schedule set forth, the firm must make a cash deposit with the Department or post a bond in the amount determined by the Commissioner. This puts teeth into the order and is a forceful means for assuring that the polluting emissions will be reduced within a reasonable time to the levels established by law.

REFERENCES

1. Laws of New York, Chapter 140, Title I, Section 1 (Environmental Conservation Law).
2. Governor's Program Bill for the Environmental Conservation Law, 1970.
3. *Ibid.*
4. Environmental Conservation Law, Article 4, Section 100.
5. *Ibid.*, Article 2, Section 15.
6. *Ibid.*, Article 2, Section 10.
7. *Ibid.*, Article 2, Section 15.
8. Interview with John R. Allen, Director of Administration, Department of Environmental Conservation, July 21, 1972.
9. Article dated October 19, 1937 in Capital District Newspapers file.
10. Article dated May 18, 1938 in Capital District Newspapers file.
11. Article dated in November, 1951 (date missing) in Capital District Newspapers file.
12. Article dated February 25, 1960 in Capital District Newspapers file.
13. Article dated February 6, 1967, *Knickerbocker News*.

14. Letter dated May 3, 1967 in the files of the Department of Environmental Conservation.
15. Letter dated June 1, 1967 in Department of Environmental Conservation files.
16. Letter dated July 12, 1968 in Department of Environmental Conservation files.
17. Letter dated September 24, 1968 in Department of Environmental Conservation files.
18. Memorandum dated December 3, 1969 in Department of Environmental Conservation files.
19. Letter dated December 12, 1969 in Department of Environmental Conservation files.
20. Article by Shirley Armstrong, Albany *Times-Union*, March 10, 1970.
21. Article in *Knickerbocker News*, March 9, 1970.
22. Letter dated August 20, 1970 in the Department of Environmental Conservation files.
23. Letter dated July 20, 1970 in the Department of Environmental Conservation files.
24. Letter dated March 15, 1971 in the Department of Environmental Conservation files.

Chapter 3

TECHNOLOGICAL FACTORS

ALTERNATIVES FOR CONTROL OF PARTICULATE EMISSIONS

The major air contaminants that Allegheny Ludlum had to control were metallic oxides. The rusty air over the steel plant was caused by particulate matter, different in chemical composition but similar in some physical characteristics to other forms of visible smoke. Air contamination by particulates may be controlled in a variety of ways. The management problem, therefore, is to identify the available alternatives and choose the air cleaning system that promises the greatest efficiency under the operating conditions of the industry.

One alternative is to reduce emissions by changing the manufacturing process. This might be feasible where new production technologies can, in fact, reduce emissions and where an existing plant or equipment is obsolete and has to be scrapped anyway. Sometimes changing the raw material in a manufacturing process or changing the fuel in a heating or power plant may clean the air. For example, the air in New York City has become measurably freer from sulfur dioxide because the law requires that low sulfur fuels must be used.

Atmospheric dispersion and dilution of contaminant emissions is another way of dealing with them. The ambient air is still used as a free dump for pollutants, but the harm to the immediate plant environment may be reduced by raising the point of emission by building a tall chimney or smoke stack. By the time the particulates reach the ground they are more dispersed and some distance away from the stack. Building tall stacks is not always an effective method of emission control, however. Cement plants without positive air cleaning equipment emit large quantities of dust through their stacks that cause property damage and nuisance to the environment. Large numbers of contiguous smoke-producing industrial plants also cause pollution from their forest of chimneys, as a visit to the steel center around Gary, Indiana easily demonstrates.

Positive methods for reducing contaminant emissions from industrial processes and operations require the installation of air cleaning equipment. Particulates can be separated from air and other gases because they behave according to Newton's law of gravitation and other laws of physics. Particles are more dense than the surrounding gases, and the heavier ones may be separated by changing their velocity or direction.

Mechanical Collectors

Most particles over 100 microns in diameter settle out of the effluent before leaving the stack. A simple gravitational device for collecting them and even smaller particles is a settling chamber, a compartment in the duct with a larger cross section. When the carrier gases reach the enlarged chamber they suddenly lose velocity and the larger particles have time to drop out. Gravitational collection is efficient for particles larger than 40 microns. The Howard dust chamber is a refinement of the settling chamber that can remove particles down to 10 microns in size. The Howard device has horizontal plates in the settling chamber that further reduce carrier gas velocity. Although the Howard dust chamber is more efficient than the ordinary settling chamber, removal of the collected dust is more difficult.

When dust particles strike a solid surface they also slow down, but in addition impingement causes the particles to agglomerate. The smaller particles thus come together as large particles and are removed from the gas stream by gravity. Baffles in a flue cause direction changes in the gas flow and impingement of particles. A more sophisticated inertial separator is the cyclone. Dust-laden gas enters a large funnel tangentially. The solid particles are whirled around and thrown against the wall of the cyclonic unit. Loss of inertial movement, impingement, and agglomeration occur. The particles fall to the bottom of the unit and discharge into a storage hopper. Cyclones can be used with high efficiencies for particles as small as 10 microns. Depending on the sizes of the particles, they catch 85 to 95 per cent of the potential pollutants.

Electrostatic Precipitators

Electrostatic precipitators have been used commercially since the beginning of the century. They are very efficient for collecting small

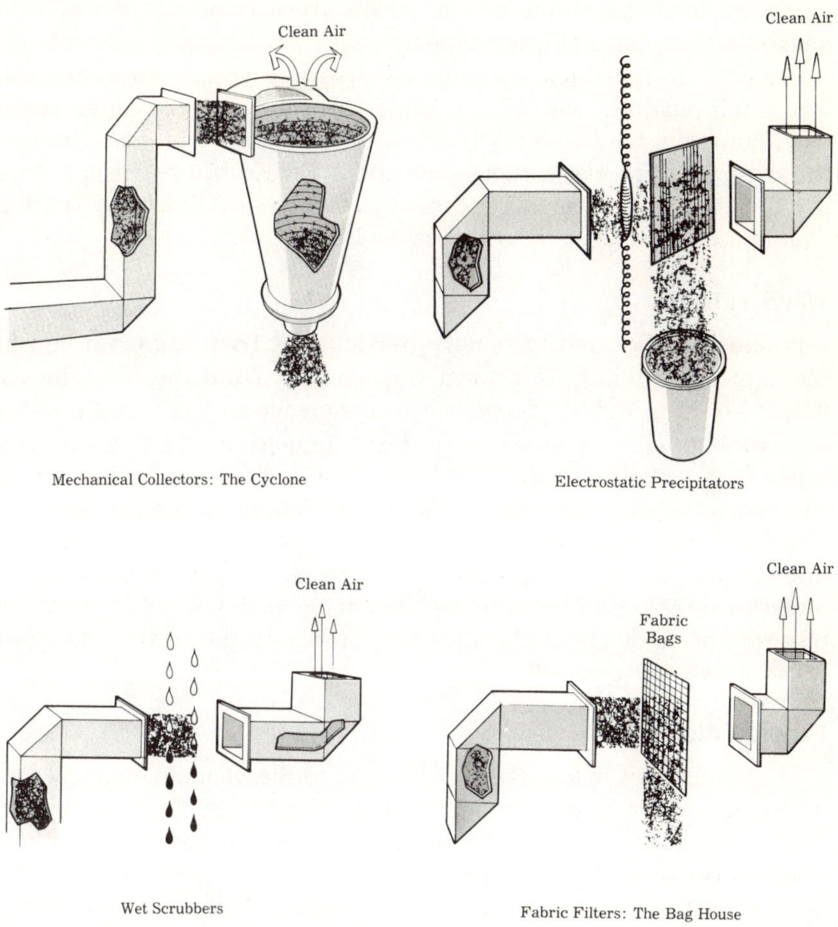

Figure 5. Particulate control equipment (Courtesy Industrial Gas Cleaning Institute).

particles down to 0.1 micron in diameter. Such particles are as small as those in cigarette smoke. The precipitators have discharge and collection electrodes. The discharge electrodes (cathodes) are wires that discharge electrons. When the gas stream is passed across the wires the electrons adhere to the dust particles, giving them a negative charge. The charged particles then migrate to the collection electrodes (anodes), which are positively charged plates. The particles are held fast to the plates, which are periodically vibrated to shake the dust into a storage hopper.

Properly designed and installed electrostatic precipitators can collect small particles with 98 to 99.9 per cent efficiency. Larger particles, however, tend to have too much momentum and pass through the charging process without collection. Electrostatic precipitators are therefore often used as secondary equipment following a settling chamber or cyclone, which catches the larger particles.

Wet Scrubbers

Liquids can be used to remove particulates from a gas stream in the same way that a rainstorm washes dust from the air. The efficiency of the scrubber depends on the violence with which the water or scrubber liquid is mixed with the incoming gas. Medium energy types such as spray towers or cyclone scrubbers can collect up to 98 per cent of the dust. The high-energy Venturi scrubber gives efficiencies of 98 to 99.5 per cent with particles as small as 0.5 micron in diameter. While this process cleans the air, it may create a water pollution problem. The scrubber liquor loaded with dirt must be disposed of. If it is simply allowed to run into the nearest body of water it will cause pollution.

Fabric Filters or Bag Houses

This equipment is the industrial cousin to the vacuum cleaner. The air loaded with particles passes through fabric bags. The dust is held back, and the bags are shaken periodically into a hopper for collection and removal. A wide variety of fabrics is used, depending on the kind of dust to be caught and the temperature of the gas. Fabrics in use can handle gases as hot as 550°F, but they must not react chemically with the effluent.

As the gas passes through the fabric a mat of trapped particulates develops that filters material far smaller than the original voids in the fabric. As the mat builds up, however, the vacuum pressure drops to the level at which fabric cleaning is necessary. Then there is a period of reduced efficiency until a new mat is formed. Nevertheless, particles as small as 0.4 micron can be removed from effluent gases with efficiencies up to 99.9 per cent. This is the system selected by Allegheny Ludlum to clean the air from its electric-arc furnaces.

Figure 6. Effectiveness of electrostatic precipitator (Courtesy Research-Cottrell).

New Technology

Scientists and engineers who are not dismayed by the accusations that technological development is the chief culprit responsible for the deterioration of the environment claim that pollution will be controlled by further technological innovation. Technology has no mind of its own. It is created and applied by men for their own purposes. Awareness of the consequences of past technological application and reappraisal of the uses of technology can redirect it from exploitation of the environment to protecting and conserving the environment. Technology has always been at the service of man. Problems arise for society when particular men are in a position to exploit technology in their own interest without regard to the social costs involved.

ALLEGHENY LUDLUM'S CHOICE

When the decision was made by the Allegheny Ludlum management to install an air pollution control system the various technological alternatives that have already been described were considered. The major factor in choosing the fabric filter bag house was the relative efficiency of the system for collecting particles of the size emitted from the electric-arc furnaces. These particles are very small, less than a half micron (0.5μ) in diameter. The consistency of the dust is about like that of talcum powder. This is too fine to be collected efficiently by cyclone and other gravity devices. The scrubber system was also rejected because disposing of the effluent from the scrubbers could cause a water pollution problem.

Electrostatic precipitators were also considered, but they have been found by the steel industry to be less useful for metallic oxide particulates than the bag house system. Electrostatic precipitators require a higher capital investment, and they are adapted to very fine particulates. Larger particles escape the system and must be collected by secondary methods such as a bag house anyway. In the steel plant the dust is collected over the electric-arc furnaces by large canopy hoods that draw in large volumes of air. This also would make for less efficiency in electrostatic precipitators. This system works best with high concentration of particulates and a constant low level of moisture in the air to be cleaned.

Narrowing the choice down to the fabric filter system resolved the pollution control problem into one of designing the most efficient and economical installation. Not only would it have to remove iron oxide emissions from present melting operations, it would also have to have capacity for future expansion to the argon-oxygen process.

The four electric-arc furnaces are spaced widely apart in the long melt shop. Each furnace is shaped somewhat like a ball with a flattened top. The huge carbon electrodes are introduced into the furnace through an opening in the top. When the charge is being melted, and especially during lancing with oxygen, the iron oxide fumes escape from the furnace through the opening around the electrodes. The fumes are collected by huge canopy hoods 400 feet square located directly over each furnace. A second hood of the same size next to the first one collects the fumes when the furnace is tipped over to pour out the melted steel. The fumes collected by the hoods are drawn into ducts that join to form an exhaust duct that is ten feet square in cross-section. Suction is provided by three huge blowers, each operated by a 700-horsepower motor. Together these blowers can move 585,000 cubic feet of air per minute.

The dust-laden air is pulled out of the melt shop by the fans and then pushed through the huge bag house. This giant vacuum cleaner has eight compartments, each containing 672 spun orlon bags. These are 20 feet long and six to ten inches in diameter. The dust is trapped on the inside of the bags. The clean air passes through the fabric into the compartment and then out through openings in the top of the bag house. Seven of the eight banks of vacuum bags are operated at one time, while the eighth goes through its vibrating cycle. The dust falls into hoppers under each compartment and is conveyed to closed containers. These are removed periodically by a specially built truck. The amount of dust collected each day varies with the scale of operations, but it may be between 2,000 and 3,000 pounds. These tons of dust are deposited in the Allegheny Ludlum landfill, where slag and other waste materials are also dumped. Because these materials are chemically rather inert, contaminants are not likely to be leached out into the ground water. The dust collection system is diagrammed in Figure 7.

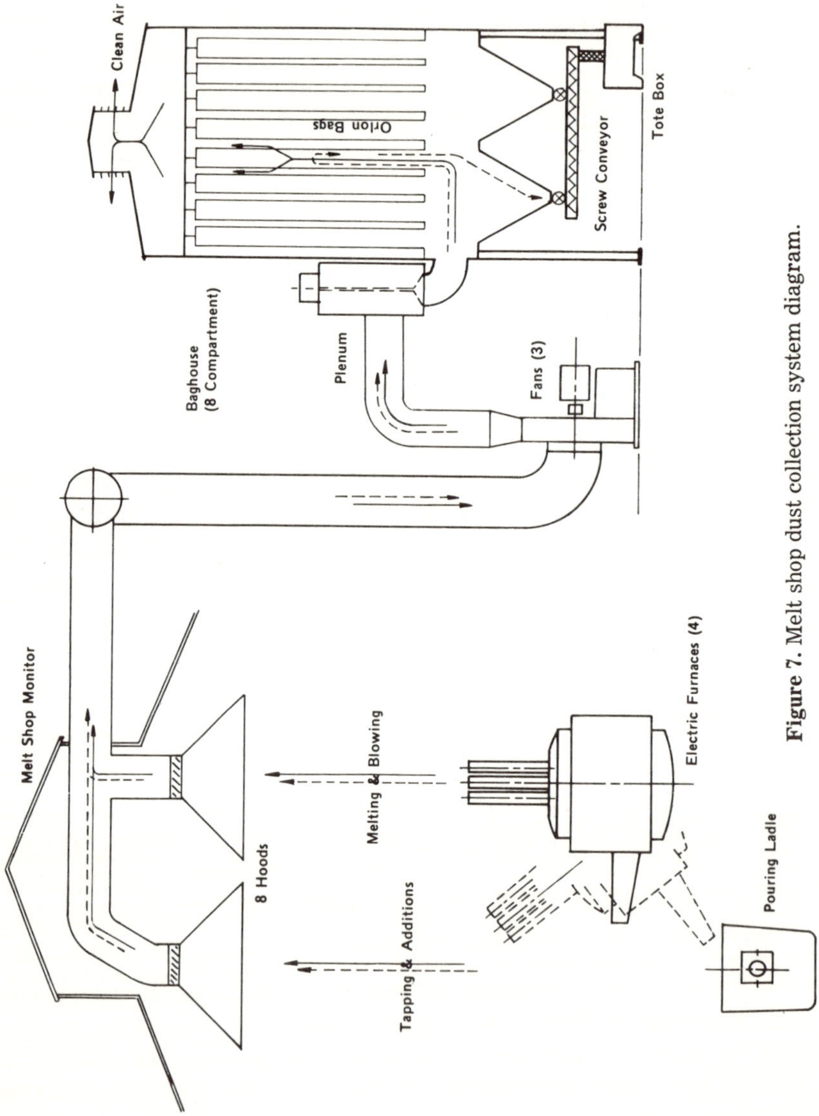

Figure 7. Melt shop dust collection system diagram.

Chapter 4

ECONOMIC FACTORS

WHO MUST PAY FOR POLLUTION CONTROL?

Problems of environmental pollution, depletion, hazards, and ugliness are not just the fault of some "bad guys". And those who wring their hands in consternation and alarm are not necessarily the "good guys". The despoliation of the natural environment would not suddenly go away if the "culprits" were either jailed or reformed.

Materials Balance in the Economy

Technological progress and affluence create problems that cannot easily be avoided. To eliminate them would probably require calling a halt to technological development and accepting a simpler and materially poorer life. Industrial production using advanced technology uses up huge amounts of natural resources, converting them into temporarily useful goods and noxious wastes. Even the useful goods eventually become mountains of junk and garbage. But in the meantime our economy thrives on material abundance and the short-term economic stimulus of rapid obsolescence.

If we are dissatisfied with the consequences of the technological revolution because of its effects on the natural environment, we must ask how many of us would be willing to go back to "the good old days" of Eighteenth or Nineteenth Century America. If we want the "good" things that come from technological progress, are we not all to some extent responsible for perpetuating the "bad" things that happen to the environment as a consequence of such progress?

It might be objected that this is too extreme a condemnation of our mass consumption society. The argument could be advanced that we simply need to manage our exploitation of the natural environment more intelligently. We can do a great deal to conserve the environment in this way. But would we be willing to bear the costs if we acted on the understanding that air and water should not be regarded as free goods? What would in fact happen to our level of living if all consumers paid the full social cost of producing everything they bought? What would happen to the prices of autos, houses and appliances, and the wealth of other products and packages on which our affluence depends if the full cost of treating industrial, power plant, municipal, and transport vehicle wastes were passed on to the consumer?

Nothing is ever used up or disappears. Matter and energy are simply converted from one form to another. Our highly productive and consumption-oriented economy is characterized by a huge flow of materials from the environment. These pass through the economic system as goods and energy, but they must inevitably return to the environment as wastes or residuals. Figure 8 presents a simplified model of the flow of materials through the economy.

Social Values and the Environment

The obstacles that confront us in moving toward paying the full cost of production are ideological as well as financial. Nature in the absence of man creates ecological communities that are "efficient" in terms of their adaptation to climatic and geological changes. But the natural ecology has disappeared from great areas of the earth's surface because man has used his technology to more effectively exploit the earth and its living creatures. Man now has the power to design and create new ecological systems, but they have not turned out very well. For one thing, man has not been able to predict all of the consequences, especially in the long run, of his tampering with natural ecological systems. For example, some species are killed off or a few survivors preserved as biological curiosities, while other species multiply and become resistant to the technology of extermination.

Another reason why man has failed to create viable new ecological systems is that he has substituted his own concept of economic efficiency for the biological efficiency of natural selection and survival of superior mutants. The grand criteria of human action have become the maximization of returns to producers and the maximization of satisfaction to consumers. Nothing else seems to matter. To maximize business profits and support such consumer affluence as we have achieved, we exploit the natural environment for raw materials and to absorb the enormous wastes produced by industrialized so-

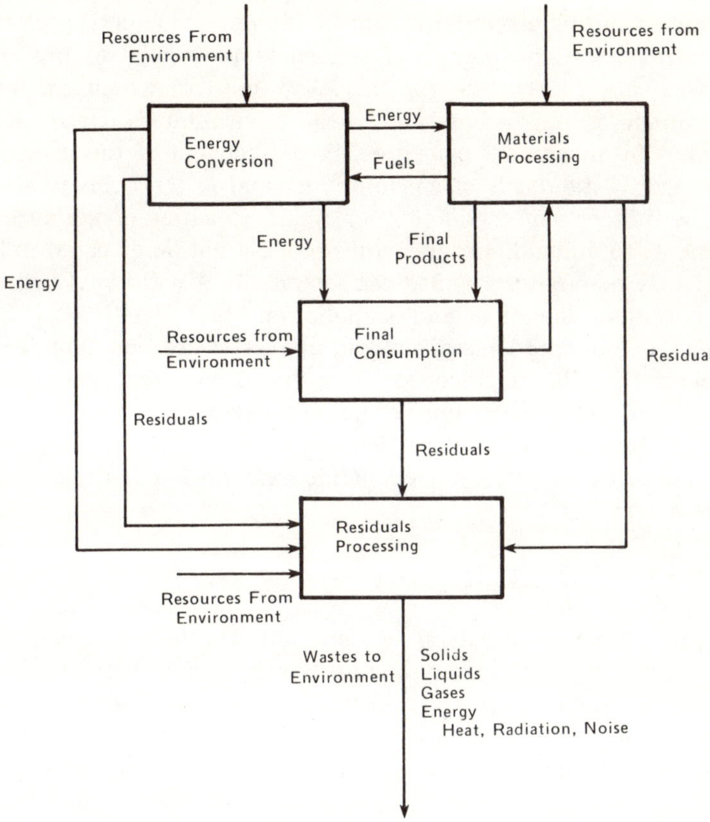

Figure 8. Materials balance model.

ciety. Not only have we depleted resources that were once regarded as inexhaustible, we have also created chemical agents and manufactured wastes that are no longer biologically degradable and become permanent environmental pollutants.

The ideal of economic efficiency, with its focus on short-run returns and consumer satisfaction, seems to stand in the way of progress by technological man to create new ecological systems that will assure the long-run survival and need satisfaction of human communities in a natural environment that can also survive and renew itself. Limitations on the perfectibility of technology may prevent this in any case; but movement in this direction will probably not occur until societies adopt new values. Consumers and governments as well as business corporations are responsible for the sorry pass to which we have brought much of our urban and rural environment. Until there are changes in investment priorities, in the concept of the good life as expressed in standards of consumption, and in the collective will to bear the full costs of production and the restoration of the natural environment, communal energies will probably not be directed to the design of new man-nature ecological systems that will avoid present evils of pollution, depletion, and despoliation.*

All of us, demanding consumers and apathetic citizens—not just a few supposedly villainous corporation executives and venal politicians—will have to change our values. If we do not do so voluntarily, we may be forced into it by the deepening threat to our communal survival posed by our drive for economic exploitation of the environment and each other.

THE CONCEPT OF EFFICIENCY

Economic efficiency results from maximizing the net benefits of economic activity, that is, maximizing the difference between benefits and costs. This principle of economics can be applied to the individual consumer or producing unit as well as to society as a whole. In a democratic society public policy making faces the problem of reconciling private costs and benefits with social costs and benefits. There is also the problem of equity, how private benefits and costs are to be distributed among individuals in the society.

Private Costs and Benefits

For the individual in society, benefit is defined as the satisfaction he derives from consuming various quantities of goods. His cost is defined as the deprivation in the amount of consumption of one good that results from his consumption of another good. Because the indi-

* Economists count as contributions to Gross National Product the expenditures required by government to counter the effects of pollution. According to the logic of these accounts, the more we pollute, the greater our national output of wealth.

vidual's resources are limited he must decide on how much he wants of the various goods available by trading off the consumption of one against the consumption of another so that the mix of goods he consumes will give him maximum satisfaction. His guides to choosing the amounts of each good he will consume are the prices set in the markets where he obtains them.

As far as the problem of pollution is concerned, the individual must not only make choices between goods available in the market, but also between these goods and goods that may be called "environmental services." These are satisfactions derived from enjoying relatively clean air, clean bodies of water, and clean and attractive natural and man-made physical environments. We recognize that air and water, like land, are not inexhaustible resources, and that air should no longer be regarded as a "free" good, available without cost as a dump for residuals. If they are to be maintained at some acceptable level of quality for human use and enjoyment, we must pay the cost of improved environmental services by giving up some other goods or services.[1]

Social Costs and Benefits

Social benefits are defined as the summation of the satisfaction received by individual members of society from the consumption of various quantities of particular commodities or goods. Social costs are, therefore, the reduction in the consumption of other goods required for increasing consumption of the commodity or good in question. Obviously, in a world of limited resources the more society consumes of one good, the less it must consume of other goods. Net social benefits are then by definition social benefits minus social costs. For the society as a whole, therefore, economic efficiency is attained by maximizing net social benefits.

How does a whole society arrive at decisions about the trade-offs involved in deciding how much of one good to utilize relative to other goods? In a purely market economy, the relative prices of goods guide individual consumption choices so that the total satisfaction derived by all individuals from the consumption of various quantities of available goods is supposed to be maximized. Economic efficiency presumably results when a particular mix of various quantities of goods consumed produces the greatest satisfaction for all the people in the society.[2]

In relation to the problem of pollution, we can divide all the goods that society consumes into two classes. One is composed of all the goods and services made available by the various economic units that produce them. The other class is the "environmental services" already referred to, that is the enjoyment of clean air, water and physical environment. If the production of goods and services is inevitably accompanied by the production of wastes that degrade the quality of the environment, then society must give up some of the waste-making production in order to enjoy more of the environmental services.

Unfortunately, the economic principles discussed so far apply only to a society in which there are uncontrolled markets for all goods. Prices for these goods, including the use of air, water and land for the disposition of the waste products of production and consumption, are not controlled in such markets by government, by individual large producers, or by limited groups of producers. We know, however, that such "perfect" markets do not exist. Particularly, there is no such market for the use of air and water resources, so production units have used these resources freely for dumping wastes. Urban communities and government producers of services have likewise used the environment for dumping their wastes. To this situation economists have applied the concept of externality.

THE CONCEPT OF EXTERNALITY

In the abstract kind of market discussed so far, producers and consumers bear directly all the costs and benefits involved in their exchanges of goods and services. In the real economic world, however, production and consumption activities may involve indirect costs and benefits to others who are not parties to them and have no voice in making the decisions about whether or not the indirect benefits are to be made available or the indirect costs imposed. Environmental pollution is a negative externality, an indirect cost (loss of environmental services) borne by all those affected by production and consumption activities of others. It could be said that for the whole society, as regards pollution, we are all victims of each other's production and consumption decisions. We each bear the indirect costs of producing and consuming goods that others want, and they in turn bear the indirect costs of our having the goods we want. If no one pays any attention to these costs, producers and consumers have no incentive to do anything about them. The environment becomes more and more degraded as we take in each other's pollution.

In the discussion of the concept of efficiency, we have seen that individuals make trade-off decisions about how much they will consume of various goods available in the market. In the economists' terminology, marginal analysis provides the logical basis for making trade-off decisions. Business firms use the same kind of marginal analysis to make decisions about their own volume of production.

If a manufacturing plant produces smoke that is simply allowed to pollute the air, the firm takes into account in deciding how much to produce only its direct costs in raw materials, labor, interest on capital, and other production inputs. It increases production until its marginal production costs (costs per unit product resulting from increasing production by an additional unit) equal the price of the product set by the market. If marginal production costs do not include control of effluents from the manufacturing process, then the dumping of contaminants into the environment is a negative externality borne as a social cost by the entire community.

Pollution can be reduced if the firm installs pollution control equipment in the plant. This adds to the cost of production, however, so that its marginal product cost will reach the market price level at a lower volume of production. If all firms manufacturing that product installed air cleaning equipment, as they would be required to do under national air quality standards, then production costs and product prices would rise for the entire industry. At higher product prices, consumer demand would decline. For both reasons, increased production costs and higher product prices, reduction of the social costs of pollution by "internalizing" them in the production process reduces production and consumption of that particular product.[3] Figure 9 illustrates the application of the principles of marginal analysis to output decisions by the firm.[4] The same effects of pollution control on quantity of production and product prices is shown by the use of simple demand and supply curves in Figure 10.[5]

Economist Robert M. Solow uses the following examples to show how externalities may cause distortion of resource use.

> If electric power is 'too cheap' to the customer, because he is not charged its full social cost, then other things will happen. Other commodities that are produced with the help of

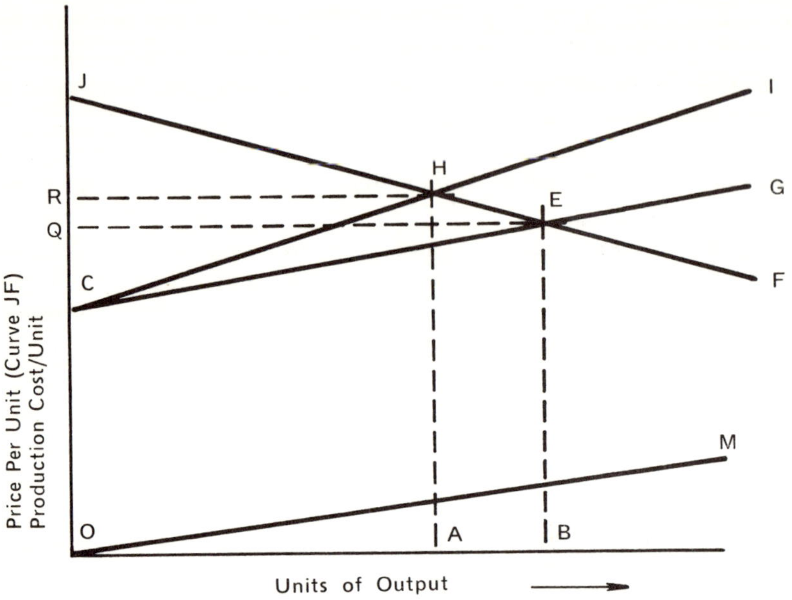

Figure 9. Marginal analysis in production decisions.

JF —market price per unit: decreases as production increases. This is the same as the marginal revenue to the firm.

CG—marginal cost of production: includes only inputs *purchased* by the firm or direct costs.

OM—marginal cost of pollution control: marginal cost to firm if it were to install pollution control equipment. This is the same as the social cost of uncontrolled pollution.

CI —total marginal cost of production: includes the "internalized" social cost of pollution. This curve is the sum of CG and OM.

B —quantity of production if firm considers only direct costs: marginal cost of production and marginal revenue to the firm are equal at BE.

A —reduced quantity of production if social costs of pollution are internalized: total marginal direct and indirect costs of production are equal to marginal revenue to the firm at AH.

Consequence of pollution control: quantity of product available to consumers is reduced from B to A and the market price of the product rises from Q to R.

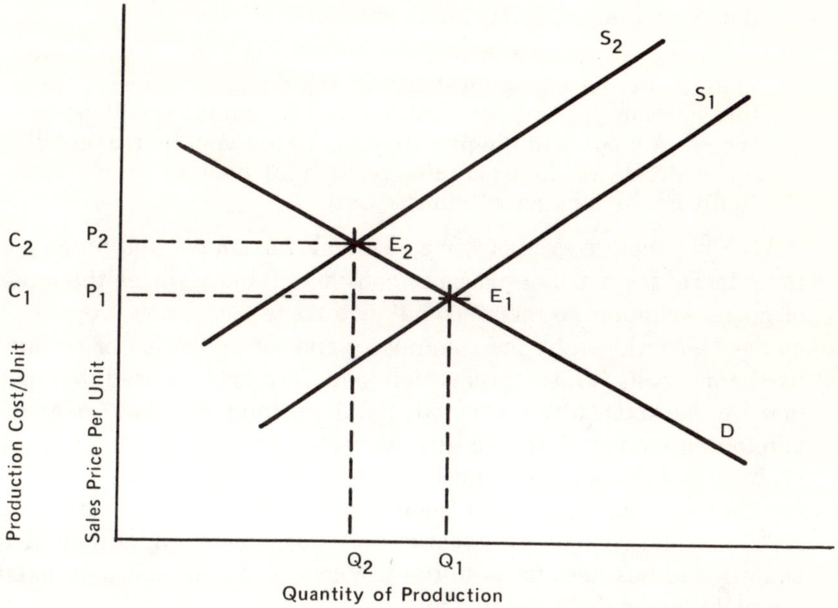

Figure 10. Demand and supply after internalization of pollution control costs.

D —demand schedule for a privately produced good.

S_1—supply schedule of producers: taking into account only direct production costs.

E_1—equilibrium position in market at which quantity Q_1 of product is being produced at unit cost of C_1 to producer and sales price of P_1 to consumer.

S_2—alternate supply schedule of producers: takes into account both direct production costs and "internalized" social costs resulting from installation of pollution control equipment.

E_2—equilibrium position in market after pollution control at which reduced quantity Q_2 of product is available to consumers at increased price P_2.

large amounts of electric power will also be cheap, and they will be overproduced. Other industries will be tempted to adopt techniques of production that use more electric power than they would if the price of electric power were higher. The rest of the society will find itself subsidizing those people

> —if they are an identifiable group—who consume a lot of electricity or a lot of goods made with a lot of electricity.
>
> Similarly, if society is in fact subsidizing the private automobile—by not charging it for all the damage it does— then the location patterns of suburbs and of industry will be affected. A change in the private costs of automobile travel will have effects on house rents, residential choices, and eventually on the location of industry.[6]

Avoiding the free use of air as a dump for smoke and other pollutants increases product prices to consumers and reduces the amount of goods available to them. To balance these costs, however, are the cleaner air enjoyed by the community and the reduction of resources used for goods whose production had formerly caused the pollution. As we have already noted, pollution, and its costs, cannot be eliminated entirely because then we would have no goods at all. The problem is to decide how much pollution is acceptable as a trade-off for the goods that a civilized society needs. We must, therefore, turn from consideration of the effect of pollution control on individual consumers and business firms to the problem of public policy in balancing pollution against production.

POLLUTION CONTROL POLICY

Markets can bring about efficient resource allocation by giving buyers and sellers information in the form of prices. With this information they can weigh the combination of quantities of different goods available that would maximize satisfaction. Concern for environmental quality also involves allocating scarce resources among competing uses. But there are no markets for air and water. Environmental services—which were identified earlier as providing a habitat for man and other forms of life, recreation and amenity, and materials input for the economy—cannot be allocated by the market to their highest value uses. Where there are no well-defined and enforceable property rights in the environment, anyone may appropriate it for his own purposes, whatever the externality costs to others.

When the market fails to allocate resources efficiently, government eventually responds to the dissatisfaction expressed by the affected members of society. Pollution control becomes an issue for public policy, and the basic problem is how to arrive at that level of pollution that may be an acceptable trade-off for the goods that people need and want. The criterion that economists have suggested for determining the most acceptable level of pollution is economic welfare.

Economic welfare is said to be maximized when the economic pie is as large as possible, that is when total economic benefits exceed total economic costs to the greatest degree.* It was suggested earlier that we can divide all the goods and services that society consumes into two classes: those made available by various producing economic units (N); and environmental services (E) or the enjoyment of clean air, water and physical environment. The benefits from these goods and services are reduced, however, by the costs resulting from the production of residuals. These costs are also of two kinds: resources (T) that must be used to process residuals and control pollution; and damage (D) to the environment caused by pollution. Total welfare (W) may be expressed simply as a function of these four variables:

$$W = (N - T) + (E - D)$$

According to this relationship, economic welfare would be maximized by that pollution control policy which minimizes the costs arising from treatment of residuals (T) and also minimizes damages to the environment (D). The optimum situation, therefore, is one where the level of pollution is such that the sum of treatment costs and environmental damage is minimized.[7]

This relationship is illustrated by Figures 11 and 12. The first shows the level of pollution (discharge rate) at which the total cost of pollution control and environmental damage is minimized. The second graph transforms the treatment and damage cost curves into marginal costs.[8]

These economic principles can be translated into ordinary language somewhat as follows. The economic welfare of society can be maximized if there is some way to find that level of production that makes available the greatest amount of the goods people want, and at the same time requires the least amount of expenditure on treatment of useless residuals and also results in the least damage to the environment. The curves in Figure 12 show how trade-offs should be made

---

* This ignores the problem of equity, or the distribution of welfare among the members of society. As consideration of equity would lead discussion too far astray from our focus on pollution control, we will assume that whenever the total economic pie is increased, society's welfare is increased. Equity considerations will be noted later on.

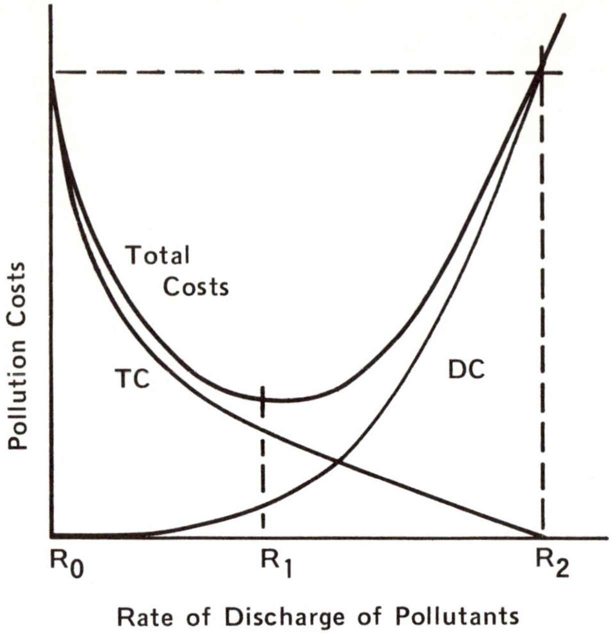

Figure 11. Pollution control optimization.

TC—*Treatment Costs:* very high at R_o where all residuals are treated or controlled; decline to zero at R_2 where there is no treatment at all.

DC—*Damage Costs:* environmental damage is zero at R_o because all residuals are treated; damage is very high at R_2 where there is no treatment.

R_1 —level of pollution at which total costs of treatment and damages are minimum. In this particular case, welfare is maximized at a pollution level where treatment costs are several times higher than damage costs. The reverse would be true if the curves were drawn differently. The only relevant criterion for level of pollution is where the economic pie is greatest—that is, where total treatment and damage costs are least.

in principle to maximize one variable, N, and minimize the sum of two other variables, T and D, in the above equation. Nevertheless, it is difficult to find the data that can be used to actually plot such

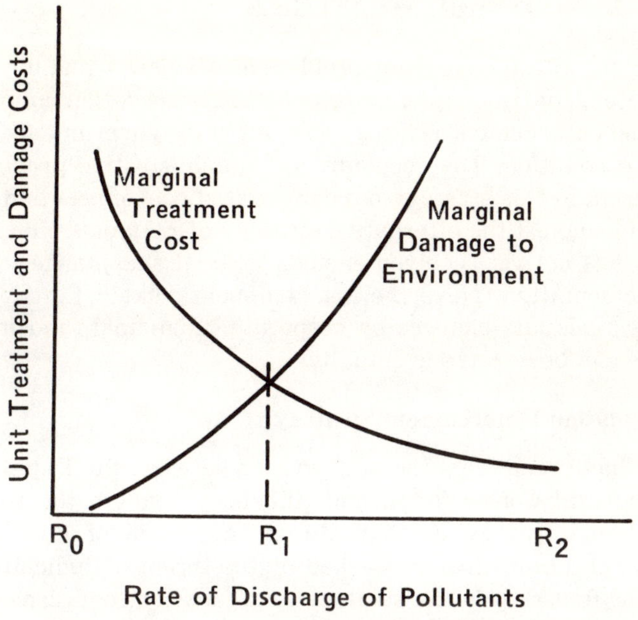

Figure 12. Marginal analysis for pollution control optimization.

The marginal treatment and damage curves show the rate of change of the corresponding curves in Fig. 12. As the level of pollution is allowed to rise from R_0, marginal treatment costs decline and damage to the environment increases. The best trade-off level is at R_1, where the two marginal costs are equal. A dollar of expenditure on treatment buys a dollar's worth of reduction in environmental damage. On either side of R_1, higher treatment costs would buy less damage reduction; lower treatment costs would cause a disproportionate increase in damage to the environment.

graphs for particular watershed or airshed regions and make the economic principles operational. For this reason there is considerable concern among environmental administrators to develop control strategies that will optimize economic welfare and minimize environmental damage in the face of great uncertainty about the cumulative regional costs and benefits of the activities of many separate private and public organizations.

POLLUTION CONTROL STRATEGIES

In dealing with the rusty air problem at Allegheny Ludlum the New York State Department of Environmental Conservation employed the regulation-enforcement strategy that all state governments now use to reduce pollution. The economic and administrative problems that are inherent in this strategy have motivated economists and political leaders to suggest the alternative strategy of residuals charges. This strategy has not yet received enough political acceptance to support its implementation. Nevertheless, it appears likely that legislation imposing residuals charges on corporate, municipal, and individual polluters will be enacted eventually.

The Regulation-Enforcement Strategy

As we have seen from the negotiations between the Department of Environmental Conservation and Allegheny Ludlum the regulation-enforcement strategy involves direct regulation of discharges by Department administrators backed by the threat of judicial enforcement. The first step in the strategy is to identify conditions and concentrations of contaminants in the air when they become injurious to life and health. Considerable scientific effort has gone into determining criteria for various states of pollution. Nevertheless, there are still gaps in scientific knowledge about pollution and its effects. An editorial in *Science* makes the following comment on the 1972 report of the federal Council of Environmental Quality.

> Implicit in the CEQ report is an even more fundamental gap in knowledge—the extent of the hazard posed by various individual pollutants. The council has been seeking an overall index for air quality. In this search, one of the problems cited is lack of knowledge concerning effects. The report rightly states that the ambient air quality standards on which most of the air pollution indices are based are still somewhat controversial.[9]

On the basis of these scientific studies, standards have been formulated for the maximum levels of concentration of contaminants in the ambient air. Concentrations above these levels are considered harmful, and legal action is considered justified against the sources of these contaminants. Sources are therefore inventoried to determine the total amount of contaminants being dumped into the airshed of the region. Rules and regulations are adopted by the pollution control agency, under authority of the law, that specify the maximum rates of emission that are permissible from various kinds of sources. If any particular source, such as an industrial plant or power plant, is found in violation of these rules, it may be subject to legal prosecution and fines.

Limitations of the Regulation-Enforcement Strategy

Although ambient air standards and rules and regulations concerning permitted contaminant emissions are based on scientific study, such knowledge is yet incomplete. In the absence of reliable scientific evidence, environmental standards are determined partly by the political process. The police power of the state is then invoked to reduce discharges from individual sources in order to attain the environmental standards. The pollution control agency must carry out continuous surveillance of dischargers to detect violations of the rules. This strategy, therefore, suffers from the difficulties associated with any direct public effort to regulate human behavior, be it concerned with pollution or automobile traffic. "In practice, the number of violations (whether or not detected) depends on the cost of compliance with the regulations, the penalties associated with being caught in a violation, and the probability of being detected in violation and having the penalties imposed."[10]

This strategy is also said to be economically inefficient because it does not minimize the costs to society of pollution control. According to the economic principles discussed earlier, minimum total cost is achieved, for both producers and consumers, when the marginal treatment costs of all dischargers are equal at the levels permitted by the environmental standards. For some products and manufacturing processes marginal costs of pollution control are higher or lower than others. If equal standards of emission control are set for all dischargers, regardless of their individual marginal costs, total treatment costs may be higher than necessary to achieve ambient air standards. Also, even if legal procedures and sanctions are able to keep discharges below the established standards, there is no economic incentive to pursue new treatment and production technologies to reduce emissions even more.

The Residuals Charges Strategy

This is a strategy of controlling pollution by creating economic incentives to do so by levying taxes or charges on sources of contaminants discharged into the environment. This strategy was advocated originally by academic economists, but it has gained some support by businessmen and political leaders. Both state and federal legislators have before them bills on pollution control based on the strategy of economic incentives, for example, proposed taxes on lead in gasoline or sulfur dioxide emissions from coal or oil combustion. Such charges would raise the cost of discharging wastes to the environment. Internalizing these costs would presumably induce the polluters to find ways to reduce their emissions.

It has already been noted earlier that markets can foster economically efficient use of resources by conveying price information by which producers and consumers may decide the relative quantities of goods to sell or buy that will give them the greatest returns or satisfaction. There are no price signals, however, for the use of environmental resources because no one owns them. When environmental resources are "free" they will be overused or abused.

> The other alternative is to reproduce the effect of private markets by charging a price or fee to those who would use the common property resource. The fee or price would then allocate or ration the resource . . . . Under a system of residuals charges, people discharging wastes are required to pay the government a certain sum for each unit of wastes discharged. Dischargers are led to compare the cost of using the environment for waste discharge—as reflected to them by the residuals charge—with the cost of handling their waste disposal problems in some other way. The choice of means for dealing with the waste is left to the discharger. And he has a wide range of options. He may treat the waste, recycle it, store it, or find methods of production which reduce the volume of wastes generated. His only guide is the relative costs of alternative procedures . . . . People generating wastes will reduce their discharges to the environment as long as the marginal cost of doing so [by waste treatment, recycling, etc.] . . . is less than the price or marginal cost of discharging the waste to the environment. The higher the residuals charge the greater the incentive to seek alternatives to direct discharge, and the smaller the flow of wastes

to the environment. In this way environmental resources can be brought back into the economic system. The incentives which induce efficiency in the use of labor, capital, and land can also effect a more efficient allocation of environmental resources.[11]

Determining The Residuals Charges

Putting a price on pollution requires that the pollution control agency must have some way of determining the charges for the various kinds of emissions. The economist would suggest the principle that the charge should equal the marginal damage to the environment caused by each pollutant. It is not now possible, however, to measure in dollar terms the environmental damages caused by contaminants. Fortunately, there is a simpler alternative. This starts out with the same first step as the regulation-enforcement strategy, setting standards for minimum acceptable levels of ambient air quality. It is only necessary to set the residuals charges high enough to induce dischargers to limit their emissions to a rate that will achieve the ambient air standard for that area. "In other words, there is a market clearing price or charge which will equate the quantity of discharges demanded with the fixed supply implied by the standard."[12]

It is not necessary to have detailed information about the marginal production costs or residuals treatment costs of the various emission sources in order to set the charges. This can be done by trial and error after charges are first established using the best information available. If these charges are not high enough to bring emissions down to the levels set by ambient air standards, then the residuals charges can be raised. These charges will not be simply licenses to pollute, because if they are set high enough the discharger will find it worthwhile to modify the production process or install treatment equipment to reduce emission rates to the level at which the marginal cost of treatment equals the residuals charge. The system would be economically efficient because all of the dischargers would face the same price for the same type of pollution. The marginal cost for abatement of the emissions would be the same for each source and the total cost of abatement at all sources would be minimized.

Administration of Residuals Charges

Advocates of this system suggest that it would be simpler to administer than the regulation-enforcement procedure. The pollution control agency has only to inventory emissions from all sources. The Department of Environmental Conservation already does this by requiring each source to file an Environmental Analysis Report. The agency would not have to know anything about the industrial plant or other source except its total emissions. It would not have to control, negotiate, threaten, or grant favors. It would not destroy the incentive to seek more efficient abatement technology that would reduce pollution payments to the agency.[13]

The residuals charge strategy has not yet been put to the test in this country. It is therefore impossible to substantiate the economic and administrative advantages claimed for it as an alternative to regulation-enforcement in the American institutional environment. Yet an economic incentives approach similar to the residuals charges strategy has been used in Germany for years. It succeeded in cleaning up the Ruhr, which drains a heavily industrialized region, so that stretches of it are safe for swimming and fish find it habitable.[14] Yet it is curious that this pollution control system has not been applied to other German rivers or to pollution problems in other European countries.

Equity Considerations

The residuals charges strategy would use the price system to reallocate resources after the internalization of pollution costs was reflected in new production levels and price schedules. It would then be considered fair that those who want to use things whose production would damage the environment should either pay for the damage or pay for avoiding it. But this reliance on the market to deal with pollution may place an unfair burden on those whose incomes are already strained or insufficient to provide the necessities of life.

> Incomes are not equally distributed, nor do they meet any other test of equity or justice. The principle of assessing environmental costs on the activities that cause them would lead to material goods (which play a relatively bigger role in the budgets of the poor) becoming dearer relative to services (which play a proportionately bigger role in the budgets of the rich).[15]

The economist's own response to this problem is to deal with each aspect separately. The environment should be protected and conserved in the most efficient way possible, which appears to be by a system of effluent charges. Correcting an inequitable distribution of income is a separate matter. It should be attacked directly by taxes on the income and wealth of the rich to provide transfer payments to the poor.

REFERENCES

1. Arthur F. Schreiber, Paul K. Gatons and Richard B. Clemmer, *Economics of Urban Problems* (Boston: Houghton Mifflin, 1971), pp. 16-22.
2. *Ibid.*
3. Robert L. Bish, *The Public Economy of Metropolitan Areas* (Chicago: Markham, 1971), pp. 122-130.
4. *Ibid.*, p. 123.
5. L. L. Wade and R. L. Curry, Jr., *A Logic of Public Policy* (Belmont, California: Wadsworth, 1970), p. 98.
6. Robert M. Solow, "The Economists' Approach to Pollution and Its Control," *Science* 173 (6 August 1971), pp. 498-503.
7. A Myrick Freeman III, *The Economics of Pollution Control and Environmental Quality* (New York: General Learning Press, 1971), pp. 11-14.
8. *Ibid.,* pp. 13-14.
9. Philip H. Abelson, "Environmental Quality," *Science*, 177 (25 August 1972).
10. A. Myrick Freeman and Robert H. Haveman, "Residuals Charges for Pollution Control: A Policy Evaluation," *Science* 177 (28 July 1972), p. 324.
11. *Ibid.*, pp. 323-324.
12. *Ibid.*, p. 324.
13. Larry E. Ruff, "The Economic Common Sense of Pollution," *The Public Interest,* No. 19 (Spring 1970), pp. 69-85.
14. Allen V. Kneese and Blair T. Bower, *Managing Water Quality: Economics, Technology, Institutions* (Baltimore: Johns Hopkins University Press, 1968).
15. Robert M. Solow, "The Economists' Approach to Pollution and Its Control," *Science* 173 (6 August 1971), p. 500.

Chapter 5

FINANCIAL CONSEQUENCES OF POLLUTION CONTROL FOR ALLEGHENY LUDLUM

The negotiations between the State Department of Health, the Department of Environmental Conservation and Allegheny Ludlum that led to successful control of the iron oxide fumes emitted from the electric-arc furnaces were described in Chapter II. The major point of contention during this period was the schedule for design and construction of the dust collection system. The pressure of public opinion that had been aroused by newly awakened interest in the problems of the environment on the part of conservation groups and the news media was perhaps the major influence on the establishment of the January 1, 1971 deadline for air pollution control that was incorporated in Part 187 of the Rules and Regulations. Allegheny Ludlum's series of requests for extensions and delays in carrying out its pollution control program could be interpreted as simply intransigence on the company's part. Nevertheless, the deadline forced a real financial crisis for Allegheny Ludlum.

It was an unfortunate coincidence that the deadline came at a time when Allegheny Ludlum was caught in the financial squeeze that affected the whole American economy—a period during which severe inflation and economic recession occurred. The labor force experienced a high level of unemployment and business faced weakened consumer and government markets. Money was tight and interest rates rose to new heights.

SCARCITY OF CAPITAL

In this situation Allegheny Ludlum had to contend with reduced demand for its products and stiff competition from low-priced imported steel, especially from Japan. Foreign steel producers were able to take advantage of the most advanced technology when their plants were rebuilt with American financial aid and technical assistance after World War II. Their American competitors were not able to modernize so readily and were faced also with rising labor and other costs of doing business.

To meet foreign competition in a depressed market Allegheny Ludlum was forced to discount 35–40 per cent from its book prices for stainless steel and other products.[1] Reduced income from sales cut back the internal generation of capital at the same time that interest rates on borrowed capital had reached 9 per cent. In the face of these financial difficulties Allegheny Ludlum had to make some hard choices about how it would use its scarce capital resources. Plant modernization to reduce production costs and to meet foreign competition, as well as other capital needs, had forced the company into a $40 million refinancing program at high interest rates. At the same time it was being forced into a pollution control deadline requiring a heavy capital investment that would drain its resources and produce no financial advantage for its operations.

Allegheny Ludlum's request to the State Department of Health for an extension of time to deal with its air pollution problems so that it could consider whether or not to shut down its melting operations in Watervliet was not just an idle threat. The Watervliet plant had a book value of $9 million. To keep it operating in conformance with state pollution control laws would require capital investments of $1.5 million to control the iron oxide emissions and an additional $1 million for water pollution control. The company had to decide if this was a reasonable way to use scarce capital when there were competing demands for modernization of production facilities. Perhaps it would be better to shut down the melting operation and use the $3.5 million required to combat air and water pollution in Watervliet on plant improvements at Dunkirk, New York and Brackenridge, Pennsylvania.

In 1907, when the Watervliet plant was first established by the predecessor company of Allegheny Ludlum, there were some advantages to its location in the Albany metropolitan area. It is still a good location from the point of view of access to markets, the availability of scrap iron and steel, its main materials, good rail and highway transportation, and skilled labor. Yet there are other locations that would provide the advantages of lower operating costs, principally from reduced taxes, workmen's compensation, and other personnel costs imposed by New York State law. The Albany metropolitan area has no particular comparative advantage for the production of specialty steel products, and it is therefore not a likely location for the establishment of new plants in this line of manufacture. Nevertheless, Allegheny Ludlum has a large investment in its Watervliet facilities that could not be abandoned lightly.

The issue for Allegheny Ludlum management finally narrowed down to the question of whether or not it was worth protecting its investment in Watervliet by diverting scarce capital from plant modernization to pollution control. Tied in with this question was the problem of site limitations that appeared to preclude the expansion of production capacity. If steel production at Watervliet would not be able to keep up with anticipated future demand, then the investment in pollution abatement facilities would appear of doubtful value.

Two factors were of considerable importance in tipping the balance of decision in favor of controlling pollution at Watervliet and keeping the plant in operation. One was the feasibility of increasing production by the new argon-oxygen process for operating the furnaces. Not only would this new technology increase production volume, it would also reduce production costs. This would put the company in a better position to meet foreign competition. The other factor was the willingness of the plant workers to adopt procedures that would increase productivity. This favorable attitude on the part of the workers at Watervliet helped to convince top management of the feasibility of maintaining operations there.

Once the decision was made implementation followed rapidly. Installation of the dust collection system to meet the state deadline was given priority over capital expenditures for the new argon-oxygen process. The dust collection system was designed with sufficient capacity to accommodate the future expanded production that would be made possible by the new process. It also appeared likely that additional capital resources would be assigned to Watervliet for conversion to the argon-oxygen system during 1973.

OPERATING COSTS

Some of the elementary principles of economics as they apply to the problems of pollution abatement were discussed in Chapter IV. If other factors are held constant, economic theory would anticipate that controlling pollution would increase manufacturing costs and product prices and reduce rates of production and consumption. This is only a conceptual premise, however, for things do not remain the same. We have already seen that prices and production rates do not respond only to changes in production costs, but also to market conditions set by competitors and to international demand for the products.

Installation of the dust collection system certainly adds to Allegheny Ludlum's production costs, but prices and production volume will be influenced by market conditions. It has already been noted that increased production costs were not an important factor in company decision making relative to air pollution control. Scarce capital resources and competing internal demands were the major considerations. Nevertheless, operating costs cannot be neglected. Monthly operating costs during the first year after the dust collection system went on line averaged $9,133.00. Operating expenditures were distributed as follows:

Electric power to operate the blowers	$7840.00
Maintenance labor	1012.00
Maintenance material (orlon bags)	20.00
Transportation of dust from bag house to landfill	261.00
Total average monthly operating costs	$9133.00

It is estimated that the direct cost of operating the dust collection system adds about $1.80 on the average to the production cost per ton of steel. This is not a significant cost increase relative to the prices of the final products, which vary from $800 to $2000 per ton, depending on the steel and the finishing processes required. These cost figures do not include interest on the use of the capital required to construct the emission control system although at the time the $1.6 million was needed, Allegheny Ludlum was paying 9 per cent to refinance its debt. In any event the anticipated direct operating cost of a pollution control system was not the major obstacle for Allegheny Ludlum. The problem was the limited availability and high cost of capital during a period when there were conflicting pressures for plant modernization and price reduction to meet foreign competition and for meeting the January 1971 deadline for air pollution control set by the state agencies.

TAX RELIEF

Industrial firms that install pollution control equipment may offset some of the capital and operating costs involved by tax relief offered by federal, state and local governments. The federal contribution takes the form of rapid amortization of the capital invested in the installation. The state permits an income (franchise) tax deduction for the capital cost of the facility. Local governments may exempt the equipment from the tax on real property.

State Income Tax

In 1966 the New York state legislature amended the Tax Law to provide benefits that might encourage business firms to construct air pollution control facilities. Article 9-A contains the Franchise Tax on Business Corporations which, in effect, is a corporate income tax. Sections 208, 612, 683, 706, and 1083 of this Article contain the relevant provisions. Section 208 is reproduced in Appendix D as it contains most of the important points.

According to the amended Tax Law, the firm may deduct from its taxable income the amount of capital expenditures during the tax year that were required to build or improve air pollution control facilities. This is only a one-time tax break, but it reduces the company's income tax somewhat during the period in which it has to pay or incur costs for installing the equipment. It so happens that Allegheny Ludlum could not take advantage of this change in the law because it had no profits to report during the year when its dust collection system was built. This is an indication of the economic pressure the company was under at the time it faced the Department of Health deadline and the choice about whether or not to continue melting operations at the Watervliet plant.

Only facilities that "remove, reduce, or render less noxious air contaminants emitted from an air contamination source" are eligible for this tax benefit. The equipment is defined as extending from a point immediately preceding the removal, reduction or treatment device to the point of discharge to the outer air. The facility must also meet emission standards set by air pollution control rules. Devices that reduce or eliminate pollution but whose primary purpose is to recover usable or marketable materials from the effluent are not eligible. Installations, such as tall stacks that "rely for their efficacy on dilution, dispersion or assimilation of air contaminants in the ambient air after emission'' are also ineligible.

Before a company can take this deduction from its income for tax purposes it must first obtain a Certificate of Compliance for Tax Relief, Air Pollution Control Facility. Application for a certificate is made on a form that describes the installation, and the certificate itself is a simple one-page document. Both forms AIR108 and AIR104, respectively, are reproduced in Appendix D. The Certificate of Compliance is issued for a completed facility for three years. The certificate may be renewed if the pollution control system is still in operation. As state income tax relief is only provided during the tax years when expenditures on emission control are actually made or incurred, there does not seem to be any need for long-term certification. The long-term consideration is applicable, however, to relief from local property taxes and the federal income tax.

Local Property Taxes

The New York State Real Property Tax Law was also amended in 1966 to encourage industrial enterprises to control polluting emissions from their plants. Normally the value of a plant's real estate is considered to increase when new buildings and permanent installations are added. Consequently its real property assessment and the property tax paid to the local government in whose jurisdiction it is located will go up. This would tend, however, to discourage rather than encourage the installation of pollution control facilities.

The amendment to the state Real Property Tax Law was enacted to enable local governments—counties, cities, towns, school districts and villages—to exempt from taxation any increase in a plant's property value resulting from the installation or reconstruction of a certified air pollution control facility. The amendment was to Article 4 Exemptions, Section 481 Tax Exemption for Air Pollution Control Facilities, which states:

> Air pollution control facilities which were constructed or reconstructed in order to comply with the provisions of the Public health law and codes, rules, regulations, permits or orders issued pursuant thereto shall be exempt from taxation and special ad valorem levies to the exetent of any increase in value thereof by reason of such conservation or reconstruction.

The state law also stipulates that the pollution control facility must have a Certificate of Compliance. The firm may then file an application for tax exemption with the local assessor. However, the exemption cannot be granted unless the local legislative body has enacted the appropriate measures. Paragraph 7 of Section 481 states that "The provisions of this section shall be applicable only to the assessment rolls of a county, city, town, or village which has adopted a local law or a school district which has adopted a resolution as provided in this section."

The Town of Colonie has not, in fact, adopted a local law to provide this form of tax relief to Allegheny Ludlum. A proposal to this effect was presented to the Town Board on February 11, 1971. The Board felt that an industrial firm should not receive tax exemption to eliminate an environmental hazard of its own creation.[2] Nevertheless, the steel plant assessment has not been raised to reflect the $1.6 million dust collection system. The town assessor has taken no action because it did not seem fair that the company should be adversely affected for doing what was required by law.[3] Because the property assessment has not been increased, Allegheny Ludlum has not been required to pay additional property tax on its pollution control system to the town or to the school district in which it is located.

Federal Income Tax

The federal income tax law provides tax relief by allowing for rapid amortization of the investment in pollution control facilities. This is provided for under Section 169 of the Internal Revenue Code of 1954, as amended. According to this procedure, the entire capital cost of the installation may be amortized in five years. This means that one-fifth of the cost may be deducted from corporate income each year with a corresponding reduction in the income tax during the years immediately following the investment.

Reduction in income taxes would help the company to offset somewhat the expenditures required to build the facility. In Allegheny Ludlum's case, however, the saving on income tax would depend on how profitable its operations were during the five-year amortization period. If there was not much taxable income, the tax itself would be low in any case. Also, there is the company's problem of balancing long-term versus short-term benefits. The company might take larger deductions for five years, but it would otherwise have been able to take smaller reductions in its income tax over a longer period.

Procedures under the federal law require not only the state certification already noted, but also certification of the pollution control facility by the U.S. Environmental Protection Agency. Application and certification forms and instructions are reproduced in Appendix D. The original copy of the application for certification and the supporting documents are submitted to the Regional Administrator of the Environmental Protection Agency and copies to the State Department of Environmental Conservation. The state agency makes its decision on certification and so notifies the EPA Regional Administrator. The federal agency then makes it decision and issues or withholds certification. The application and certification documents are then attached to the federal income tax return that the company sends to the Internal Revenue Service.

For a company the size of Allegheny Ludlum the various forms of tax relief provided by state, local and federal governments may be welcome but of little financial importance. In the circumstances confronted by the company at the time it had to assess its alternatives for meeting the pollution control deadline set by the state regulations—install the dust collection system or shut down melting operations in Watervliet—tax relief was a minor consideration. Even if it could save a few thousand dollars a year in taxes, this would be a small offset to the financial burden of a $1.6 million investment and additional operating costs of almost $10,000 per month.

REFERENCES

1. Information about the financial situation faced by Allegheny Ludlum and the factors that influenced management decision making was obtained from Thomas J. Gorman, Vice President of Operations.
2. Letter dated February 15, 1973 by Robert P. Heywood, Town Attorney.
3. Interview with Edward Wagner, Assessor, Town of Colonie.

Chapter 6

STEEL PLANTS AND IRON FOUNDRIES IN THE ALBANY METROPOLITAN AREA

The rusty air problem in the Albany metropolitan area was not caused by Allegheny Ludlum alone. The Adirondack Steel Casting Company in Watervliet, Republic Steel Corporation and the Ross Valve Manufacturing Company in Troy, and the Ravena Iron Company in Ravena also produced iron and other metallic oxides from their plants. The consequences of State Department of Health and Department of Environmental Conservation enforcement of New York State laws to control air pollution were not the same in all cases, however. The Adirondack Steel and Ross Valve companies succeeded in practically eliminating the emission of metallic oxides and absorbing the necessary capital and operating costs. Republic Steel and Ravena Iron were not so successful. Enforcement of air pollution laws resulted in the closing of these plants, but this was only one factor in the situation. Plant obsolescence, financial problems, and market conditions were already almost too much for these marginal operations.

THE ADIRONDACK STEEL OPERATION

Adirondack Steel was not a primary steel producer like Allegheny Ludlum. Rather it used alloy steels obtained from the primary producers to make steel castings to order. Adirondack Steel had a smaller scale but complex problem of controlling particulate emissions. The variety of operations and the disposition of equipment in the plant did not lend themselves to emission control by means of a single large fabric filter bag house.

The first step in making steel castings is to prepare a wood pattern or model of the final product. The woodworking shop produces large amounts of sawdust and wood flour. From the wood patterns, sand molds and resin cores are prepared. Processing and handling the sand produces sand dust, and the ovens where the cores are baked also cause some emissions.

The steel and alloying metals are melted in electric-arc furnaces. Lancing with oxygen produces the iron oxides that cause the same rusty air problem as the Allegheny Ludlum furnaces. After the castings are cooled, they are removed from the molds in a "shakeout," where much of the sand is removed from the casting surface. The remaining sand and metal scale are removed by shot blast cleaning equipment. These steps also produce particulate pollutants. The castings are inspected for flaws, and if they are found acceptable go on to the annealing and draw furnaces. Here they are heated to relatively high temperatures and allowed to cool slowly in order to eliminate internal stresses and hard spots and to make machining easier. After final finishing and inspection, the castings are ready for shipment.

Adirondack Steel already had emission control equipment on some of these operations. The sawdust and wood flour from the woodworking shop were collected in a cyclone that usually operated at about 95% efficiency. The foundry sand dust was collected in a fabric filter bag house. The shot blast equipment was connected to a separate bag house that was rated 98% efficient.[1]

Particulate emissions that were not controlled came from the electric-arc melting furnaces and the shakeouts. An abatement schedule was negotiated by the company, the Albany County Health Department and the state agency. This called for new equipment to control emissions from these operations and also the upgrading of the existing bag houses and other air cleaning equipment to meet Department of Environmental Conservation requirements. The schedule called for completion of construction by July 1971.[2] Delays in obtaining equipment and in construction required revision of the abatement schedule to call for completion of the installation by January 1972.[3] Nevertheless, all Department of Environmental Conservation requirements were met, and Adirondack Steel joined Allegheny Ludlum as prime examples of the technical and financial feasibility of controlling particulate emissions from steel production and casting plants.

THE REPUBLIC STEEL PLANT IN TROY

The experience of Republic Steel is in sharp contrast to the successful air pollution control at Allegheny Ludlum and Adirondack Steel. On April 16, 1969 the State Health Department ordered the Republic Steel plant to stop operating its blast furnace immediately. A 90-day extension was later granted by the New York State Commissioner of Health, but this only postponed final shutdown. Republic Steel could not justify investment in pollution control equipment to keep its aged plant going.

The blast furnace in Troy had been in operation as far back as 1930. The Troy Furnace Company had leased it from the Hudson Valley Fuel Corporation, a subsidiary of New York Power and Light. Republic Steel leased the plant in June 1940 so that the firm could increase its production to fulfill a contract with the federal government for armor plate. This was the eve of World War II, and this perhaps was the basis for the rumors that the Troy plant would be expanded to three times its size.[4] When Republic Steel took over, it had one blast furnace that could produce 500 tons of pig iron a day. At that time it employed 200 men.

There were good reasons why Republic Steel chose this location. The plant was served by the New York Central Railroad and had its own docks on the Hudson River. Coke could be obtained from the adjacent plant of the Hudson Valley Fuel Company, and native limestone was available. More important, high-grade iron ore was available from the mines operated by Republic Steel at Port Henry, Mineville, and Lyon Mountain in the Adirondacks.

Six months after leasing the blast furnace, Republic Steel purchased the plant. It also signed a contract with the Hudson Valley Fuel Corporation to take at least 50 per cent of the coke output. In September 1941 the Federal Defense Plant Corporation loaned Republic Steel $58.3 million to expand ore production in the Adirondacks and to build four new blast furnaces in Buffalo and Cleveland.[5] The rumored expansion of the Troy operation was apparently not to take place after all. Ten years later, in June 1951, Republic Steel bought the coke plant from the Niagara Mohawk Power Corporation, successor to New York Power and Light. The power company had converted to natural gas from gas extracted from coal, which had produced coke as a by-product. Republic Steel bought the coke plant which adjoined the blast furnace property in order to assure a continued supply of coke for its pig iron production.[6]

As the decade of the 1950's advanced the Troy operation ran into problems. First, the coke ovens had to be shut down in 1955. The coke plant had a battery of 31 ovens, but production costs were not competitive. Sharp competition in the steel industry required Republic Steel to cut pig iron production costs in Troy by bringing in coke from cheaper sources than its own plant. The coke plant shutdown resulted in the loss of 170 jobs, but with pig iron production still competitive, 160 men were kept on at the blast furnace and the Port Henry and Lyon Mountain mines were still operating.[7]

By 1957 the coke plant had been dismantled. Republic Steel had petitioned for its property tax assessment to be reduced by $1.8 million for the yars 1955, 1956 and 1957. A favorable referee's decision for Republic Steel required the City of Troy and the School District to refund part of the taxes paid for 1955 and the first half of 1956. The City of Troy had to borrow $200,000 to make this restitution.[8]

From 1958 on, the blast furnace was also shut down periodically because of uncertain demand for its pig iron. In January 1958, 135 men were laid off at the furnace and 350 men at the Adirondack mining and sintering operations. This happend again in December 1960 and three times during 1961. Until it closed permanently in 1969 the plant could no longer be maintained as a year-round operation.[9]

During the prosperous years of Republic Steel operations in Troy, there were apparently no serious objections to the smoke produced by the furnace. It may be conjectured that as their economic stake in Republic Steel declined, the people of Troy could become more pollution conscious. State Health Department records of complaints go back to 1966. These came from residents in the area who objected to the fallout of metallic particles, excessive smoke and sulfur odors. It was also claimed that the finish of automobiles and aluminum trailers had been pitted by the rusting of metallic particles in the dustfall.

In response to these complaints the Rensselaer County Health Commissioner requested the Air Pollution Control Board of the State Department of Health to order an investigation. This was carried out in June 1966 by the Air Pollution Unit, Division of Industrial Hygiene, State Department of Labor. The investigators described the blast furnace operations and noted that it had been built in the 1920's. In 1943 a dust collection system was installed that consisted of a cyclone and wet scrubbers. However, when high pressures developed in the furnace, dust-laden gases were released directly to the outer air through a bleeder line.[10] A second investigation made by the Rensselaer County and State health departments showed that in 1966 an additional bleeder line was installed from the scrubber exhaust duct about 30 feet higher than the first one.[11] A third investigation made in June 1968 showed that there had been no attempt by Republic Steel to control the emissions.[12]

These investigations led to hearings on April 20 and September 18, 1968. The hearing officer filed his report on March 18, 1969. Shortly afterward, on March 31, 1969, Commissioner of Health Hollis S. Ingraham signed an order that (1) adopted the hearing officer's report; (2) ordered Republic Steel to terminate immediately the operation of its blast furnace in Troy; (3) required Republic Steel to continue suspension of operations until it filed a declaration of intent to install air pollution control equipment, a compliance schedule, plans for the system, and dates for beginning and completion of construction; (4) required the firm to post a bond in the amount of the cost of planning and completing the compliance program or $25,000, whichever was less (See Appendix C).

At the September hearing an engineering consultant testified as a witness for the company. He said that the Troy facilities were so old it would not be feasible to modernize them. During 1968 the plant had been in operation for only five months because demand for its pig iron had dwindled in recent years.[13] Nevertheless a Republic Steel spokesman said that a letter of intent had been sent to Dr. Ingraham and that plans and a compliance schedule would follow.[14] On May 12, 1969 the Commissioner signed another order modifying the original one that postponed the mandatory closing date until July 16, 1969. The amendment said the reason for the extension was to avoid hardship on the plant employees, who numbered 165 at the time.

In spite of the extension and the declaration by Republic Steel that it would file a compliance schedule, the blast furnace shut down for good in July 1969. A public relations official at the Cleveland headquarters said that the company was not in a battle with the State Department of Health. Shutting the blast furnace down had nothing to do with pollution. If the market for pig iron improved, the furnace might even reopen with full compliance with the state health laws.[15] Plant obsolescence, production costs, and market factors were the main reasons for closing the Republic Steel plant in Troy. It could not stand the costs involved in controlling pollution. It might have limped along for a while, but it would probably have closed eventually even if there had been no Commissioner's order to do so.

Abandonment of the plant has had serious economic effects for its former workers and the Troy tax base. Nevertheless, an optimistic note was struck in December 1971. Republic Steel announced that it might redevelop its 70–80 acre property as an industrial park. This was only one alternative being considered, although the company had already carried out such projects on its properties in Cleveland and Birmingham.[16] No action has been taken on redevelopment, but the air over Troy is perceptibly cleaner since the old plant was phased out of operation.

REFERENCES

1. Environmental Analysis Report, March 1970.
2. Letter dated June 4, 1970 in Department of Environmental Conservation files.
3. Letter dated March 1, 1971 in DEC files.
4. Article dated June 24, 1940 in the files of Capital District Newspapers.
5. Article dated September 23, 1941 in CDN files.
6. Article dated June 29, 1951 in CDN files.
7. Article dated March 23, 1955 in CDN files.
8. Article dated August 13, 1957 in CDN files.
9. Articles dated December 23, 1957, May 2, 1958, December 2, 1950, February 14, 1961, August 30, 1961 in CDN files.
10. Letter dated September 21, 1966 in DEC files.
11. File Report on April 13, 1967 investigation, DEC files.
12. File Report on June 24, 1968 investigation, DEC files.
13. Article dated April 24, 1969 in CDN files.
14. Article dated April 18, 1969 in CDN files.
15. Article dated February 20, 1970 in CDN files.
16. Article dated December 4, 1971 in CDN files.

PART II

GRAY AIR: CEMENT DUST

Chapter 7

ATLANTIC CEMENT COMES TO TOWN

One of the world's largest cement manufacturing plants was built in the Albany Metropolitan Area in the early 1960's. It was welcomed as a great economic boon to the Town of Coeymans and the Village of Ravena located about 12 miles south of Albany near the Hudson River. When limestone quarrying and cement production began, however, property owners in the immediate neighborhood of the plant began to protest against the noise and dust. Lawsuits by eight of these neighbors involved Atlantic Cement in a decade of litigation, costly penalties, and the award by the courts of "servitude" or easement rights to pollute neighboring lands. The New York State Department of Health, and later the Department of Environmental Conservation, also became involved in the problems of measuring air pollution, assessing the environmental damages caused by it, applying available technology to abate the cement dust emissions, and enforcing the pollution control law.

ESTABLISHMENT OF THE ATLANTIC CEMENT COMPANY

Newspaper accounts in February 1961 first brought the new enterprise to the attention of residents in the Albany metropolitan area. It was formally announced at a press conference in New York City on March 16, 1961. Industrial executives, engineers, architects and real estate brokers had already been quietly at work for a year organizing the company, designing the plant, and taking options on the 2,000 acres of land that would be needed for the limestone quarries, conveyor systems, stock piles and residuals dumps, and the plant itself. The corporate parents of the new company were the Cerro Corporation and the Newmont Mining Corporation. The New York State Department of Commerce assisted in the birth by helping to find a suitable location for the plant, and area banks participated in financing the venture.

The Ravena location had several advantages. Extensive deposits of limestone could feed the cement kilns for 100 years at full production. Equally important were the availability of excellent rail service, the New York State Thruway for short-haul shipping of bagged and bulk cement, and tidewater docking on the Hudson River for low-cost water transportation to cement markets along the entire Atlantic coast. By the same token fuel for the kilns and gypsum and other raw materials for cement manufacture could readily be obtained.

The natural resource and locational advantages of the site were to be exploited by constructing a technologically advanced high-volume production plant whose efficiency would make possible the sale of the cement at about a penny a pound. The limestone would be quarried from hills west of the plant site and transported by a 4,000-foot conveyor to stockpiles at the plant. The landscape scars caused by quarrying would not be visible from the Hudson River, the Thruway or Route 9-W, the major road near the plant, for the quarries were located beyond the escarpment west of these north-south transportation arteries. It was therefore necessary to dig a 1,000-foot tunnel through this range for the limestone conveyor. From the manufacturing plant, the cement would be transported on another conveyor 7,000 feet to the ship-loading facilities on the Hudson River.

Cement plants are generally widely scattered for they produce to meet market demand within a limited 250-mile radius. Costs for transportation by rail or truck make wider distribution uneconomical. With water transportation, however, Atlantic Cement would find it economically feasible to ship to markets in sixteen seaboard states. Ten distributing plants would be built at Boston, Middletown, New York, Bayonne, Baltimore, Norfolk, Savannah, Jacksonville, Port Everglades and Tampa to serve regional markets. Company officials aimed at capturing 10 per cent of the cement market on the Atlantic seaboard and estimated that the whole market would grow by 3 to 4 per cent each year.[1]

Local Welcome to the New Enterprise

A vice president of Atantic Cement, Sam Webb, was reported to have remarked that from the company's point of view the site was ideal because of the spirit in which it had been welcomed by Ravena, the Town of Coeymans, and the whole capital metropolitan area. Town and village officials had been genuinely friendly to company personnel.[2] The friendly attitude was motivated by the economic fallout which was the only one anticipated by the local taxpayers and town officials. Ralph C. Pape, Supervisor of the Town, said "Cement spells gold to Coeymans taxpayers these days. It'll change the face of the town."[3] Town officials expected that the completed plant would have an assessed valuation almost equal to the total for the rest of the town. Pape talked of plans to install new storm and sanitary sewers, build a garage for a new ambulance, install street lights, and beef up the police force. "We couldn't do most of these things if it wasn't for the plant," he said, "and we're building three new schools here too."[4]

The Atlantic Cement plant, the limestone quarry, and the materials handling and transportation facilities were estimated to cost $42 million. The Coeymans town assessment was expected to increase by $12 million, more than one-and-one-half times its 1962 assessment of about $7,052,000. This addition would almost equal the Ravena-Coeymans-Selkirk (RCS) school district assessment of about $14,157,000. On the basis of this new assessment, Atlantic Cement would pay $537,000 a year to the town and $686,500 to the RCS school district. The Atlantic Cement investment was not limited to the $42 million for the Ravena facilities, however. The ten coastal distributing plants would require $22 million more. Another anticipated economic benefit from the town was the million-dollar annual payroll that would go to workers and merchants.

At the groundbreaking ceremony in June 1961, Governor Rockefeller was the principal speaker. A tent to accommodate a large audience had been set up. The new Atlantic Cement President, Dr. Ulrich, in extending his invitation to the Ravena area residents said that the ceremony would be "a community-wide event to be commemorated jointly by Atlantic and its hospitable neighbors." He also praised the "generous cooperation and wholehearted support of officials, landowners, businessmen, and the community-at-large."[5]

THE CEMENT PLANT AND ITS PRODUCTION PROCESS

Two years after groundbreaking, in May 1963, the plant was dedicated. The giant system was now beginning to produce its 10 million barrels of cement per year. Every day the plant would turn out about 30,000 barrels, which is equivalent to 120,000 bags or 11,520,000 pounds. Average annual output of other eastern seaboard cement plants is only about 2.3 million barrels. During the planning stage, Atlantic Cement officials had assured the people of the town that plant operations would not create an air pollution problem. There would be no pall of cement dust over the area.[6] The plant was located one mile north of the Village of Ravena. The immediate area was rather sparsely populated, but a large new junior-senior high school was built just across Route 9-W, several hundred yards from the plant. Company officials said that air pollution would be prevented by the installation of a $3 million dust recovery system.[7]

It is inevitable, however, that disturbances to the environment occur from beginning to end of the cement production process. Obtaining the limestone involves blasting, crushing, and transporting by conveyor to the plant stockpiles. A series of mills pound and grind the limestone into progressively smaller pieces at the quarry. At the plant the stone is ground to powder and mixed with water in large slurry tanks. Cement manufacture requires not only the calcareous materials from limestone, but also alumina and silica-bearing minerals found in clay or shale as well as iron ore. The composition of the slurry is controlled to create the proper mix of these materials.

The slurry is fed to two horizontal rotating kilns, great steel pipes lined with fire bricks. At Atlantic Cement they are 580 feet long, 20 feet in diameter at each end, and somewhat smaller in diameter in the middle. The kilns slope slightly so that the slurry, and the clinker formed from it, move by gravity from one end to the other as the kilns are rotated. The slurry is introduced at the high end and hot gases from burning coal are fed into the lower end.* A 350-foot chimney at the slurry end removes the combustion and dust products of the reaction in the kilns.

As the slurry moves down the rotating kiln it is dried and the residue is burned by the hot furnace gases. During this process carbon dioxide is driven out of the calcareous materials, and the remaining lime combines with the alumina and silica materials. They partially fuse to form small glass-hard balls called clinker. The clinker is ground to a fine powder and mixed with small quantities of gypsum, which regulates the setting time of the finished portland cement. The final product is stored in silos thirteen stories high in reserve for bagging or bulk shipment.

---

* Oil was substituted for coal in 1970.

Figure 13. A working face of the Atlantic Cement quarry.

If the cement dust is not trapped and collected, up to 5 per cent of the kiln output could pour out the chimney. At a daily production rate of almost 12 million pounds, 576,000 pounds of cement dust could go up the chimney every day. Fortunately, mechanical or electrostatic precipitators can reduce this dust emission considerably. As we shall see, however, Atlantic Cement's neighbors were not satisfied with the control measures installed and were disturbed by other production process nuisances.

ATLANTIC CEMENT AND ITS NEIGHBORS

Once the cement plant began operating in earnest, the public relations fanfare and the golden goose fantasies were laid to rest. The plant was dedicated in May 1963. In July the owners of Albano's Drive-In Theatre sought in the Supreme Court a temporary injunction restraining Atlantic Cement from blasting operations at the quarry. The outdoor theatre owner, Sylvester Albano, also brought a $200,000 damage suit. He claimed that the explosions prevented the theatre from opening that year. During the previous season explosions had disrupted movie performances, forced patrons to leave, and damaged theatre equipment.[8] The suit was dropped when the property was purchased by the RCS Board of Education for the new Junior High School.[9]

Figure 14. Conveyor of crushed stone from the quarry as it emerges from the tunnel through the escarpment and crosses Route 9-W.

When Sylvester Albano went to court other neighbors complained about the explosions. Arthur and Robert Albright said their garage and home were shaken by the blasts and that a car that was being repaired had slid off its jacks. Sam and Laura Wilkes said their infant granddaughter fell out of her high chair as a result of the explosions. These and other property owners along Route 9-W were to become plaintiffs in later suits.

In August 1963 a freak accident occurred as a result of blasting in the quarry. A large boulder came out of the sky and buried itself in the grounds of the Junior-Senior High School. The boulder landed almost 100 yards from the school buildings and, fortunately, no one was injured. The entire community became concerned about the safety of the school children. The RCS Board of Education had previously protested to Atlantic Cement about the blasting that was severe enough to shake the buildings. As a consequence of this incident the company abandoned the area of the quarry closest to the school.[10]

Noise was another problem for residents along Route 9-W opposite the cement plant. Robert Albright lived 350 yards from the overhead conveyor that carried the crushed stone from the quarry to the stock piles. He complained that the conveyor operated late at night and the machinery was very noisy. Several months later Ralph Schimmel, a neighbor of Albright, also complained in court about the noise. The judge found Atlantic Cement guilty of disorderly conduct and fined it $50. The company filed an appeal.[11] In August 1964 Albright and Schimmel complained again, this time that they were awakened at 4:20 A.M. by a bulldozer working on a stone pile. In response to the complaint the State Police arrested the bulldozer operator. Albright told the newspaper reporter that his wife had become a nervous wreck. The neighbors said they had proposed to Atlantic Cement that the company buy their homes and businesses so they could move away, but the idea was rejected.[12] Albright and some of his neighbors then brought suit against the company. Eight years later the court ordered Atlantic Cement to pay Albright $70,000 in damages. By the time all the suits were settled, the company had paid about $900,000 in damages to the property owners, who still retained their properties. Had Atlantic Cement acquired the properties along Route 9-W in 1964 it might have saved a great deal of money and avoided a lot of bad publicity.

Complaints about air pollution were received by the State Department of Health and the Albany County Health Department from people who lived some distance from the plant. They were in Ravena and the hamlet of Coeymans south of the plant and in Selkirk to the north. The cement dust settled on houses, cars, terraces, and gardens and even sifted through doors and windows into homes more than two miles from the plant. Some of the residents also feared their health was being affected by breathing the dust. Complaints were received as early as 1963 and were still coming in at the end of the decade in spite of attempts by the Department of Health and later the Department of Environmental Conservation to induce Atlantic Cement to reduce dust emissions.

The dust control problem at the giant plant was complex and diffi-

Figure 15. The conveyor, T-bar and crushed stone stockpiles.

cult to resolve. There were multiple sources of dust at the quarry, dust dump, clinker cooler and storage, and cement kilns. Spray equipment and precipitators were subject to breakdown and had to be shut down periodically for maintenance. Plant operations also had to be halted because of equipment failures. Dust collectors at the kiln stack could not be turned on again until the kilns had reached a suitable operating temperature, so there were periods during which stack emissions could not be controlled at all. How these problems were eventually resolved will be described later on.

In mid-1964 the Coeymans Town Board found it necessary to respond to the residents' complaints. Albright, Schimmel and other neighbors complained that because of the noise and cement dust pollution their homes were not marketable, and they could not maintain their businesses either. The Town Board appointed a three-member committee to investigate the complaints. One month later in July 1964 the committee filed its report. It recommended that the Town Board exert "special pressures" on Atlantic Cement to control the air pollution, for there was no town ordinance that could be the basis for a legal attack on the problem.[13]

Figure 16. The slurry tanks, rotating kiln, precipitator house and main stack.

At the Town Board meeting at which the committee report was given, Oscar Boomer, another neighbor and future litigant, exhibited evidence of the air pollution. He said he was a dealer in used cars and used auto parts, but the casual passer-by would have called the operation an auto junk yard. In any case, Boomer displayed body parts encrusted with a hard, grey substance, presumably caused by the limestone and cement dust. He also had 96 color slides that showed the clouds of dust coming from the plant chimney. Nevertheless, it was made known at the meeting that the New York State Air Pollution Control Board had certified Atlantic Cement as complying with its air pollution control requirements. In fact, the firm had volunteered to have the formal review of its operations.[14]

Complaints against Atlantic Cement continued to dominate Town Board meetings. The residents protested that the special committee of the Board did not do a thorough job of investigating the nuisances and that its report did not contain all the relevant facts. Supervisor Pape tried to meet with the company president in New York, and Oscar Boomer threatened the Town Board with political reprisal if they did not take action. Boomer repeated the complaints of cracked

Figure 17. Storage silos for finished cement.

walls and floors in buildings, cement dust on cars, windows, and outdoor furniture, and offensive odors from smouldering stock piles of coal that fueled the plant furnaces.[15]

Meanwhile plant engineers were trying to deal with the neighbors' complaints. They said there was no way to improve blasting operations in the quarry and that they were carried out in accordance with federal mining laws. They were also trying to reduce the dust emissions. About 500 tons of dust was produced every day, but most of it was returned to the kilns. Some of the dust was too alkaline to be used again in the cement process, so a centrifuge and bubbler were being installed to leach the alkali from the dust. The wastewater from this process would also have to be treated to neutralize the alkali so that it would not pollute the Hudson River into which it drained.[16]

At the same time that the town fathers were troubled with complaints about nuisances and air pollution, they had another reason for dissatisfaction with Atlantic Cement. They had believed this golden goose would be assessed at $12 million and pay $537,000 in taxes to the Town of Coeymans and $686,000 to the RCS School Dis-

Figure 18. Office building flanked by rotating kiln and mill building.

trict. The plant was actually first assessed at $4.1 million, but the company protested this figure. After a two-year court battle the assessment was reduced to $3.8 million.[17] In 1968 the plant was assessed at $3,870,700 and paid $117,750 in taxes to the Town and $258,601 to the School District. It provided other local economic benefits, however, for it employed 433 workers who received an annual payroll of $3,352,134.

The company had its own financial problems, however. In 1969 it finally anticipated that it might hit its break-even point where income would match costs. Since 1963, when the plant opened, it had not shown any profit at all. To obtain working capital, the firm had to raise $8 million from the Prudential Insurance Company by pledging part of its limestone deposits. The Town of Coeymans claimed that this was a mortgage and demanded that the company pay a $40,000 mortgage tax. The State Tax Commission agreed. This time the Appellate Division and the Court of Appeals found in favor of the Town and ordered payment of the tax plus $16,000 interest.[18]

The was not the end of Atlantic Cement's problems with the Town Board. In January 1969 the Board held a public hearing on a proposed zoning amendment that was intended to curb air pollution. The amendment would prohibit stone crushing, grinding, and stockpiling in all zones except I-1 industrial, and then only by special permit to be issued by the Zoning Board of Appeals. Atlantic Cement objected to the proposed amendment on the grounds that the company had brought economic benefits to the town, plant expansion would be prevented, and the company would lose the Interpace Concrete Pipe Company as a potential customer for its cement and crushed stone. As the only land in I-1 industrial zones was already owned by Atlantic Cement and the brickyard on the Hudson River, the Interpace Concrete Pipe Company would be unable to find a site for its operations. The crucial provision in the proposed zoning amendment was the prevention of stockpiling of crushed stone on new sites. Interpace would have to stockpile the stone at its new plant in order to manufacture the pipe.[19]

The attorney representing Atlantic Cement at the hearing said that "if the company had known such restrictions were going to be imposed, it would not have located in the community."[20] He also maintained that although the technology for complete control of dust emission at cement plants was not yet available, the company was ready to sign a contract for a new $1.5 million system to collect dust from the clinkering operation. The attorney for the residents near the plant who were plaintiffs in a damage suit against the company countered with the argument that the zoning amendment was not strong enough. He said, "The Town Board must make a decision on whether Coeymans is going to be an industrial wasteland or a place where private citizens can live in peace."[21] A member of the RCS School Board also urged strict dust control because the Junior-Senior High School was affected by the quarrying, crushing and conveying of limestone. The Town Board was apparently reluctant to lose a potential industrial taxpayer, however. It adopted the zoning amendment in January 1969 but eliminated the prohibition on stockpiling. The Interpace Concrete Pipe Company would, therefore, be able to obtain and store crushed stone from Atlantic Cement.[22]

This was not the Town Board's last word, however. At a meeting of the Board the following September, Supervisor Pape reported that town engineers were working with experts from the State Health Department to prepare a new air pollution control ordinance. At a Board meeting in October an attorney for the State Air Pollution

Control Board recommended that the town enact a general ordinance providing "that no person shall permit particles to be emitted into the outside atmosphere that would be harmful to personal health or property."[23] The Air Pollution Control Board had a similar regulation, but it could be enforced only after a hearing before the State Commissioner of Health. Supervisor Pape wanted a town ordinance that could be enforced in the Albany County Court. State methods of pollution control are slow and awkward and the maximum penalty under state law was only an initial fine of $1000 for each violation and $200 for each additional day. At the Town Board meeting Oscar Boomer said, "A fine of $200 a day would be just a drop in the bucket . . . . They would be happy to keep on operating and emitting dust for $200."[24]

Noise and dust were not the only impacts of the cement plant on the environment. Odor was also a problem, but not from the manufacturing process. Bituminous coal was stockpiled for firing the cement kilns. Normally the stored coal was used and replenished about every two weeks. When a railroad strike was expected in the summer of 1963, Atlantic Cement stocked up in advance with a several-month supply of coal. Unfortunately, when bituminous coal is stored in a damp condition for an extended period it may combust spontaneously. After almost six months in storage the coal deep within the stockpile caught fire. The smouldering coal produced offensive odors, especially when the weather was stable and the smoke was not dispersed. Opening the pile would only feed more oxygen to the fire and aggravate the problem, so water spraying and compacting the coal pile with bulldozers was begun.[25] The problem was not completely solved, however, for the fires could only be suppressed temporarily.

In mid-1970 Atlantic Cement gave in to complaints about smoke and odors caused by the smouldering coal stockpiles and converted the firing of its kilns from coal to oil. The operation had required 300,000 tons of coal per year, which were brought in by rail. The furnaces would now burn 1,200,000 barrels of oil, about 50 million gallons. The oil would come by ship and be stored in large tanks on the Hudson shore. The Hudson River Valley Commission became involved at this time and asked that landscaping be provided to minimize the disfigurement of the river bank. The company agreed to paint the tanks and reforest the entire sixty acres around the plant facilities.[26]

REFERENCES

1. Article dated September 3, 1961 in the Capital District Newspaper Files.
2. Article dated February 18, 1962 in the Capital District Newspaper Files.
3. Article dated June 14, 1962, CDN files.
4. *Ibid.*
5. Article dated June 18, 1961, CDN files.
6. Article dated March 18, 1961, CDN files.
7. Articles dated March 15, 1961 and January 16, 1963, CDN files.
8. Article dated July 22, 1963, CDN files.
9. Letter dated June 14, 1973 from the Atlantic Cement Company.
10. Articles dated August 1 and August 10, 1963, CDN files.
11. Articles dated December 16, 1963 and March 17, 1964, CDN files.
12. Articles dated August 21, 1964, CDN files.
13. Articles dated July 22, 1964, CDN files.
14. *Ibid.*
15. Article dated October 6, 1964, CDN files.
16. Article dated September 19, 1965, CDN files.
17. Article dated December 22, 1964, CDN files.
18. Article dated January 6, 1971, CDN files.
19. Article dated January 21, 1969, CDN files.
20. Article dated January 22, 1969, CDN files.
21. *Ibid.*
22. Article dated January 31, 1969, CDN files.
23. Article dated October 3, 1969, CDN files.
24. *Ibid.*
25. Letter dated December 3, 1963 from L. U. Spellman, Manager, Technical Services and Distribution, Atlantic Cement, in Department of Environmental Conservation files.
26. Articles dated June 28 and July 23, 1970, CDN files.

Chapter 8

DAMAGE SUITS FOR AIR POLLUTION

At an August 1964 meeting of the Coeymans Town Board attorney Edward Uthe, who had been retained by the Board, reported that there were no local laws that could be invoked to control dust and noise caused by Atlantic Cement. He believed that the dust problem should be dealt with as a civil issue between the complaining residents and the company.[1] However, it was not until May 1967 that eight property owners brought suit for an injunction to stop the plant from producing damaging fallout of cement dust and other property damage caused by quarrying. These were the plaintiffs:

Oscar H. Boomer — auto parts, used cars, junk yard
Avie Kinley — farm and home
Kenneth R. Livengood — home
Charles J. Meilak — home and garage
James McCall — home
Floyd W. Millious — home
Theodore J. Richard — restaurant
Joseph L. Ventura — home

Robert Albright filed a separate suit, although he had his home and garage on the same stretch of Route 9-W as the plaintiffs in the other case.

THE TRIAL AND APPEALS

The trial was held in the Albany County Courthouse with Acting Supreme Court Justice R. Waldron Herzberg presiding. At the non-jury trial expert witnesses for the plaintiffs contended that their homes were coated with cement dust and that their business operations could not continue. In addition to the injunction, which if granted would shut down the cement plant, the plaintiffs also sought temporary damages covering losses they claimed to have incurred from the time the plant began operating in September 1962 until the time of the trial in June 1967.[2] Atlantic Cement spokesmen testified that operations were carried out to minimize disturbance to the environment. A seismograph was used to measure earth movements during blasting in the quarry. Limestone stockpiles were sprayed with water in the summer and with calcium chloride in winter to keep the dust down.[3] It has already been noted that most of the cement dust produced in the kilns was collected and recycled.

After a 30-day trial, Justice Herzberg in August 1967 denied the injunction against the quarrying and cement manufacturing activities on the grounds that more than $40 million had been invested in the plant, that the company paid large amounts of taxes to the Town and School Board, and that it had "installed at great expense the most efficient devices available to prevent the discharge of dust and polluted air into the atmosphere." Justice Herzberg did find, however, that Atlantic Cement operations constituted a nuisance. He awarded temporary damages based on the loss of rental value or loss of usable value per month resulting from the dust and blasting as follows:[4]

Oscar H. Boomer	$ 50.00
Avie Kinley	150.00
Kenneth R. Livengood	40.00
Charles Meilak	50.00
James McCall	40.00
Floyd Millious	40.00
Theodore J. Richard	125.00
Joseph Ventura	40.00

Permanent damages were based on the drop in market value of the properties between 1962 and 1967 caused by the nuisances.[5]

	Reasonable Market Value 9/1/1962	*Reasonable Market Value 6/1/1967*	*Permanent Damage*
Boomer	25,000	12,500	12,500
Richard			
Property	30,000	12,000	18,000
Business	40,000	16,000	24,000
Kinley	140,000	70,000	70,000
Livengood	18,000	7,000	11,000
Millious	20,000	8,000	12,000
Ventura	25,000	12,500	12,500
McCall	22,000	11,000	11,000
Meilak	26,000	12,000	14,000
		Total	$185,000

In making his decision, Justice Herzberg reasoned as follows: The dust and blasting deprived the plaintiffs of the reasonable use of their properties and the enjoyment of life and liberty on them. However, equity forbids the granting of an injunction. On balance it would produce great public hardship because of "the defendant's immense investment in the Hudson River Valley, its contribution to the Capital District's economy and its immediate help to the education of children in the Town of Coeymans through the payment of substantial sums in school and property taxes."[6]

If the plaintiffs and the defendant agreed to accept the permanent damages within thirty days, Atlantic Cement would be required to pay the stipulated amounts, with costs. However, neither the plaintiffs nor any successor in title to their properties could bring any further action against the company. Justice Herzberg also limited his decision to the specific complaints raised by the plaintiffs, leaving the door open for future public or private action. He wrote, "This decision in no way makes any findings in respect to the conduct of Atlantic in the operation of its plant between September 1, 1962 and June 1, 1967, except in so far as the plaintiffs herein are concerned. Further, I make no findings in respect to the operation by Atlantic of its plant subsequent to June 1, 1967."[7]

The parties to the trial did not agree to the permanent damage awards, so the case was appealed to the State Supreme Court, Appellate Division. In November 1968, fifteen months after Justice Herzberg's trial court decision, the Appellate Division affirmed his findings. Justice Aulisi, in his opinion for the five-man court, recognized the evidence that the plant had, in fact, created a nuisance to the plaintiff's properties. Nevertheless, the trial court had "carefully considered, weighed, and evaluated the relative equities, relative hardship and interests of the parties to this dispute and the public at large. Reexamining the record, we note the zoning of the area, the large number of persons employed by the defendant, its extensive business operations and substantial investment in plant and equipment, its uses of the most modern and efficient devices to prevent offensive emissions and discharges, and its payment of substantial sums of real property and school taxes. After giving due consideration to all of these relative factors, the trial court struck the balance in defendants' favor and we find no reason to disturb that determination."[8]

The parties failed to agree again after the Appellate Division affirmation of Justice Herzberg's decision. The case therefore went to the Court of Appeals, the highest in the state. The earlier decisions were reversed by a conditional injunction against Atlantic Cement. The injunction could be lifted after payment of permanent damages, the amounts to be reconsidered by the Supreme Court. The Court of Appeals accepted the trial court's finding of a nuisance and granted the injunction on that ground alone.

Justice Francis Bergan, in his opinion for the court majority, recognized the growing public concern with air pollution, but he noted that this case involved private litigation between the individual property owners and a single plant. He wrote, "The threshold question . . . is whether the court should resolve the litigation between the parties now before it as equitably as seems possible; or whether, seeking promotion of the general public welfare, it should channel private litigation into broad public objectives."[9] The court is primarily concerned with deciding the rights of parties before it. Judicial power should, therefore, not normally be used "in private litigation as a purposeful mechanism to achieve direct public objectives."[10] The trial court had denied the plaintiff's suit for an injunction, although it found that there is a nuisance and that property owners have been damaged substantially, on the ground that the economic consequences of forcing the plant to close far outweigh the value of the damages to plaintiffs. The Court of Appeals overturned the trial court decision on this vital point. Justice Bergan wrote of the trial court's decision:

> This theory cannot . . . be sustained without overruling a doctrine which has been consistently reaffirmed in several leading cases in this court and which has never been disavowed here, namely that where a nuisance has been found and where there has been any substantial damage by the party complaining an injunction will be granted. The rule in New York has been that such a nuisance will be enjoined although marked disparity be shown in economic consequence between the effect of the injunction and the effect of the nuisance."[11]

The Court of Appeals here affirmed its adherence to the precedent long established that the small property owner's rights would not be limited because his opponent at law was a large corporation with a multimillion dollar investment.

SERVITUDE ON THE LAND

Although the Court of Appeals reversed the trial court's and Appellate Division's departure from a settled rule of law, it wanted to avoid the drastic remedy of closing down the plant at once. Two alternatives were considered. One would be to postpone the effect of the injunction, say for 18 months, to give the company an opportunity to develop techniques that would eliminate the nuisance. The other alternative would be to grant the injunction, but to lift it on payment by Atlantic Cement of permanent damages to the property owners that would compensate them for their total present and future economic loss caused by the cement plant operations. The second alternative was the one chosen by the Court of Appeals.

The court rejected the first alternative because it felt that the problem of effective control of air pollution was far from solution. It would require research in great depth, carefully balanced consideration of the economic impact of strict regulation, and proof of its actual effect on public health. If the effect of the injunction were postponed for 18 months, there would be no assurance that Atlantic Cement could solve the technical problems of abating the pollution. The company could apply to the Supreme Court for extensions of time on the showing of good faith efforts to perform technical research. "For obvious reasons the rate of research is beyond control of defendant. If at the end of 18 months the whole industry has not found a technical solution a court would be hard put to close down this one cement plant if due regard be given to equitable principles."[12]

Choosing the second alternative, granting the injunction unless the company paid the property owners permanent damages as fixed by the courts, would presumably be a just solution because all of the plaintiff's economic losses would have been redressed. Furthermore, "it seems reasonable to think that the risk of being required to pay permanent damages to injured property owners by cement plant owners would itself be a reasonable effective spur to research for improved techniques to minimize nuisance."[13] Justice Bergan was also careful to point out that granting permanent damages to the plaintiffs without at the same time requiring that the plant air pollution be abated did not mean that the pollution would continue indefinitely. This decision did not "foreclose public health or other public agencies from seeking proper relief in a proper court."[14] The

State Department of Public Health and later the Department of Environmental Conservation were, in fact, holding hearings and putting pressure on Atlantic Cement to reduce the cement dust emissions from the plant.

Justice Bergan based the decision to grant permanent damages on the theory of "servitude on the land" of the property owners imposed by the cement plant's nuisance. "This should be placed beyond debate by a provision of the judgement that the payment by defendant and the acceptance by plaintiffs of permanent damages found by the court shall be in compensation for a servitude on the land."[15] This would preclude future recovery by plaintiffs or their grantees.

Servitude is defined in Ballantine's Law Dictionary as "the term of the civil law for easement. The right of the owner of one parcel of land, by reason of his ownership, to use the land of another for a special purpose of his own." New York Jurisprudence amplifies this definition by noting that, "the most important characteristic of an easement is that its burdens fall upon the possessor of the servient land regardless of his identity or the circumstances under which it was created or under which the servient owner entered into possession."[16] The "special purpose of his own" would presumably apply to the future right of Atlantic Cement to use the neighboring properties as a depository for cement dust emissions. By the imposition of a servitude, these properties must bear that burden forever, regardless of who owns them. No future owner can have a clear title, because some of the rights in those lands belong to the owners of the Atlantic Cement property. The servitude was imposed on the properties by the Court of Appeals, which in fact condemned those particular rights of the eight neighbors. Atlantic Cement did not want these rights, but the court required the company to accept them and pay for them anyway. The important legal point here is that the condemnation was for a private use by Atlantic Cement, not for a public purpose, which is the justification for the taking of private land.

Applying the "servitude on the land" theory in this case established a legal precedent. It amounted to condemnation by a manufacturing firm of certain rights to private property. The usual application of this legal theory had been to cases where a railroad or public utility caused some damage to private property, but these were uses imbued with the public interest. In this case, Atlantic Cement had involuntarily acquired under court order a permanent "easement" or right to pollute the private properties in question.

The Court of Appeals decision was not unanimous, for Justice Matthew Jasen wrote an opinion that partially dissented from the majority. Justice Jasen agreed that the lower court decisions should be reversed by granting an injunction that would require the plant dust pollution to be abated. What he objected to was "the newly enunciated doctrine of assessment of permanent damages" to remove the injunction. "It has long been the rule in this State, as the majority acknowledges, that a nuisance which results in substantial continuing damage to neighbors must be enjoined. To now change the rule to permit the cement company to continue polluting the air indefinitely upon the payment of permanent damages is, in my opinion, compounding the magnitude of a very serious problem in our State and Nation today."[17]

Citing the State Air Pollution Control Act and evidence that particulate contamination, especially by suspended particulates fine enough to remain in the air for a long time, is hazardous to health, Justice Jasen felt that the cement plant emissions were not only damaging to the plaintiffs' property, but also harmful to the general public. In permitting the injunction to become inoperative upon the payment of permanent damages, the majority is, in effect, licensing a continuing wrong. It is the same as saying to the cement company, you may continue to do harm to your neighbors as long as you pay a fee for it. Furthermore, once such permanent damages are assessed and paid, the incentive to alleviate the wrong would be eliminated, thereby continuing air pollution of an area without abatement.[18]

There is some disagreement with these points in the minority opinion. At a public meeting held at the RCS Junior-Senior High School in April 1969 Dr. John A. Lyons, Albany County Health Commissioner, referred to studies on the effect of breathing cement dust. He was reported to have said, speaking as a physician, "There is no evidence that it produces silicosis or tuberculosis. I know you won't believe this, but we have the evidence."[19] Silicosis is caused by inhaling silicon dioxide, which is present in stone, sand or flint dust. An article in the *Albany Law Review* on this case also notes that there is no evidence that cement dust is hazardous to health. Thomas H. Quinn, Director of Environmental Health Services in the Albany County Health Department, told the author of the article that cement dust particles are large in size and readily filtered out before reaching the lungs. An article was also cited, written by Gardner *et al.* in a 1939 issue of the *Journal of Industrial Hygiene and Toxicology*, which reported on a study of workers in cement plants scattered throughout the country. It was found that finished cement dust contains practically no free silica, which could cause lung damage; and the incidence of tuberculosis and other chronic infections of the lungs was less among the cement workers than in the general population.[20]

With regard to Justice Jasen's second point, it has already been noted that the majority opinion does not simply sanction the indefinite pollution of the air around the cement plant on the payment of permanent damages to the property owners. Justice Bergen had written that the decision did not foreclose action by public health or other governmental agencies to enforce pollution abatement under New York State law. This point was echoed by Alexander Rihm, Jr., director of the air pollution control program of the State Environmental Conservation Department, at a September 1970 workshop sponsored by the New York State Assembly Standing Committee on Conservation. Rihm pointed out that the Court of Appeals decision "did not interfere with the right of government agencies to further control pollution from this source [Atlantic Cement] . . . The public interest is still there . . . . If there was a license to pollute forever, we would not be initiating another action against Atlantic, which we are."[21]

A legal objection to the majority opinion was also raised by Justice Jasen. The "servitude on the land" theory had been used in earlier cases where an injunction against a nuisance was denied and permanent money damages awarded instead, where continuation of the use producing the nuisance was primarily for the *public* benefit. Justice Jasen wrote:

> . . . it is clearly established that the cement company is creating a continuing air pollution nuisance primarily for its own private interest with no public benefit . . . . Inverse condemnation should only be permitted when the public is primarily served in the taking or impairment of property. The promotion of the interests of the polluting cement company has, in my opinion, no public use or benefit. Nor is it constitutionally permissible to impose servitude on land, without consent of the owner, by payment of permanent damages where the continuing impairment of the land is for private use.[22]

In Justice Jasen's view, the only way the injunction should be lifted against Atlantic Cement is by the abatement of the nuisance by the company within 18 months. He was aware that the trial court had found that dust control devices had been installed in the plant, but he wrote, "I submit this does not mean that better and more effective dust control devices could not be developed within the time allowed to abate the pollution."[23] This is similar to the point of view expressed by the federal Environmental Protection Agency about auto emissions. The automobile manufacturers were given a specific deadline to perfect and install emission control devices in 1975 cars. This is somewhat like insisting that Atlantic Cement perfect the technology of cement plant dust control in 18 months. Nevertheless, as Justice Bergan pointed out, the rate of accomplishment of research objectives is beyond the control of any one company, and Atlantic Cement would be justified in petitioning the court for extensions of time on the basis of its good faith in actually conducting research. This is what the automobile companies have done and may succeed in getting their deadline pushed back.

No mention was made in the minority opinion of damages to be paid the property owners. Presumably, if the "servitude on the land" doctrine was not to apply, the plaintiffs would not receive permanent damages—only temporary damages to the time the pollution would be abated. They would, therefore, have to endure the dust pollution nuisance for perhaps another 18 months, or longer if the company could have the deadline extended, and would receive less compensation for damages. Under the majority decision, the plaintiffs would receive full compensation and still retain ownership of their properties. At the same time, public agency efforts to abate the pollution would continue. It therefore appears that the court imposed on Atlantic Cement the double penalty of paying extensive damages to private property owners and also making the capital investments required by law to finally abate the dust pollution. At the same time the property owners received the double benefit of substantial awards for damages and the prospect of recovering the full market value of their properties when the pollution was, in fact, abated by the company under pressure from the Department of Environmental Conservation.

It has already been noted in Chapter 4 that pollution control policy focuses on the trade-off of avoiding injury to human, plant or animal life against the economic advantages to a community of having a source of tax income and local employment. The trial court found that Atlantic Cement did produce pollution, but that on balance the economic benefits to the Town of Coeymans and the large investment made by the company outweighed the nuisance to a few neighboring property owners. The interests of these property owners were not ignored, however, for they were compensated for damages and loss of market value.

Nevertheless, there was considerable dismay in some legal circles at the decision not to curtail pollution, but rather to award damages to property owners. State Attorney General Louis Lefkowitz declared that the Court of Appeals Decision was "a license to pollute," for although it offered monetary relief to the residents in the area, there was to be no protection against further pollution.[24] The *Albany Law Review* called the decision "regrettable."

> Contributions made by industry to their communities, such as providing employment and paying taxes, are not readily ignored. But results such as *Boomer* may perpetuate environmental pollution to the detriment of future generations. It has been remarked that many polluters "have adopted the callous attitude that it is cheaper to pay claims than to control pollution.[25]

The Boomer v. Atlantic Cement decision cannot be defended if it is unconstitutional, but it should not be assumed that it represents a victory of big business over the small property owner. Industrial firms are now open to damage suits from any property owner who thinks he can collect. It is possible that attorneys are already using this decision to drum up business by encouraging property owners in the vicinity of industrial plants to sue.[26] The only defense a firm would have, if in fact pollution control technology to stop residuals emissions altogether is not available, is to buy up in the open market all the property within an indefinite distance from the plant.

FINAL PROPERTY SETTLEMENTS

After the trial in the Albany Supreme Court, Justice Herzberg had awarded the eight Boomer case litigants a total of $185,000 in permanent damages. Ownership of the properties would remain with the plaintiffs, however. The Court of Appeals sustained the trial court finding of a public nuisance caused by cement dust pollution, but it asked the Albany Supreme Court to reexamine the damage awards. As the consequence of these negotiations, Atlantic Cement finally purchased seven of these properties; Avie Kinley was awarded a large damage settlement, but he retained ownership of the farm and buildings.

The final settlements were as follows:

Boomer — auto parts and junkyard	$185,000
Richard — Coach House restaurant	70,000
Kinley — farm and buildings (damage award only)	175,000
Meilak — garage and home	87,000
McCall — home	30,000
Ventura — home	39,000
Livengood — home	28,000
Millious — home	31,750
Total	$645,750

Albright had filed a separate suit for damages to his garage and home. The suit was settled out of court when Atlantic Cement purchased the property for $70,000.[27]

It is interesting to note that the plaintiffs in these cases claimed they could not comfortably live in their homes or carry on their businesses because of the cement dust fallout. Yet after the suits were finally settled, the properties were, with one exception, still being put to their original uses. The Coach House Restaurant has been leased by Atlantic Cement to the PUB Restaurant. Meilak has leased back from the company the property he formerly owned and continues to use it for his business and residence. The Boomer junkyard has been leased to the Matlock Trucking company. All of the homes acquired by Atlantic Cement, including Albright's, are rented to company employees as residences. Kinley still owns and operates his farm after receiving $175,000 in damages, but Atlantic Cement has appealed this award.[28]

Five additional residences were purchased by Atlantic Cement to round out its own property boundaries or for quarrying operations. These purchases were:

Swilkes	$ 15,000
Ferguson	62,000
Kelly	18,000
Schoonmaker	45,000
Butn	17,000
Total	$157,000

Altogether, Atlantic Cement has had to spend $872,750 for property acquisition and damages since it began operations.[29]

REFERENCES

1. Article dated August 6, 1964, Capital District Newspapers files.
2. Article dated May 25, 1967, Capital District Newspapers files.
3. Article dated June 6, 1967, Capital District Newspapers files.
4. *Boomer v. Atlantic Cement Co.,* 55 Misc. 2d 1023, 287 N.Y.S. 2d 112 at p. 115.
5. *Ibid.*
6. *Ibid.*, p. 114.
7. *Ibid.*, p. 116.
8. *Boomer et al. v. Atlantic Cement,* 30 App. Div. 2d 480, 294 N.Y.S. 2d 452 at p. 453.
9. *Boomer et al. v. Atlantic Cement,* 26 N.Y. 2d 219, 309 N.Y.S. 2d 312, at p. 314.
10. *Ibid.*
11. *Ibid.*, p. 315.
12. *Ibid.*, p. 317.
13. *Ibid.*
14. *Ibid.*
15. *Ibid.*, p. 319.
16. *New York Jurisprudence,* V. 17, p. 252.
17. *Boomer et al. v. Atlantic Cement,* 309 N.Y.S. 2d 312 at p. 320.
18. *Ibid.*, p. 321.
19. Article dated April 18, 1969, Capital District Newspapers files.
20. M.M.N., "Environmental Control—Judicial Grant of Easement to Pollute—An Unwelcome Precedent for New York Environmental Law," *Albany Law Review,* 35 (1970), p. 154.
21. Article dated September 4, 1970, Capital District Newspapers files.
22. *Boomer et al. v. Atlantic Cement,* 309 N.Y.S. 2d 213 at p. 321.
23. *Ibid.*, p. 322.
24. Article dated September 4, 1970, *Albany Times Union,* p. 14.
25. M.M.N., "Environmental Control—", *op. cit.*, p. 152.
26. Interview with field staff of the N.Y. State Environmental Conservation Department.
27. Letter dated June 14, 1973 from the Atlantic Cement Company.
28. *Ibid.*
29. *Ibid.*

Chapter 9

THE STATE AND THE COMPANY: EMISSION CONTROL NEGOTIATIONS

Although the Atlantic Cement Company had intended to create a pollution-free operation, neither the company nor the residents of Ravena and Coeymans were prepared for the plant's actual impact on the environment. At a public meeting in the RCS Junior-Senior High School, Donald M. Halstead, then President of the company, pointed out that the latest technologies for controlling dust were included in the original plant design. About $3.1 million, almost 10 per cent of the total capital outlay for the plant, had been invested in pollution control systems.[1] The Mayor of Ravena testified at a later hearing on the pollution problem at Atlantic Cement that he and other Town and Village officials had gone to Canada to visit the plant of the St. Lawrence Cement Company, which was managed by the founders of Atlantic. The local officials were impressed by what they saw. "We were told that we would see the cleanest cement plant in this part of the country," the Mayor said, and he was proud that he had been instrumental in the selection of Ravena for the site of the new plant.[2]

New York State agencies were also anxious to see the plant established. It has already been noted that the Department of Commerce provided information and industrial location assistance. It is also important to note that the State Department of Health, as well as other agencies, reviewed the plans for the cement plant and gave them the official stamp of approval. Several other cement plants were located in the Hudson Valley, so the Health Department personnel should have been guided in their plan reviews by years of prior experience with such operations.

Plans for the cement plant included a great variety of pollution control devices adapted to the various operations in the production process. The equipment and the original installation costs make up a long list:

Primary crusher	$ 54,500
Spray systems, scrubber dust collectors, Johnson-Marsh pumps	
Secondary crusher	70,500
Spray system, four bag house dust collectors	
Raw mills	15,000
Two scrubber dust collectors	
Finish mills	144,000
Three dust suspension systems, six cyclone dust collectors, three water spray systems	
Raw materials silo and feeders	14,788
Two bag house dust collectors	
Finish silos and feeders	12,300
Three cyclone dust collectors	
Kilns	
Electrostatic precipitators	2,000,000
Dust control spray system	13,700
Dust leaching system	554,000
Clinker cooler	102,000
Cyclone dust collectors and dust traps	
Buffer silos	45,500
Six bag house dust collectors	
Customer silos	66,700
Thirteen bag house dust collectors	
Packhouse	19,000
Two bag house collectors	
Dock and conveyor belt	42,700
Four bag house collectors	
TOTAL	$3,154,688

For years after the plant began operations, including the period during which the company was fighting damage suits by neighboring property owners and dealing with pollution control demands by the Department of Environmental Conservation, Atlantic Cement spent $5.3 million more on additions and improvements to its pollution control facilities. This was over $2 million more than the cost of the original equipment. These are the items:

Primary crusher	20,000
New Johnson-Marsh system, 1969	
Raw mills	30,600
Replaced scrubber with bag houses, 1966	
Finish silos and feeders	
Bag houses replaced cyclones, 1966	73,000
New dust suspension system, 1967	17,840
Clinker cooler	1,700,000
Bag houses replaced cyclones, 1969	
Kilns	
Conversion from coal to oil, 1969	1,107,000
Oil storage facilities and lines, 1970	1,900,000
Road paving to reduce fugitive dust	301,000
Precipitator improvements	134,000
TOTAL	$5,283,440

Perhaps it was the unprecedented scale of the new plant and the complexities of its operation and management that accounted for the unexpected environmental problems. The dust collection systems in the plant itself were apparently not as efficient as expected. Furthermore, noise and dust were not anticipated from blasting and drilling operations at the quarry as well as from conveying and stockpiling the crushed stone for use by the plant.

The Atlantic Cement experience points to the need for careful environmental impact studies before large development projects are approved and built. Federal government agencies are required by the National Environmental Policy Act of 1969 to prepare such studies for proposed public works. The state of California enacted an Environmental Quality Act in 1970, but this one required environmental impact studies for private projects also. Such studies must be prepared if the proposed development involves building permits, zoning changes or subdivision maps. The act was upheld by the California Supreme Court.[3] Careful environmental analyses could prepare both industry and community for the consequences of new plants. They would then be in a good position to realistically assess the environmental costs as well as the economic benefits of the proposed operation.

DEFINING THE PROBLEM

As far back as 1963, a year after Atlantic Cement started up its cement production, Dr. Norbert P. Ringleman, then Commissioner of the Albany County Department of Health, responded to complaints from area residents. He asked the State Air Pollution Control Board to order an investigation. Following procedures in force at that time the investigation was carried out for the Board by the Department of Labor's Division of Industrial Hygiene, Air Pollution Unit. A report indicating that there was indeed an air pollution problem at the Atlantic Cement plant was forwarded to the County Health Department. Nevertheless, years of negotiations had to pass after this official finding before the Commissioner of Health and the Commissioner of Environmental Conservation issued Orders in 1968 and 1972 requiring the company to abate the pollution to meet the standards set by the New York State Rules and Regulations.

The report of a field inspection made by the State Health Department in November 1966, again in response to one of the long series of complaints, summarized the air pollution sources and the existing equipment available to control them:[4]

The Quarry

The large boulders loosened from the bedrock by blasting are reduced to smaller-sized stones by the primary crusher. There is a manually operated spray at the dumping area where the rock is piled before crushing. A Johnson Marsh spray system also operates at the primary crusher and the conveyor belt that carries the crushed stone through the tunnel from the quarry, across Route 9-W, and to the stockpile at the plant. The conveyor terminates in the "T-bar," a tall structure from which the stone pours on to the conical stockpile. If the crushed stone is not sprayed properly at the primary crusher, it emits clouds of dust as it rides the conveyor and then falls on the stockpile.

Raw Mills

These are gyrating drum mills that grind the limestone and other raw materials with water into a consistency fine enough to form the proper slurry for feeding to the kilns. Before the limestone is fed to the raw mills it goes through secondary and tertiary crushers. The finely crushed stone, shale, and iron ore are stored in silos before being fed to the mills. As the grinding in the raw mills is a wet process, there are no dust emissions. The feeder, conveyor and elevator, however, are vented through scrubbers that exhaust through the mill building.

Kiln Building

Dust from the kilns is collected by electrostatic precipitators. For certain types of cement all of the dust may be returned to the kilns by either of two processes. Pugging is a wet process and returns the dust to the slurry end of the kilns. Insufflation is a dry process whereby the dust is blown into the firing end of the kilns. If the dust is too alkaline, it must be taken by truck from the precipitators to the dust dump. Should the precipitators go out of service for any reason while the kilns are still operating, considerable amounts of dust pour out of the main stack.

Clinker Coolers

The clinker formed from the kiln process is dropped into the clinker coolers and then stockpiled in the great open clinker storage hall. The coolers are vented through stacks preceded by multiclones (multiple cyclones) that collect the dust by gravity.

Finish Mills

From storage the clinker is ground in dry mills to the proper fineness for finished Portland cement. The elevator, mill separator, and collecting conveyor are vented through a cyclone and bag house.

Dust Dump

Great amounts of dust are collected from the main kiln precipitators and the various cyclones and bag houses at the coolers, mills, silos and other installations. The dust is disposed of at a dump east of the plant, but sometimes returned to the air in the process of transporting, dumping and spreading at the disposal area.

The result of this comprehensive investigation of the cement manufacturing process was the simple finding that the company was in violation of Rule 176.1 of the Compilation of Rules and Regulations. This rule requires that

> Any person planning to . . . make modifications to an existing installation which will or might reasonably be expected to

> increase the amount or change the effects or the characteristics of the air contaminants discharged, or planning to install an air cleaning device shall submit a report and/or plans and specifications to the commissioner for approval prior to initiation of construction.*

The basis for this allegation by the investigators was that the company had not submitted plans for the system for returning dust to the kilns by pugging or for the loading, hauling or dumping of dust at the disposal area. The company also apparently failed to file plans for improving its grinding mills, which would increase production. The State Health Department report does not mention air pollution.

The report was prepared in November 1966. At a conference during January 1967 representatives of Atlantic Cement agreed to comply with Part 176.1 by filing the plans. But in a letter the following June the State Department of Health had to warn the company that if the plans were not received by the Division of Industrial Hygiene by July 7, 1967 the matter would be referred to the Office of Counsel for legal action. The deadline was extended however to September 10, 1967.[5] In connection with the operations cited in the investigator's report, the technical director of Atlantic Cement noted that about 5,000 tons of kiln waste dust were dumped on company property every month. Plans included the installation of a sprinkler system to keep the dust down while the dump was being worked. The area would eventually be covered with soil like a sanitary fill.[6]

By March 1968 the Environmental Analysis Report submitted by Atlantic Cement had received an engineering review in the State Health Department. The review noted that no tests had been made on the main kiln stack when both kilns were in operation. A Certificate to Operate would be given if particulate level in the stack gas was acceptable for a "B" rating. Nevertheless the plant was operating and the kilns were obviously being fired even without the Certificate to Operate.

The review also noted that there were excessive emissions from the two clinker coolers. This condition would be corrected by the installation of new bag houses at the cooler exhausts. Plans had already been approved and Permits to Construct were to be issued. It was noted, however, that the open clinker storage hall might also be a source of air contamination.[7]

---

* 10 NYCRR 176 at 176.1 (See Appendix A).

DEVELOPING A STATE STRATEGY

In March 1968 Atlantic Cement was again inspected by engineers from the State and County Health Departments. This time they were looking for air pollution and found that eight items of dust control equipment were not operated to comply with state health standards. Here was evidence collected by health engineers rather than by complaining laymen. Now, perhaps, was the time to formulate an enforcement strategy aimed at inducing Atlantic to comply with the state air pollution rules.

This was a difficult problem for the state officials. It is not possible to document how they perceived the problem at that time, but one may imagine some of their concerns. It was well known that state agencies and local officials had promoted the location of Atlantic Cement in Coeymans. The State Health Department had approved the plans for the plant and its pollution control systems. After the plant had been in operation for some time new air pollution rules were incorporated into the New York State Rules and Regulations. These were still untried in practice and had not yet been tested in the courts. The elements of an enforcement strategy, therefore, entailed selection of the particular rules whose violation would be charged, the collection of evidence to substantiate the charges, and the choice between pressing for a public hearing or avoiding legal proceedings in favor of continued informal negotiations.

The First Commissioner's Order: Dust Control of Materials Handling

After considering the March 1968 survey by the state and county engineers, the Department of Health attorneys decided that action to correct the polluting emissions, under a Commissioner's Order, would be more effective than legal proceedings to close the plant by injunction.[8] In contrast to the strategy pursued by Boomer and the other plaintiffs in the nuisance and damage suit who sought a court injunction to close the plant, the State Department of Health chose to follow administrative procedures.

The first step in this state strategy was to issue a Notice of Hearing and Complaint signed by Dr. Hollis Ingraham, Commissioner of Health. This was dated May 27, 1968, and the hearing was called for June 24, 1968. There were two charges in the complaint. One was that Atlantic Cement had violated Section 179.2 of Part 179 of the New

York State Rules, on specific dates, by failing to maintain and operate its air pollution control equipment in a satisfactory manner. The other charge was violation of Section 186.1 of Part 186 of the Rules which contained a general prohibition against causing air pollution.*

The Notice of Hearing was directed mainly at the complaints by Albright and neighboring residents on Route 9-W, who were then concerned about dust coming from the conveyor between the quarry and the limestone stockpiles, from the stockpiles themselves, and from the dust dump and other sources of fugitive dust around the plant. Complaints about dust from the main kiln stack by residents who lived further away from the plant were not the focus of attention in this Notice.

The hearing originally scheduled for June 24 was postponed four times and never did take place. In a Stipulation dated September 3, 1968 Atlantic Cement acknowledged that there were sufficient grounds for the issuance of a Commissioner's Order; the company waived rights to a hearing and accepted the terms and conditions of the Order.**

The Order, signed by Commissioner Ingraham on September 4, 1968, ratified and confirmed the Stipulation. According to the terms of the Order, the company must use the Johnson Marsh spray equipment during the operation of the primary crusher at the quarry, the conveyor to the stockpiles, and related materials handling equipment. If at any time this dust control equipment does not operate properly, crushing and stone handling operations must be shut down. The Johnson Marsh system would be monitored by the Albany County Health Department. If the equipment was found incapable of meeting Air Pollution Control Board standards for dust control, then Atlantic Cement would be expected to install additional air cleaning devices.

The Continuing Pollution Problem

Complaints continued to come from residents of Ravena and the area within a mile or two of the cement plant alleging damages to their homes and cars. Replies to these complaints could now cite the Commissioner's Order and the monitoring of the plant by the County

* See Appendix A for the text of Parts 179 and 186 and Appendix C for the Commissioner's Notice of Hearing and Complaint.

** See Appendix C.

Health Department. Nevertheless, the Order referred only to the spray equipment that controlled dust in the immediate environs of the plant. The Health Department assurances to the complainants were not really addressed to the cause of their problems, the emissions from the main kiln stack. Some of the residents in the area pointed this out to a newspaper reporter. They said the Commissioner's Order was too limited because it did not deal with the major dust problem of emissions from the main stack and the clinker cooler stacks.[9]

During this same period state and county health agencies issued a report on an extensive study of air pollution in Albany, Schenectady and Rensselaer Counties. The report showed that process emissions from cement and stone industries accounted for about half of the 2,400 tons of particulates falling on Albany County each year. A newspaper comment on this report also noted Ravena residents found that the dust coming from Atlantic Cement had not noticeably abated since the Commissioner's Order, because it did not cover two of the main sources of pollution, the plant stacks and the dust dump.[10]

In December of 1968, three months after issuance of the Commissioner's Order on the operation of the Johnson Marsh spray equipment, the Albany Regional Office of the State Health Department noted in a memorandum to the Division of Air Resources in the central office that in dealing with the public in response to complaints, and informing them about state action, it is first necessary to arrive at a clear-cut definition of the problem. This would help to determine which rules apply and should be enforced. Three alternatives were suggested:

Part 179, Section 179.2. This section refers to efficient maintenance and operation of existing air cleaning systems. Applying it to the kiln stack emissions would require more information about the operation of the electrostatic precipitators.

Part 187. This is the same rule that applied to the emissions from the Allegheny Ludlum steel plant. The rule concerns contaminant emissions from manufacturing processes and exhaust and ventilating systems. Atlantic Cement was apparently in compliance with Part 187 according to its Environmental Analysis Report. The results of the kiln stack emission tests had not been transmitted to the state, however. Additional stack tests might be needed to define proper maintenance of the electrostatic precipitators under Section 179.2 and to determine compliance with Section 187.3, which specifies permissible emission rates.

Part 186. This was the general prohibition against air pollution that could be applied to the problem of fugitive dust from the open storage piles caused by wind turbulence. Violations under this rule are difficult to prove and enforce, however, and the legal ramifications of applying this rule should be investigated.[11]

During the following month, January 1969, a series of meetings and memoranda covered aspects of the state's developing strategy. One meeting that included personnel from the central and regional offices of the State Health Department and the County Health Department reviewed the sources of dust at the cement plant and the status of abatement action.

Dust Dump. Plans for a new dust dump, haul road, and sprinkler system had been submitted and reviewed. A Permit to Construct had already been issued. Future action on dust from dumping could be taken under Part 179, Section 179.3, which dealt with the efficient disposal of material collected from dust control equipment.

Clinker Storage. Action on this and other sources of fugitive dust should be deferred until procedures could be developed to apply Part 186 effectively.

Clinker Cooler. Atlantic Cement had already agreed to replace the inefficient multiclones on the cooler stacks by new bag house installations. Plans and specifications had already been received and were under review.

Kiln Stack. The Environmental Analysis Report required by Part 187 had already been submitted by the company, and it reflected its own stack test for particulate emissions. Additional stack tests would be required, however, and the State Health Department would begin to carry out stack tests beginning in March 1969. Kiln stack emissions would have to comply with the abatement schedule of Part 187 and meet the January 1, 1967 deadline for cleaning up existing sources of particulates.[12]

An "immediate action plan" was suggested against the dust dump. A joint inspection by county, regional and central office staff was scheduled for the end of the month. If voluntary compliance with Section 179.3 could not be obtained, evidence gathered by the inspection would be used to document a request for a formal administrative hearing. An "intermediate action plan" was also suggested against the other sources of fugitive dust, including the open clinker storage piles. Action under Part 186 would be necessary as there were no other rules to apply against such sources. Evidence would be gathered on these dust sources for a possible second administrative hearing.[13]

The chief of environmental engineers at the County Health Department disagreed with this strategy. He thought the attack on the air pollution problem at Atlantic Cement should not be fragmented by attempting to hold different hearings on different alleged violations. He noted the distinction between the localized dust problem from the dust dump, clinker storage piles, and clinker cooler building that affected residents in the immediate vicinity of the plant and emissions from the main kiln stack that brought valid complaints from Ravena and residents who lived as far as 2-½ miles from the plant. Although the company was preparing plans for a new dust dump and cooler bag houses, no measures were contemplated to deal with dust from the storage piles. The kiln stack was emitting dust because the precipitators were probably not operating at maximum efficiency at all times as the result of maintenance and repair problems.[14]

As the consequence of this discussion of strategy alternatives the State Department of Health wrote to the president of Atlantic Cement about the long series of complaints that had been received since 1962. Complaints had been confirmed by investigations, but cooperation by the company had resulted in the elimination of some dust sources. There were continuing problems with the kiln stack and clinker storage, however. The Health Department therefore wrote, "In keeping with our policy of attempting to first secure voluntary compliance with our rules and regulations before initiating legal action, we would like to meet with you to discuss the solution of the control of these two sources."[15]

Officials of the Department and the company met in March 1969. The company representatives noted that plans and specifications had already been submitted for a new dust dump and new clinker cooler bag houses. These facilities should be completed during the following summer. In spite of these assurances, dust problems continued to plague Atlantic Cement, the residents around the plant, and the state agencies. Construction of the bag houses for the clinker coolers was delayed by late delivery of structural steel and other problems. The company made several requests for time extensions of the scheduled completion date. Finally, in July 1970, a year late, the two bag houses went on line. They were inspected and stack tests were conducted on the cooler stacks. Inspection and test reports indicated compliance with Part 187.[16] Evidently one element in the complex dust control problem at Atlantic Cement had been solved.

The Problem of the Kilns

Dust from the kiln stack was the result of unavoidable shut-off of the electrostatic precipitators before and after kiln shutdowns for equipment repair and maintenance. The temperature in the kilns must be high enough (350°F) to exceed the dew point of the gas stream, which would eliminate vapor condensation and cementing of the precipitator electrodes. Another reason for the minimum kiln temperature was to eliminate combustible gases that could be exploded by sparking in the precipitators. The kiln shutdown and start-up cycles each required 24 hours, and uncontrolled dust emissions had to occur during that part of the cycles when the temperature in the kilns was too low. The company therefore agreed to make available records of kiln and precipitator shutdowns.[17]

Plant records showed that during 1969 the two kilns had to be shut down 27 times. On each such occasion there were periods of uncontrolled dust emission from the stack both before and after shutdown. During 1970 one or the other kiln was shut down 34 times.[18] A regional office analysis of kiln operating data showed that from January 1969 through August 1971 one or the other kiln had been shut down 240 times. This was close to an average of eight shutdowns per month.[19] These were the periods when residents and businesses some distance north and south of the plants received heavy dustfalls from the stack. The company no doubt regretted this more than the people who were troubled by the dust, for each time a kiln is shut down, thousands of pounds of cement production are lost. Production losses and repair costs may mount up to several thousand dollars per hour of shutdown.

Stack dust increases pollution of the ambient air. A follow-up report on air quality completed in April 1971 came to these conclusions: (1) settleable particulates were grossly exceeding standards for ambient air; (2) standards for suspended particulates were also being exceeded in the Ravena-Coeymans area; (3) the Atlantic Cement Company is a significant contributor to the degradation of air quality in the area.[20] Kiln dust was therefore contributing to violation of Parts 186, 501 and 504 pertaining to the ambient air.

At about this time the state was also conducting stack tests on the kiln stack. These tests were made to verify compliance with Parts 187 and 195. Part 195 contained an interim standard for older cement plants that could not meet the higher standards in Part 187 by its January 1, 1971 deadline. Cement plants in this category were to improve their emission controls according to a time schedule set by the Commissioner, but had to meet Part 187 standards no later than January 1, 1981.* It was alleged in one memorandum that a stack test showed an emission rate of 1,000 pounds per hour, which greatly exceeded the limits of Parts 187 and 195. Stack tests conducted in the fall of 1970 showed particulate emission rates of 396 lb/hr as compared to the limit of 375 lb/hr prescribed by Part 195. These were complete tests conducted while the plant was operating under normal conditions.[21] If the electrostatic precipitators were not operating efficiently enough to meet the standard of Part 195, the higher standards of Part 187 were certainly being exceeded.

Meanwhile, preparations were being made for particulate emission tests on the main kiln stack. There was some question about tests that had already been made by the company. New stack tests were requested by the County Health Department. The level of emissions with both kilns operating should be low enough for a "B" rating under the standards in Part 187. A test was performed in August 1969 while engineers from the County and State Health Departments were present. Dust emission was found to be 36.1 pounds per hour or 0.0161 pounds of dust per 1,000 pounds of gas at 829,000 cubic feet per minute passing through the stack at a temperature of 428°F. This rate of emission was well within the compliance limits set by Part 187.[22] Nevertheless the central office of the Health Department was not satisfied with the company's stack test. After months of trying to obtain data about the test, the Department decided to run its own test in August 1970, a year after the previous one.[23] The status of emissions from the main stack was therefore uncertain as the company and the new Environmental Conservation Department headed for the showdown hearing that would be scheduled for December of that year.

---

* See Appendix A.

Completion of the new dust dump was also delayed for many months after the plans were approved. It was to have been ready in June 1969, but manpower and equipment shortages caused delays in completing the haul road and the sprinkler system. The Health Department approved several time extensions, but the dump continued to be a serious source of dust. One Sunday in September Assistant Commissioner Rihm was driving on the thruway and saw a huge cloud of dust coming from the plant at ground level. He was later informed that it came from the dump, for which pollution abatement was behind schedule.[24] More than a year after the new dump was to have been available for use the state began collecting evidence to include violation of Part 179, Section 179.3, as one of the items in its formal complaint.

Other factors also contributed during 1969 and 1970 to the decision of the Department of Environmental Conservation to call Atlantic Cement to a public hearing. The predecessor Health Department had completed in March 1969 an ambient air study in the Town of Coeymans. It had placed high-volume air samplers at strategic locations in the town. The materials collected on the filters indicated that Atlantic Cement was a significant contributor to the contravention of state Ambient Air Quality Standards.

> Settleable particulate results . . . . indicate that dustfall in the Ravena-Coeymans area must be reduced by two-thirds to attain Ambient Air Quality Standards. Similarly, dustfall reductions of more than 90% will be required adjacent to Atlantic Cement . . . to comply with the Standard.[25]

This report appeared to reinforce the spate of new complaints about dust that arrived at about this time from residents near the plant, from trailer courts some distance away, and from an auto dealer in Ravena who had to keep washing his new cars with acetic acid. One of the complaints came from Robert Albright that the conveyor from the quarry was emitting dust. A county health engineer inspected the equipment and found that this was indeed the case. A spray nozzle on the Johnson Marsh system at the primary crusher was clogged, and the condition improved after the nozzle was cleaned.[26] This was in September 1969. In March and June 1970 Albright was back with more complaints about dust from the conveyor and limestone stockpile on which it deposited the crushed stone from the quarry. After the June complaint another engineer from the regional office went out to investigate. Again the Johnson Marsh equipment was not working, but crushed stone continued to be transported in contravention of the Commissioner's Order of 1968.[27]

This inspection by an engineer was the first technical evidence of violation of the Order. Allegations from complaining laymen were not considered acceptable by the regional office as legal documentation for such a charge.[28] This seems odd, because almost three years earlier Justice Herzberg had found that Atlantic Cement was causing an air pollution nuisance on the basis of evidence presented by eight plaintiffs, who were all laymen. In any case it was in June 1970 that steps were being taken to document violation of the 1968 Order concerning the transporting and stockpiling of crushed stone and also the possible violation of Part 179, Section 179.3 relating to operation of the waste dust dump.[29] When this documentation was combined with what appeared to be adequate evidence that ambient air standards were also being contravened, the information was sent to the Office of Counsel for the preparation of a formal Notice of Hearing and Complaint to be served on Atlantic Cement.

THE LONG HEARING

Years of investigating complaints, testing the ambient air and dust emission sources, negotiating with the company, and testing enforcement strategy finally led the newly-created Department of Environmental Conservation to serve Atlantic Cement with a Notice of Hearing and Complaint in November 1970. The complaint alleged that the Commissioner's Order of September 1968, which required the continuous operation of the Johnson Marsh spray equipment whenever the primary crusher, conveyor from the quarry, and related materials handling equipment were in operation, had been violated on specific dates during 1969 and 1970. Alleged violation of Part 179, Section 179.3 referred to the fugitive dust resulting from improper disposal of contaminants collected from air clearing devices—the electrostatic precipitators, bag houses, and cyclones—and failure to provide a satisfactory dust dump. Part 186 was alleged to have been violated by frequent shutdown of air cleaning devices, especially the kiln stack precipitators, causing pollution of the atmosphere with cement dust, injuring property, and interfering with the comfortable enjoyment of life and property at the homes of named residents of Pantages Mobile Home Park near Selkirk, among others. Parts 501 and 504 contain ambient air standards for settleable particulates for the Coeymans area. The complaint cited specific air sampling locations and the excessive amounts of dust collected there during particular months in 1969 and 1970.

In addition to citing these specific complaints the Notice convened a public hearing for December 1, 1970. The hearing would follow courtroom procedures—all witnesses would testify under oath, witnesses could be subpoenaed and cross-examined, and the proceedings would be recorded. If the Hearing Officer found violation of the Commissioner's Order, it would be punishable by a civil penalty up to $1,000 and $200 for each day of violation.*

The first substantive session of the hearing was held on December 18, 1970. Dr. Emmanuel Bund, Professor of Law at Columbia University, was the Hearing Officer, Nicholas Silletti represented the Department of Environmental Conservation, and Thomas F. Tracy represented Atlantic Cement. The hearing dragged on for a year and a half. Sometimes a month or more would pass between sessions. The record contains what appears to be inconclusive testimony and cross examinations of expert witnesses and residents in the area. The attorneys wrangled about procedural points, and there appeared to be deliberate legal maneuvers to drag out the hearing—either to wear down the company or to wear out the Department of Environmental Conservation before it could actually prove a single violation.

Witnesses against Atlantic Cement included Robert Albright, who had already brought suit for damages, and residents in trailer courts and private homes in the vicinity of Selkirk. They all repeated familiar complaints about cement dust falling on homes, autos, outdoor furnishings and swimming pools, and even sifting into the houses. When the dust was moistened by dew it hardened into cement and was difficult or impossible to remove completely. The attorney for the company apparently tried to impugn the credibility of witnesses and make it appear they did not know what they saw in the way of pollution coming from the plant or when they saw it.[30]

At a session held in Ravena, witnesses testified in favor of the company. They were all women who said there was not much of a dust problem. One lived only 500 feet from Boomer's Garage, but noticed no cement dust at all, not even from the main kiln stack. The others, who lived in Ravena, said they were not troubled by dust in-

* See Appendix A for Parts 501, 504, 179, 186. Appendix C contains the Notice.

side or outside their homes. One elderly woman said pollution had been much worse when the railroad with steam locomotives had active facilities in Ravena and a local cider mill fouled the air with black smoke and odors. She pointed out that with the passing of these activities Ravena and Coeymans fell on hard times. Not until Atlantic Cement was established did jobs and commercial prosperity return to the area.[31] This testimony paralleled the action of a group of over 40 women who organized to improve the image of Atlantic Cement and the Town of Coeymans. Many of their husbands worked at the plant. They were grateful to the company for bringing prosperity back to the area, and they said they did not experience any dust problem.[32]

Engineers from Environmental Conservation testified about their inspections of the plant and the clouds of dust they saw on those occasions from the crushed stone stockpiles and the dust dump. One of these technically qualified witnesses was asked by the Atlantic Cement attorney about what measures the Department was taking to abate pollution at other cement plants in the Hudson Valley. The witness said that the primary abatement goal in those cases was compliance with the emission standards in Part 187, which applied specifically to particulates coming from exhaust and ventilating systems on industrial processes, and Part 195, which governed emissions from cement plants. These actions did not include alleged violations of Part 186, which concerns nuisance and the comfortable enjoyment of life and property.[33]

This testimony points to odd legal and administrative contradictions. The plaintiffs in the Boomer *et al.* suit had no problem proving nuisance and property damage in the State Supreme Court. Yet a newspaper reporter who had followed the hearing and other events connected with Atlantic Cement wrote, "Observers of the long hearing had noted from time to time that legal evidence to prove air violations . . . was weak."[34] Another reporter noted that some Environmental Conservation officials admitted they could not prove the air pollution case against Atlantic Cement.

> To prove its charges of violating a 1968 Commissioner's Order and state air rules, ECD officials said they would have had to show that Atlantic exceeded ambient air (average) quality standards by collecting weekly dust measurements in the plant's vicinity for a solid year and computing the annual

> dustfall average. Instead, they note, the state proceeded under a "nuisance rule" which applies only "where no other specific rule is applicable." And they offered test results from dust samples taken sporadically over the last two years . . . . The year-long sampling wasn't done, ECD officials say, because of a "lack of manpower."[35]

In spite of the tactical problems involved in proceeding against Atlantic Cement under the nuisance provisions of Part 186, Environmental Conservation chose to pursue an "ambient air" strategy rather than following up on previous successful experience with cement pollution abatement under the "stack emission control strategy" written into Parts 187 and 195. The Department witness who brought up this point testified that Marquette, Lehigh, and a third cement plant in the Cementon-Alsen area, which had been found in violation of emission standards Part 187 and Part 195, had already submitted plans for updating their emission control systems.[36]

The technical difficulties of proving ambient air violations were illustrated by the testimony of other expert witnesses.

> Edward Davis, Jr., an air pollution engineer with ECD Division of Air Resources, testified that . . . dustfall near the cement plant was one of the five heaviest concentrations in the state . . . . He added that specific studies within the Town of Coeymans showed concentrations far in excess of ambient air standards . . . . Mr. Davis conceded under questioning by Mr. Tracy, however, that "no one source" could contribute all the dust found in testing jars.
>
> Sanitary Engineer Gary Neighmond testified that higher values of suspended particulates were found in samples taken south of the cement plant. Although he said the company's exact dust contribution could not be determined without further testing, he termed it a "significant portion."
>
> Barbara Kladatos, senior chemist at Griffen Laboratory . . . said the presence of calcium did not specifically prove that the dust was from a cement plant but that it was "supporting evidence."[37]

In attempting to identify dust in air samples analyzed by Barbara Kladatos, Environmental Conservation Department Senior Research Scientist Dr. William D. Balgord performed X-ray diffraction tests. These tests could show that not only was calcium present, but that the dust contained Portland cement in specific proportions. Three dust samples were tested, two from the Oscar Boomer property and one from the Pantages Motor Court. One sample from the Boomer property contained about 40–50 per cent cement, while the other one showed only 5 per cent cement. The Pantages sample contained only 5–10 per cent cement.[38]

The Atlantic Cement attorney could cast doubt even on this evidence. The State Geological Survey had also performed X-ray diffraction tests on the same samples and found cement in only one of them. Dr. Balgord could only surmise that this finding was the result of deterioration of the samples or the age and inferiority of the Geological Survey equipment.[39] Mr. Tracy asked Dr. Balgord if he knew who had collected the samples. When? What happened to the samples after they were collected? How long had the dust been present in those locations before collection. Dr. Balgord had to admit that dust could have been there for as long as 8–10 years, even before the cement plant began operations.[40] After persistent questioning, Dr. Balgord even admitted confusion about the sites where the samples were taken.[41]

At a hearing session in November 1971, almost a year after the Notice was first issued to Atlantic Cement, Mr. Tracy informed the Hearing Officer that attorneys and engineers working for the company and the Department had discussed ways of bringing the hearings to an early conclusion. A consent agreement had been drafted acceptable to both parties, but at a subsequent meeting Deputy Commissioner Biggane had substituted a different draft consent order that was not acceptable to the company. Tracy said, "Our door is open and will remain open to discuss this problem in the hopes of arriving at something that will be satisfactory to the state . . . and satisfactory and economically feasible to my client."[42]

Environmental Conservation decided not to enter that open door, however, so the hearings dragged on for another six months. At the session of December 2, 1971 the first anniversary of the hearing was celebrated with a birthday cake. In January Tracy indicated he would need 25 more days of hearings. At the rate of one session per month, the pace of past meetings, the hearings could go on for another two years.[43] By the following May only the State had presented its case. Atlantic Cement could have taken many more months to present its side. Nevertheless, by this time both sides had had enough and finally worked out a consent agreement. The company had not been proved guilty of any violations, nor had any penalties been assigned to it.

The Commissioner's Order of Consent was dated May 11, 1972. Under it, Atlantic Cement agreed not to use its old dust dump and to operate the new one according to terms and conditions set by a Certificate to Operate. Bag house collectors and precipitators were to be in operation at maximum efficiency whenever the production facilities were in operation. On kiln start-up, the precipitators must be turned on within 30 minutes after feed is introduced. If dust collectors become inoperative, the production level of the kilns and clinker coolers would be reduced so that emission levels would be no higher than those under full efficiency. If this standard could not be met, the kilns and coolers would be shut down. The company must regulate emissions from the plant so as to conform to the ambient air quality standards adopted for Albany County and prevent fugitive dust from leaving the boundaries of the Atlantic Cement property.

A noteworthy provision of the Order required the company to modify or repair its facilities to control dust emissions so as to conform with the environmental ratings assigned under Part 187 of the air pollution control rules. The original Notice of Hearing and Complaint never alleged violation of this rule. Environmental Conservation, therefore, had to finally incorporate the "stack emission control" strategy along with its original "ambient air" strategy to assure dust abatement from the kiln and clinker cooler stacks. In order to pursue both strategies, Atlantic Cement was required to perform at its own expense for one year stack tests on the kiln stack to demonstrate compliance with Part 187 and an ambient air quality study to demonstrate control at the materials handling facilities and dust dump as well as other sources of fugitive dust. If by May 1, 1973 such dust control could not be demonstrated, the company would have to either install additional control equipment or modify its production process. The schedule was later extended: (1) On July 15, 1973 the results of the ambient air study would be submitted to the Department; (2) By August 1, 1973 the company would submit satisfactory abatement schedules for all sources not meeting air pollution control rules; (3) By October 1, 1974, all work required by the abatement schedule for compliance with ambient air standards would be completed.

REFERENCES

1. Article dated April 18, 1969, Capital District Newspapers files.
2. Transcript of hearing on February 15, 1972, p. 1022.
3. September 21, 1972 in the case of Friends of Mammoth vs. Board of Supervisors of Mono County.
4. Report dated November 22, 1966 by Lauber, Better, and Goranson.
5. Letters June 3, 1967 and July 13, 1967, Department of Environmental Conservation files.
6. Letter dated November 7, 1967, DEC files.
7. Memorandum dated March 7, 1968 in DEC files.
8. Article dated March 8, 1969 in CDN files.
9. Article dated September 6, 1968 in CDN files.
10. Article dated October 3, 1968 in CDN files.
11. Memorandum dated December 23, 1968 in DEC files.
12. Memorandum dated January 10, 1969 in DEC files.
13. Memorandum dated January 28, 1969 in DEC files.
14. Memorandum dated February 5, 1969 in DEC files.
15. Letter dated February 18, 1969 in DEC files.
16. File Report dated August 1970 and Memorandum dated August 27, 1971 in DEC files.
17. Memorandum dated March 10, 1969 in DEC files.
18. Letter dated December 4, 1970 in DEC files.
19. Memorandum dated September 14, 1971 in DEC files.
20. Atlantic Cement Environment Study II, Report of Findings January 1971-March 1971, Report No. BAQS-29, April 1971.
21. Stack Test Report on Atlantic Cement, March 1971 and Memorandum dated February 17, 1971 in DEC files.
22. Letter dated August 7, 1969 and Memorandum dated August 24, 1969 in DEC files.
23. Memorandum dated June 30, 1970 in DEC files.
24. Memoranda dated October 3 and 8, 1969 in DEC files.
25. Atlantic Cement Company Environmental Study, Coeymans, New York, N.Y. State Department of Health, Division of Air Resources, Report No. BAQS-9, March 1, 1969, p. 5.
26. Memorandum October 2, 1969 in DEC files.
27. Memorandum June 5, 1970 in DEC files.
28. Memorandum dated June 17, 1970 in DEC files.
29. Form AIR 109 dated June 22, 1970, Memorandum of same date, File Report dated August 19, 1970.
30. Record of the Hearing for December 18, 1970; March 8, 1971; March 23, 1971; April 20, 1971.
31. Record of the Hearing for February 15, 1972.

32. Article dated July 6, 1970 in Capital District Newspaper files.
33. Record of Hearing for September 15, 1971.
34. Elle Pankin in article dated May 24, 1972 in CDN files.
35. Peg Breen in article dated May 24, 1972 in CDN files.
36. Testimony by Jack D. Lauber, Record of Hearing for September 15, 1971.
37. Peg Breen in article dated July 9, 1971 in the CDN files.
38. Record of Hearing for January 5, 1972.
39. Article dated January 26, 1972 in CDN files.
40. *Ibid.*
41. Record of the Hearing for February 10, 1972.
42. Record of Hearing for November 4, 1971.
43. Memorandum dated January 17, 1972 in DEC files.

Chapter 10

THE ROLE OF THE ATTORNEY GENERAL IN AIR POLLUTION CONTROL

The regulation-enforcement strategy for air pollution control relies on two legal remedies: injunction and damages. The legal foundation for these remedies is the common law of nuisance, state statutes, and the rules and regulations issued by authority of the statutes. Three legal routes, or tactical approaches, are available by which to pursue this strategy.

One tactical route is available to citizens and property owners directly affected by a source of pollutant emissions. This is the route that Boomer *et al.* took against Atlantic Cement. They filed suit in the Supreme Court at Albany for injunction to stop the emission of dust from the plant and disturbances from the quarry as well as personal compensation for damage to their properties. They had no difficulty in proving nuisance in court; but on payment of damages, the injunction against the company would be lifted. In this case the law of nuisance was successfully invoked to obtain damages, but not to abate the pollution. It has already been noted that by the court-ordered payment of damages, Atlantic Cement involuntarily purchased the "right" to pollute the properties of the plaintiffs forever.

The two other routes to pollution control are through state action against the polluter. One of these is followed by the Department of Environmental Conservation. In response to citizen complaints and on its own initiative, the Department gathers evidence that might confirm violation of state air pollution rules. It then tries to negotiate an abatement schedule with the alleged polluter. If it fails to do this within what might be considered a reasonable time, it may summon the company to a public hearing. This is what happened with both Allegheny Ludlum and Atlantic Cement. In the first instance, the steel company decided to avoid the hearing and negotiated abatement of the "rusty air" problem without the issuance of a Commissioner's Order. Atlantic Cement, however, was issued a Commissioner's Order in 1968 to stop dust from the primary crusher, conveyor belt from the quarry, and the limestone stockpiles. On subsequent alleged violation of this Order and of specific state air pollution rules, the company was summoned to another hearing that lasted a year and a half. It has already been noted that the Department of Environmental Conservation had difficulty in proving the existence of nuisance to property around the plant and finally negotiated a Consent Order.

The third tactical route to air pollution abatement is through the Office of the Attorney General. This route is open to both complaining citizens and the Department of Environmental Conservation. The Department may call on the Attorney General's Office to prosecute an alleged polluter who failed to comply with a Commissioner's Order. In such cases, the Attorney General acts as counsel for the Department in seeking both injunction and penalties in court. On finding evidence of violation of the 1968 Order of the Commissioner of Health to abate pollution at the quarry, conveyor, and limestone stockpiles, the Commissioner of the Department of Environmental Conservation could have requested the Attorney General to take Atlantic Cement to court. Instead the Department chose to combine this violation in a complaint with other alleged violations against particular air pollution rules. The Department, therefore, summoned the company to a new public hearing rather than asking the Attorney General to cause the company to be summoned into court. The result of this choice was the long inconclusive hearing. Had the Commissioner turned to the Attorney General, however, he might have achieved the same quick legal success as a group of Cohoes citizens who complained about pollution from a different cement company, Universal Atlas Cement, a subsidiary of United States Steel.

Atlas Cement did not actually manufacture cement in Cohoes. It produced a light weight aggregate for concrete called Norlite. The aggregate is produced from a particular kind of shale obtained at a quarry about 600 feet from the processing plant. The shale beds are fragmented by drilling and blasting into rocks suitable in size for transporting to the plant by truck. Here the large chunks of shale are crushed, conveyed to a rotary kiln and heated. The shale is expanded by heating similar to the way in which popcorn is made from the original corn grains. The expanded shale is cooled and conveyed to a storage pile, whence it is again conveyed to the final crusher. The resulting Norlite aggregate is then screened to various sizes and stored, partly in silos and partly in outdoor stockpiles. From storage, the aggregate is conveyed to hoppers for loading into railroad cars or trucks for shipment.[1]

The blasting operations produce noise, vibration, and dust; and the processing operations also produce dust emissions, primarily from the primary crusher and the kiln. Loading, conveying, and stockpiling are also sources of dust. Residents near the quarry and plant experienced nuisances similar to those complained of by Atlantic Cement's neighbors. Fine stone dust settled on autos, homes and outdoor furnishings. It also sifted into the houses and caused perpetual housecleaning problems. Some residents also complained about the noise caused by blasting and claimed that houses were damaged by the vibration.[2]

In response to these complaints to the Attorney General's Office, a formal Complaint and Summons to the State Supreme Court at Albany were issued November 11, 1971. Only five months later, on April 21, 1972, Justice Edward S. Conway handed down a judgement ordering the parent United States Steel Corporation to adhere to a fixed schedule for the installation of dust emission control equipment. Should subsequent quarrying, materials handling and processing operations create a public nuisance, the firm was ordered to immediately eliminate the noise, vibration and dust emissions or to suspend operations. Thus in a few months the state, acting through the Attorney General in behalf of complaining citizens, obtained the kind of abatement schedule and injunctive relief that had taken Boomer *et al.* and the Departments of Health and Environmental Conservation many years to obtain through the other tactical routes of private court action and public hearings.

The complaining citizens, however, did not receive compensation for alleged damages to their homes and other property. These were demanded in a private suit in Albany Supreme Court. In July 1971, several months before the Attorney General's action, 25 residents of the Maplewood section of Cohoes brought suit against Universal Atlas Cement for $2 million in damages. One million dollars was asked for damages to homes and garages caused by blasting and for fright and nervous shock to the residents. The other $1 million was sought for damages caused by dust as nuisance and health hazard to the homeowners. One of the plaintiffs, John Bilinski, told a news reporter the suit was brought "when we realized a precedent had been set down the river," referring to the successful suit of Boomer *et al.* against Atlantic Cement.[3]

THE STATE OF NEW YORK V. UNITED STATES STEEL CORPORATION

Legal procedures against United States Steel, parent company of Universal Atlas Cement, by the Attorney General's Office began with the November 11, 1971 Summons and Complaint. Attorneys in the Water and Air Resources Bureau of the Attorney General's Office prepared the documentation. The plaintiff under this procedure was the State of New York. The complaining citizens were not parties to the action, for the state as a "body politic and sovereign entity" brought the action

> . . . on its own behalf and, as *parens patriae*, trustee, guardian and representative, on behalf of all residents and citizens of the State of New York, particularly those residents and citizens who reside in and about the City of Cohoes and the Town of Colonie, County of Albany, in and near the most southerly portion of the City of Cohoes.

The Attorney General acts as the lawyer for the State, which is the plaintiff.

There is no statutory basis for this kind of action. It rests rather on the common law of nuisance. The common law powers of the Attorney General were pursued "to require defendant to cease and abate conduct which constitutes a public nuisance."[4] The action was brought, therefore, for

> an injunction to restrain defendant from conducting operations at its plant, quarry and related facilities . . . unless and until it has installed such devices and instituted such practices as will prevent such operations from causing a public nuisance and which will be sufficient to enable defendant to comply with Part 187 of the New York State Air Pollution Control Rules and all applicable local, State, and Federal law.[5]

The Summons is a one-page document that simply required the

defendant corporation to deliver to the Attorney General within 20 days an answer to the Complaint, a separate longer document that specified the allegations against the corporation. The Complaint seeking the injunction set forth three causes of action: First, the dust and grit emitted from the defendant's quarry, plant and related facilities settled on the persons and property of nearby residents, thereby creating a public nuisance. Second, the defendant's blasting operations at the quarry caused considerable noise and vibrations adversely affecting a considerable number of nearby residents, thereby also creating a public nuisance. Third, the defendant's blasting operations, noise and dust, which created a public nuisance, were due to defendant's negligence, carelessness and failure to take necessary remedial measures.[6]

In reply to the Complaint by the Attorney General, attorneys for United States Steel filed a Verified Answer denying all of the charges. They did admit, however, that devices and procedures were available to prevent or control dust and grit emissions as well as noise and vibrations from blasting. The defending attorneys also declared that the corporation had entered into an agreement with the Albany County Health Department on an abatement schedule, which would be completed before July 1, 1972.[7]

The Attorney General's Office took the answer into account and prepared documentation to support a motion in the Albany Supreme Court for a summary judgement. This is a formal motion that the judge issue a judgement in the case in favor of the plaintiff without going to trial. If he agreed to this motion, the judge would issue an injunction against the nuisances, specify the abatement actions to be taken, and order the schedule to be followed, all without lengthy trial or public hearings.

Testimony for the State would be in the form of written affidavits. The judge could decide whether or not Universal Atlas Cement was creating a public nuisance on the basis of this evidence alone. A sheaf of affidavits was able to accomplish in three months what the Department of Environmental Conservation's hearing, with its multitude of technical and citizen witnesses, was unable to do in a year and a half, namely, prove the existence of a nuisance caused by air pollution and other environmental disturbances from an industrial operation.

By this procedure, the Attorney General served on the defense attorneys a Notice of Motion for Summary Judgement for Plaintiff dated January 20, 1972. The Notice declared that on the basis of accompanying affidavits he would move the Supreme Court on January 28 for summary judgement in favor of the State against United States Steel on the grounds that the defendant "has no meritorious defense to this action and that upon the evidentiary facts set forth in the annexed affidavits, as a matter of law, there are no triable issues of fact . . ."[8]

The affidavit of Olin Harper LeCompte, Assistant Attorney General acting in the case, summarized the earlier proceedings and the testimony in the other affidavits. Thirty-six residents in the area of the quarry and plant in their affidavits

> . . . state unequivocally that they have seen the dust and grit emitted from the various operations of the defendant . . . . Their affidavits show that such dust and grit is so pervasive that it finds its way into their eyes, mouths, and throats and that it invades their homes even through closed windows and doors . . . . Damage to property, increased labor and expense in property maintenance and the unreasonableness of the interference with comfortable enjoyment of life and property is eloquently set forth in the annexed affidavits.[9]

Statements were also made by these residents about the noise and vibration caused by blasting in the quarry. Nevertheless, the defense attorneys opposed the motion for summary judgement, mostly on the ground that the affidavits "include conclusions and opinions which the affiants are not competent to make." For example:

> In the affidavit of John G. Wells, he states that his wife has an asthmatic condition which is aggravated by the alleged 'dust and grit' . . . . This is clearly a medical matter which the deponent is not competent to determine. Furthermore, there is nothing in his affidavit to show how he concludes that whatever dust and grit comes into his home originates with the defendant's plant. In paragraph 4 of his affidavit he alleges that the green aluminum siding of his house has been turned to gray because of this dust and grit. This again is a field of expertise and cannot be sustained on the naked opinion of this lay person.[10]

Objections in the same vein were made to the written testimony of other residents whose eye-witness accounts and personal experiences were not deemed reliable—in spite of the statement by a physician, Dr. Hans D. Weiss, that

> I can state with reasonable medical certainty that the Saratoga Site Project of the Cohoes Housing Authority, because of the great amount of dust and grit to which its residents are subjected, is not a healthful place for people to live, and it would be especially undesirable for anyone with a pulmonary or respiratory condition to reside there.[11]

Furthermore, the State's motion for a summary judgement was supported by expert written testimoy by Patrick J. Lavin P. E., Senior Public Health Engineer in the Albany County Health Department. Mr. Lavin stated that during his inspections of the plant and quarry he had observed the dust emissions. He also pointed out the devices and procedures that could be installed that would abate the pollution. He also stated:

> For approximately the past two and one half years, I have been communicating with representatives of the United States Steel Corporation with respect to the . . . sources of dust emissions from its Norlite plant and premises and have recommended steps to control such emissions.[12]

This statement by a professional engineer in the Albany County Health Department was the basis for Assistant Attorney General LeCompte's assertion that the defendant was negligent and careless in permitting for years the continuation of nuisances that could have been avoided by available technology and management of operations.[13]

The defense attorneys had stated in their Verified Answer to the original Summons and Complaint that the steel corporation had agreed to an abatement schedule with the Albany County Health Department. This was denied, however, by Alexander B. Grannis, an attorney in the Office of Counsel in the Department of Environmental Conservation. He pointed out that "the only way in which such an abatement or compliance schedule can be established is by an Order of the Commissioner of Environmental Conservation." Furthermore,

> I know from my own knowledge, as well as from a search of the records of this office, that with respect to defendant and air pollution control at its Norlite plant in Albany County, there has been no hearing, there has been no stipulation, there has been no order of the Commissioner . . . and there has been no 'agreement.'[14]

JUDGEMENT

The attorneys for United States Steel filed their own affidavit in opposition to the Attorney General's motion for a summary judgement. The affidavit, filed February 8, 1972, declared that on the previous day the steel company had formally accepted a plan for controlling dust emissions from the plant which was prepared by representatives of the Department of Environmental Conservation and the Albany County Health Department. This was in effect similar to a stipulation to an Environmental Conservation Commissioner's Order.

On the basis of this agreement, arrived at after lengthy negotiation between the parties, Supreme Court Justice Conway handed down a consent judgement which did not accuse the company of violating any laws or assess penalties against it. Nevertheless, the judgement contained detailed and specific measures that would have to be taken at the Norlite plant to abate the nuisances, and it also specified the dates by which these measures had to be accomplished.* For example, Justice Conway

> ORDERED, ADJUDGED AND DECREED, that the defendant shall, on or before the dates hereinafter set forth, complete the following repairs, installations, and changes in operating procedures at its lightweight aggregate plant, related facilities and shale quarry at 628 South Saratoga Street, Cohoes, New York:
>
> a. Repair the raw storage silo roof and install a bagged vent for such silo by April 22, 1972;
> b. Install a roof and bagged vent on the large finished product silo by May 27, 1972;
> c. Install a belt cleaning device and collection hopper on the belt feeding the screens at the finished product silos by April 22, 1972;
> d. Partially enclose the truck loading area by April 22, 1972, in accordance with the understanding reached with representatives of the Albany County Department of Health;
> e. Install a triple telescoping spout at the rail car loading area by April 22, 1972;
> f. Install screw feeders at the ball mill and remove from service the existing blower by June 1, 1972;

* See Appendix F.

g. Adopt procedures, by May 1, 1972, to minimize airborne dust from the stockpiles by adequately dampening the work faces of same;
h. Submit to the New York State Environmental Conservation Department, through the Albany County Department of Health, by April 22, 1972, stack test reports on the cooler stack showing whether there is compliance with Part 187 of the New York Air Pollution Control Rules.[15]

The court's judgement also ordered the defendant to submit plans and specifications for air contaminant control systems at the primary crusher and kiln and to complete installation by July 7, 1972. The company was also required to conduct a detailed inspection and maintenance program for all pollution control devices and to operate blasting at the quarry so as to avoid nuisance caused by noise and vibration.

Furthermore, if the measures prescribed in the judgement do not result in compliance with the requirements of Part 186 or Part 187 of the New York State Air Pollution Control Rules, the defendant company would have to devise and expeditiously carry out a new or modified program that would result in compliance with the rules. If because of accident, malfunction or otherwise, emission control devices fail to perform properly or blasting at the quarry causes noise and vibration, thereby causing a public nuisance, these operations must be suspended until the condition can be corrected.

The documents cited in this account indicate some analogies between the common law nuisance procedures available to the State Attorney General and the administrative procedures followed in the Department of Environmental Conservation. Affidavits by professional and lay persons in the former procedure appear to correspond to testimony at public hearings in the latter. Written agreement between the alleged polluter and the department is similar to a stipulation in the administration procedure. And judgement by the court contains the same kinds of provisions as a Commissioner's Order. The main difference seems to be that the nuisance procedure is much more swift and carries the added legal punch that the alleged polluter is enjoined to suspend operations if he should fail to meet the requirements of the court's judgment and order.

The comparison between the Atlantic Cement hearing and the judgement against U.S. Steel is somewhat unfair to the extent that the cement company hearing was unusually long. It was not at all typical of Department of Environmental Conservation proceedings. There is also no assurance that every public nuisance action by the Attorney General can be successfully terminated as quickly as the U.S. Steel case. The comparison simply demonstrates the alternative legal strategies available to the State in its efforts to reduce air pollution.

REFERENCES

1. Patrick J. Lavin, Affidavit in Support of Plaintiff's Motion for Summary Judgement, January 20, 1972, State of New York v. United States Steel Corp.
2. Affidavits of residents of Cohoes incorporated in Plaintiff's Motion for Summary Judgement.
3. Article dated July 29, 1971 in Capital District Newspapers files.
4. Olin Harper LeCompte, Assistant Attorney General, Affidavit in Support of Plaintiff's Motion for Summary Judgement, The State of New York v. United States Steel Corp., January 20, 1972, p. 1.
5. *Ibid.*
6. Complaint, State of New York v. United States Steel Corp., Supreme Court, County of Albany, November 11, 1971.
7. Verified Answer, DeGraff, Foy, Conway and Holt-Harris, December 15, 1971.
8. Notice of Motion for Summary Judgement for Plaintiff, People of the State of New York v. United States Steel Corporation, Supreme Court, County of Albany, January 20, 1972, pp. 1-2.
9. Affidavit of O. H. LeCompte, pp. 5 and 7.
10. Affidavit of William F. Conway, February 8, 1972, p. 2-3.
11. Affidavit of Olin Harper LeCompte, p. 7.
12. Affidavit of Patrick J. Lavin, January 20, 1972, p. 4.
13. Affidavit of Olin Harper LeCompte, p. 14.
14. Affidavit of Alexander B. Grannis, January 20, 1972, p. 2.
15. Edward S. Conway, Justice, Supreme Court, County of Albany, Judgement, Index No. 3256-72, April 21, 1972, pp. 2-3.

Chapter 11

CONCLUSIONS

Analysis of two cases concerned with control of one kind of comparatively easily-abated air polluting residual, namely settleable particulates from industrial processes, cannot produce much in the way of generalization. Nevertheless, these cases show how one state government is going about meeting its legislated responsibility for dealing with air pollution, and how it is developing a record of successful encounters with pollution sources. The effectiveness of early pollution control endeavors against visible contaminants from industrial plants in New York State stems partly from the multiple tactical routes available for legal action. They were not established by a planned grand strategy for environmental improvement. In fact, they are adaptations of administrative and legal procedures long familiar in governmental practices. These cases demonstrate their continuing viability and efficacy for dealing with the new focus of popular attention on an aspect of the public interest—maintenance and improvement of environmental quality.

The three tactical routes toward air pollution control that were examined in these cases were those pursued by: (1) the State Department of Environmental Conservation and its predecessor in environmental concerns, the State Department of Health; (2) the Office of the State Attorney General; (3) the State Courts—responding to the demands of citizens and property owners for relief from the effects of pollution and for compensation for the damages sustained from it. The successes achieved by these tactics by no means indicate that the problem of air pollution is on the way to rapid solution. Perhaps the problem never will be solved, but after only a relatively short period of aroused public concern there is reason to believe that government will be able to cope with some aspects of the pollution problem.

THE DEPARTMENT OF ENVIRONMENTAL CONSERVATION

Government is mandated to protect and promote the public interest by one of its fundamental powers, the police power. This is the power that legitimates the right of government to act to protect public health, safety, and welfare. The general principle is clear enough, but serious problems arise in making it operational. Implementation of the police power raises the thorny question of how to define the public interest. The most casual observation of the political process demonstrates that there are many publics in American society and many interests, some of them conflicting, especially where pursuit of economic advantage is concerned.

It is the responsibility of legislatures, the courts and administrative agencies to establish the rules and the institutional structure for the interaction of contending interests out of which the general public interest may be identified. Out of this process two kinds of operational powers, under the general police power mandate, have been identified by which public bodies may regulate private activities in the public interest. One is the power to license activities to assure that they conform to standards established directly or indirectly by the legislative process. For example, entrepreneurs who wish to establish industrial plants must obtain approval of their plans by governmental bodies. The location may have to be approved under a zoning ordinance, structural plans must comply with building codes, and industrial processes and equipment may be regulated by public health standards for conditions inside and around the plant. If the responsible public agencies are satisfied that the proposal conforms to established standards, permits to construct and permits to operate may be issued. Before Atlantic Cement could proceed with the construction of its facilities near Ravena it had to obtain the permits required by laws and regulations in force in the early 1960's, including formal approval by the State Health Department of measures for air pollution control.

The other operating power public agencies have is to issue orders directing responsible officers of private organizations to comply with particular laws or rules. The agency may act on the initiative of a complaint from a citizen or property owner or on the basis of the findings of its own technical personnel. After appropriate legal procedures that have to be followed, the agency may order particular persons or industrial firms to cease actions determined to be injurious to public health, safety or welfare. Order-issuing is related to rule-making. With this power, agencies can require all persons or companies in various kinds of enterprises to operate in particular ways so as to meet the standards set forth in the rules.

Rule-making and order-issuing are quasi-legislative and quasi-judicial powers. Rules fill in the details of general legislation, and orders make possible enforcement of the rules. Since these are powerful administrative tools, their use and application in particular cases is subject to review by the courts. Power to make rules and issue orders is vested in the Commissioner of Environmental Conservation by the New York State Environmental Conservation Law.

The quasi-legislative rules that set standards for the ambient air and for industrial plant emissions by which the Department proceeded against Allegheny Ludlum and Atlantic Cement were adopted under the Environmental Conservation Law with the advice and approval of the State Environmental Board after proper notice and public hearings. The quasi-judicial power of the Commissioner to hold hearings, subpoena witnesses, and issue final orders that may require alleged polluters to cease activities that violate rules published in the Official Compilation of Codes, Rules and Regulations of the State of New York, or to adhere to a schedule for pollution abatement action, was also delegated by the state legislature under the Environmental Conservation Law.

THE STATE LEGAL SYSTEM

The state courts provide an alternate recourse against sources of air pollution. This route provides the opportunity for direct action by affected citizens. Air pollution is a form of common law public nuisance. Property owners may bring suit in the State Supreme Court against industrial firms they believe to be interfering with the comfortable enjoyment of life and property. Their objective may be court injunction to order the company to abate the pollution or cease operations. They may also seek monetary compensation for damages to their property.

Boomer *et al.* followed this course successfully against Atlantic Cement, but several years were required for the case to pass through the trial and appeals courts. The Court of Appeals did order that the company be enjoined from continuing its nuisance to the properties concerned, but the injunction was lifted when Atlantic Cement agreed to pay permanent damages to the property owners. Two points about this lawsuit are noteworthy. First, the plaintiffs were able to prove the existence of a damaging nuisance to their properties in fairly short order in the trial court, whereas the Department of Environmental Conservation hearing dragged on for a year and a half without conclusive proof of pollution. Second, the private lawsuit did not result in abatement of the cement dust pollution, for Atlantic Cement obtained a permanent easement to continue polluting these properties.

It is interesting to observe that there are a curious parallel and an odd paradox in the outcomes of the proceedings against Atlantic Cement. In the Boomer case the Court of Appeals reversed the Supreme Court, but the result was the same. The trial court had denied an injunction against the company; the appeals court granted it. Nevertheless, the outcome of both decisions was identical, for on payment of permanent damages, the company could continue to operate and emit cement dust without abatement.

This parallel is matched by the paradox that had the minority opinion prevailed in the Court of Appeals, the outcome would have been similar to the result of the Department of Environmental Conservation's formal hearing. The appeals court minority agreed with the injunction against the public nuisance of cement dust pollution, but would require abatement of the emissions within 18 months as the condition for lifting the injunction. The Commissioner's Order after the long hearing required practically the same condition in exchange for averting accusation of rule violations and imposition of penalties. The Commissioner gave Atlantic Cement a year to measure its own emissions and their effect on the ambient air, and then to devise effective abatement measures.

The majority opinion in the Court of Appeals had assumed that there was no short-term prospect of technological improvements that would stop the dust emissions. Investigation by the state health and environmental conservation engineers indicated, however, that technological limitation was not the obstacle to abatement. Pollution control equipment had been installed in the plant originally. The problem was that the equipment was not operated effectively. The Commissioner's Order, therefore, was really aimed at improving the cement company's management practices. The Johnson Marsh equipment was required to be maintained in good working order; and if it failed, crushed stone handling was to be suspended until repairs were made. The dust dump was to be operated with a sprinkler system when the material was being deposited and spread. The electrostatic precipitators were to be turned on no more than one-half hour after kiln start-up to minimize uncontrolled emissions from the main stack. Again, cement production was to be suspended in the event of equipment failure. Had the Court of Appeals had the same evidence and followed the same line of reasoning as the Department of Environmental Conservation, the "easement to pollute" precedent under the servitude on the land doctrine might never have been set.

The Office of the Attorney General offers another route for citizen access to the state courts. By this procedure the citizens do not sue the alleged polluter directly. Instead, the Attorney General prepares the brief and acts in the name of the people of the State of New York. He also seeks court injunction to abate the pollution nuisance as well as penalties. Penalties are limited by law, however, and the money goes to the state rather than to the complaining citizens. Nevertheless, this is a worthwhile route for citizens to follow for experience in the Universal Atlas Cement case indicates that it produces rapid results. The Attorney General may also act for the Department of Environmental Conservation should he be asked to bring an alleged violator of a Commissioner's Order into court.

Perhaps the most interesting aspect of the multiple-route strategy for air pollution control that is available to the people and government of New York State is that these routes are not mutually exclusive. An alleged industrial polluter may be hit by all three forms of abatement action. Successful suit by Boomer *et al.* did not preclude the Department of Environmental Conservation from seeking to enforce its air pollution control rules; nor did it preclude the Department from asking the Attorney General to take Atlantic Cement to court and seek an injunction and penalties on the ground that it had violated the 1968 Health Commissioner's Order to abate dust emissions in the conveying and stockpiling of crushed stone. Suit by the aggrieved citizens in Cohoes for damages to their properties following the Boomer case precedent did not preclude the Attorney General from asking the Supreme Court to enjoin Universal Atlas Cement and its parent company, United States Steel, from causing dust pollution in the area. And they have, in fact, done just that. It would appear from the availability of this multiple-tactic pollution control strategy and its successful application against Allegheny Ludlum, Atlantic Cement and United States Steel that New York State is about to lick the problem of air pollution. This is obviously not so, however, because of the uncertainties and political factors that must still be reckoned with.

UNCERTAINTIES AND POLITICAL CONSIDERATIONS

Although we observe the effects of air pollution on the environment and know that we have reached the point in the accelerating process of industrialization and urbanization where air may no longer be considered a free good, we are not yet able to measure precisely the quality of the ambient air or establish invariant cause and effect relationships between sources of pollution and their consequences for human health or ecological systems in the environment. We know that it is now necessary to control air pollution and we are developing crude standards and regulations to cope with the problem. This is presently a trial-and-error approach by which governmental bodies assemble the best scientific and technical information available and establish codes of acceptable practice as well as institutions to enforce them. The problem remains of defining what is "acceptable." We know that this cannot be zero emission of residuals, for this requirement would put an end to production and consumption as we know it in economically advanced societies. We are therefore engaged in a process of political moves and countermoves between public agencies responsible for pollution abatement and control and private enterprise. Acceptable trade-offs between pollution control and production are defined in the political arena. When the tensions between these two forces result in strains that become politically unacceptable, we find the equilibrium point for defining the standards that become, for the time being, acceptable pollution levels and control practices. As scientific knowledge, available technology and the array of political forces change, we may expect redefinition of pollution/production trade-off values and standards.

The problem of reconciling environmental quality and economic development goals has been admirably stated by Edward S. Mason:

> The attainment of a sensible trade-off between growth and environmental preservation is currently hampered at every stage by ignorance—by lack of physical and chemical knowledge of the effects of various discharges on atmospheric changes or rates of change in water composition; by ignorance of the biological . . . effects of various types and levels of pollution on human beings, plants, and animals; by

ignorance because of the lack of market tests, of what valuation people put on an improvement or worsening of levels of various types of pollution; and by ignorance of certain economic considerations that could tell us something about how various pollution measures would affect relative prices, outputs, and employment in particular industries and the location of business enterprises. We grope, not in complete darkness, but in a rather dismal sort of gloom. As I have emphasized, reconciliation of diverse energy goals takes place through a political process. But the kind of reconciliation that could emerge in the present state of our ignorance might involve either irreparable damage to the environment or, on the other hand, a sacrifice of growth possibilities to unreasonable and unnecessary environmental precautions. The kind of reconciliation we must aim toward is one arrived at by a political process of decision making based on technical knowledge of what the trade-offs between growth and environmental protection really amount to. It would still be a political reconciliation but one having some hope of being influenced by fact and rational analysis.[1]

POLLUTION CONTROL AS A BARGAINING PROCESS

Legislators, elected executives, administrators and business executives are in positions of power and responsibility for devising institutions and laws to deal with air pollution. They are representatives of contending constituencies whose political interaction determines the balance between public and private interests. The laws and procedures that were formulated in recent years for maintaining and improving the quality of the environment have been fought over in the political arena by men and women with pragmatic objectives of winning their causes or protecting their interests.

Now social theorists have analyzed the recent course of events in the field of environmental management and formulated inductive propositions and models to help explain the observed patterns of behavior. As is usually the case in public affairs, men of action and responsibility rely on their experience and judgment to deal with the problems that confront them. Then the theorists "discover" and articulate the social laws or models of behavior that the protagonists in the field of action presumably followed. The theoretical formulations and hypotheses not only help us to understand what has already happened, but also give us a more sophisticated approach to forecasting the shape of future events. New social theories have not necessarily been developed to explain what is happening in environmental management, for available behavior models may readily be applied to this area.

A rational model for regulatory decision making in pollution control has been suggested by Matthew Holden, Jr.[2] The model contains three premises: (1) the normative premise that there is an identifiable public interest; (2) the empirical premise that the public interest, however it may be defined, is most likely to be advanced and protected by a public agency that has both technical competence and legal authority to deal with the pollution problem; (3) the procedural premise that optimal results can be achieved by dividing the large problem of pollution control into smaller problems (suboptimization), each with relatively clear objectives, and arriving at decisions for dealing with the sub-problems that are consistent with decisions about the whole problem.

The model also contains three operational elements: (1) regulation is effected through prior clearance of private activities, without which they are formally illegitimate; (2) the cleared activities are supervised by the regulatory agency; (3) subsequent inspection determines whether what was done was consistent with the permit, and penalties or remedies are required for serious deviation.

The problem with this model, according to Holden, is that it does not work. There are several possible reasons for this. One is that the regulating officials may be corrupt or incapable of enforcing the rules. Another is that the regulatory agency may be poorly organized and managed. More important, regulation is a political activity; it is concerned with the distribution of advantages and disadvantages. The regulatory agency cannot simply ordain that private enterprises shall conform to established rules and standards. Regulation depends for its effectiveness on the consent of those who are regulated. Regulated interests can lobby against the whole regulatory process, the standards that are proposed and imposed, and the manner and timing of enforcement. Mass violation of the rules can make enforcement difficult, and experience with government regulation of various industries has demonstrated that those who are regulated can capture the regulatory agency.

In view of these constraints on the regulatory process, agencies tend to engage in some kind of bargaining process with the regulated parties until they find a settlement that is mutually tolerable. The bargaining process requires the agency to make three kinds of choices. First, out of all the sources of pollution in the jurisdiction, which ones should be singled out for investigation and enforcement action? This may be called the process of "picking a victim," who may be set as an example for others or whose emissions are so bad the agency can make its findings stick. The second choice is how long to wait before imposing the regulations. The timing of enforcement may be vital to the future effectiveness of the whole program. Delay may be a useful strategy where there are no precedents for action and uncertainties about the reaction to it. The regulators may prefer to wait until some pressure builds up so that they may have some guidance as to who the relevant constituencies are and what they want. It may also be advantageous to be forced by their critics among the environmental activists to do what they wanted anyway. The third choice is what degree of compliance with the rules to accept. Bargaining may produce abatement schedules that give the polluter some leeway, and delays may be requested and approved. Good intentions and partial abatement may be accepted as in earnest of future complete compliance.

Another model of regulatory behavior is suggested by George Hagevik based on game theory.[3] This model also depicts regulation as a bargaining process, but suggests that this may be a contribution to rather than a constraint on effective regulation. Bargaining is a process that involves common interest as well as conflict between parties. Both parties would prefer to cooperate, because they would both be better off with a solution than without one. Nevertheless, while they agree that they want a solution they disagree about the content of particular solutions.

Hagevik suggests that bargaining in pollution control regulation may be something like a continuous game—chess, for example. Bargaining operates best when negotiations can be broken down into parts that can be considered one after the other. The process thus becomes incremental in nature, like a series of moves in a game. The tempo of negotiation is comparatively slow, positions can change by degrees, and both parties can notice and learn from each other's mistakes. Continuous games also develop certain rituals, which help to structure the bargaining process. One of the objectives of institution building for pollution control is the arrangement of effective rituals. Hagevik notes that legal procedures may be too inflexible to permit the development of bargaining rituals. Nevertheless, legal proceedings are themselves rituals; and administrative hearings, such as the one held for Atlantic Cement, demonstrate that plenty of time may be allowed for maneuver.

Officials in the State Department of Health and the Department of Environmental Conservation as well as the executives in Allegheny Ludlum and Atlantic Cement were well aware that they were bargaining to the limits of their capabilities in trying respectively to enforce the air pollution rules and avoid being issued a Commissioner's Order to comply. In both cases, the parties negotiated consent orders that avoided accusations and penalties. The Universal Atlas Cement problem that was taken directly to court by the State Attorney General also ended in a consent agreement. Although these experienced negotiators did not need theoretical formulations to tell them what they were doing, or to guide them in doing it, nevertheless, members of the concerned public and students preparing for careers in environmental resources management will find these concepts helpful for understanding what happens in the state house and court house. They will also better understand why the course of development and implementation of air pollution controls is so long and tortuous.

REFERENCES

1. Edward S. Mason, "A Reconciliation of Goals," *Resources*, 42 (September 1972) published by Resources for the Future, Washington, D. C.
2. Matthew Holden, Jr., "Pollution Control as a Bargaining Process: An Essay on Regulatory Decision-Making," Cornell Water Resources Center, Ithaca, N. Y., October 1966.
3. George Hagevik, "Legislating for Air Quality Management: Reducing Theory to Practice," *Law and Contemporary Problems*, 3 (Spring 1968), 380-397.

APPENDIXES

Due to varying sizes of the original forms, some adjustments have been made in the sizes of the forms as reproduced in the appendixes, but the method and content remain the same.

Appendix A

Official Compilation of Codes, Rules and Regulations of the State of New York

PART 176

Reports, Plans and Specifications

Section 176.1 New sources and modifications of existing sources of air contamination—approval required. Any person planning to construct a new installation which will or might reasonably be expected to contribute to air pollution or make modifications to an existing installation which will or might reasonably be expected to increase the amount or change the effects or the characteristics of the air contaminants discharged, or planning to install an air cleaning device shall submit a report and/or plans and specifications to the commissioner* for approval prior to initiation of construction.

176.2 Waiver of approval prior to construction. In the event that the requirement for approval prior to construction will create an undue hardship to the applicant, the applicant may request of the commissioner a waiver to proceed with construction. The application for a waiver shall explain the circumstances which will cause such undue hardship.

176.3 Approval after waiver is granted. If a waiver is granted, the applicant shall submit a report and/or plans and specifications for approval as soon as is reasonably practical. The applicant, after a waiver is granted, proceeds with the construction at his own risk; and if after construction, modification, relocation or installation has begun or been completed, the report and/or plans and specifications and completed installations do not meet the commissioner's approval, the alterations required to effect such approval shall be made within a reasonable time, as specified by the commissioner.

176.4 Submission of reports and/or plans and specifications.

(a) Applications for approval shall be filed with the commissioner accompanied by an expected performance report and/or plans and

* Plans for air cleaning devices on exhaust and ventilation systems in industrial establishments are reviewed for the commissioner by the State Industrial Commissioner.

specifications in duplicate. Application forms furnished by the board shall be signed by the applicant or his authorized agent.

(b) Reports shall include the following information:

(1) Expected composition of effluent stream, both before and after any air cleaning device, including emission rate, concentration, volume and temperature.

(2) Expected physical characteristics of particulates.

(3) Type of air cleaning device, if any.

(4) The location and elevation of the emission point and other factors relating to dispersion and diffusion of the contaminant in the outer air, and the relation of the emission point to nearby structures, window openings, and other information necessary to appraise the possible effects of the effluent.

(5) Where necessary to ascertain compliance, the tests to be made of the completed installation by the applicant. The commissioner may not require testing of all new installations if operating performance of similar installations indicates this is not needed.

(6) Any other reasonable and pertinent information that may be required by the commissioner.

(c) Plans and specifications shall include the following information:

(1) Expected composition of effluent stream, both before and after any air cleaning device, including emission rate, concentration, volume and temperature.

(2) Expected physical characteristics of particulates.

(3) Size, type and performance characteristics of air cleaning devices.

(4) The location and elevation of the emission point and other factors relating to dispersion and diffusion of the air contaminant in the outer air, and the relation of the emission point to nearby structures, window openings, and other information necessary to appraise the possible effects of the effluent.

(5) Where necessary to ascertain compliance, the location of planned sampling points and the tests to be made of the completed installation by the applicant. The commissioner may not require testing of all new installations if operating performance of similar installations indicates this is not needed.

(6) Any other reasonable and pertinent information may be required by the commissioner.

176.5 Action on applications.

(a) The commissioner will acknowledge receipt of reports or plans and specifications within one week of receipt and will estimate the time necessary for processing. The commissioner will notify the applicant in writing of his approval, or denial. In cases where delays would cause undue hardship to the applicant or materially handicap his need for proceeding promptly with the proposed installation, modification or relocation, a request for priority consideration and the justification therefor shall be submitted. When a priority is granted, the application, if practicable, will be processed within 30 days after receipt of the request for priority.

(b) Reports or plans and specifications shall be approved, and a permit to construct issued, only when it appears that they are in accordance with engineering guides acceptable to the commissioner or within modifications of such guides as the commissioner may consider to be proper in the case of a particular installation.

(c) In the event of the denial of an application, the applicant shall be notified in writing of the reasons therefor. All denials shall be without prejudice to the applicant's request for a hearing before the commissioner or for filing a further application after revisions are made to meet the objections specified as the reasons for the denial.*

(d) After the completion of the construction for which an application and a report and/or plans and specifications were approved, and subject to the provisions of Part 178, the person making such installation shall receive from the commissioner a certificate to operate. A certificate shall continue in effect as long as the installation performs in accordance with the conditions upon which the certificate is based, except that the commissioner may, after a hearing, rescind or modify the certificate whenever he determines that such action is necessary to provide for compliance with the provisions of article 12-A or the rules and regulations issued pursuant thereto. Permission to operate under the certificate shall not be affected by conditions beyond the reasonable control of the operator, such as mechanical and power failures which can be and are readily repaired or corrected.

(e) A permit to construct or a certificate to operate shall not be transferable either from one location to another or from one piece of equipment to another.

---

* An order or determination of the commissioner is subject to review by the Air Pollution Control Board in accordance with section 1283-a.

PART 179

Compliance, Air-Cleaning Devices, Collected Contaminants

Section 179.1 Performance. Air cleaning devices shall be selected so as to afford the highest efficiency or the lowest discharge rate that is reasonable and practicable. Reasonableness and practicability shall take into account cost, the air contaminant concentration in the emission gas stream, particle characteristics and other properties of the contaminant and of the emission gas stream.

179.2 Installation and maintenance. All devices used to effect compliance with this Subchapter shall be installed and maintained and operated in a satisfactory manner and in accordance with this Subchapter and existing laws.

179.3 Removal of collected air contaminants from air cleaners. Collected air contaminants shall be removed and disposed of in conformity with this Subchapter and existing laws and at such intervals as may be necessary to maintain the equipment at the required operating efficiency. Collection and disposal shall be performed in a manner so as not to reintroduce contaminants to the outer air.

PART 186

General Prohibition

Section 186.1 Prohibition. No person shall permit or cause any air contamination source to produce air pollution as this term is defined in article 12-A, section 1267(4) of the Public Health Law.

186.2 Application. To the extent that there is a rule which applies to the control of a specific air contaminant or a specific air contamination source, section 186.1 shall not be applied and the other rule shall take precedence over and shall be applied in place of the general prohibition.

PART 187

Contaminant Emissions from Processes, and Exhaust and Ventilation Systems

Section 187.1 Applicability. This Part shall apply throughout the State of New York to contaminant emissions from processes, and exhaust and ventilation systems, except that when another Part applies to a specific air contaminant or a specific air contamination source, that Part shall take precedence and shall be applied in place of this Part.

187.2 Definitions.

(a) Environmental rating. A rating indicated by the letter A, B, C or D considers the environmental effects of an air contamination source. A rating takes into account properties and quantities of contaminants emitted; effects on human, plant, or animal life, or property; meteorological parameters, stack heights, characteristics of the community; and ambient air quality classification of the area in which the source is located or which it affects.

(b) Emission rate potential. The rate in pounds per hour at which air contaminants would be emitted to the outer air in the absence of air pollution control facilities or other control measures. The emission rate potential for cyclic operations shall be determined by considering both the instantaneous emission potential and the total emission potential over the time period of the cycle.

(c) Emission source. Any point at which air contaminants enter the outer air from processes, and exhaust and ventilation systems.

(d) Exhaust and ventilation system. Any system which removes and transports any gaseous or gas borne products from their point of generation to the outer air.

(e) Permissible emission rate. The maximum rate in pounds per hour at which air contaminants are allowed to be emitted to the outer air.

(f) Process weight. The total weight of all materials introduced into any specific process which may cause any discharge into the atmosphere. Solid fuels used in the process will be considered as part of the process weight, but liquid and gaseous fuels, uncombined water and combustion air will not.

(g) Process weight per hour. The total process weight divided by the number of hours in one complete operation from the beginning of a cycle to the completion thereof. For continuous processes, process weight should be determined on a daily basis.

187.3 Prohibitions.

(a) No person shall cause, permit or allow the emission of air contaminants from an emission source resulting from an operation begun or modified, after the effective date of this Part, which exceeds the permissible emission rates specified in tables 2 and 3‡, for the environmental rating as determined in accordance with table 1‡.

(b) On January 1, 1971, or such later date as established by an order of the commissioner, the permissible emission rates specified in subdivision (a) shall become applicable to emission sources in existence on or prior to the effective date of this Part.

(c) The provisions of this section shall not be construed to allow or permit any person to emit air contaminants in quantities which alone or in combination with other sources would contravene any established air quality standards.

187.4 Abatement.

(a) The commissioner may require the person operating or maintaining emission sources to provide pertinent data concerning emissions so as to show compliance with the requirements of section 187.3.

(b) When required by the commissioner, the person operating or maintaining emission sources in operation before the effective date of this Part shall submit a detailed report including emission data, pertinent environmental factors and a proposed environmental rating so as to show conformity with this Part of proposed corrective measures and schedule for compliance. If this report is acceptable, the commissioner will so notify the person operating or maintaining the emission source. If the report is not acceptable, the commissioner will notify the person operating or maintaining the emission source as to the reasons together with an environmental rating that is acceptable and a time schedule for compliance. Upon petition to the commissioner within 30 days of such notice, the commissioner shall grant a hearing to the petitioner.

(c) Persons beginning or modifying operations after the effective date of this Part are required to submit to the commissioner or his representative, either prior to* or concurrently with submission of plans and/or specifications, an appraisal of the items mentioned in table 1 in the form of a report including the proposed rating to be used for design purposes.

---

‡ See Appendix 4 of the Official Compilation of Codes, Rules and Regulations of the State of New York.

* It is recommended that for large installations the report be submitted prior to submission of plans. Following approval of the preliminary report, final detailed plans and/or specifications will be completed and submitted to the commissioner or his representative for approval.

(d) The commissioner may seal any process equipment or prohibit any operation in accordance with a determination made under the provisions of section 1282 of article 12-A of the Public Health Law. The seal may be removed from the equipment only upon receipt of written notice from the commissioner.

APPENDIX 4 TABLE 1: Environmental Rating

Rating	*Criteria*
A	Includes processes and exhaust and ventilation systems where the discharge of a contaminant or contaminants results, or would reasonably be expected to result, in serious adverse effects on receptors or the environment. These effects may be of a health, economic or aesthetic nature or any combination of these.
B	Includes processes, and exhaust and ventilation systems where the discharge of a contaminant or contaminants results, or would reasonably be expected to result, in only moderate and essentially localized effects; or where the multiplicity of sources of the contaminant or contaminants in any given area is such as to require an overall reduction of the atmospheric burden of that contaminant or contaminants.
C	Includes processes, and exhaust and ventilation systems where the discharge of a contaminant or contaminants would reasonably be expected to result in localized adverse effects of an aesthetic or nuisance nature.
D	Includes processes, and exhaust and ventilation systems where, in view of properties and concentrations of the emissions, isolated conditions, stack height, and other factors, it can be clearly demonstrated that discharge of the contaminant or contaminants will not result in measurable or observable effects on receptors, nor add to an existing or predictable atmospheric burden of that contaminant or contaminants which would reasonably be expected to cause adverse effects.

The following items will be considered in making a determination of the environmental rating to be applied to a particular source:

a) properties, quantities and rates of emission
b) physical surroundings of emission source
c) population density of surrounding area, including anticipated future growth
d) dispersion characteristics at or near source
e) location of emission source relative to ground level and surrounding buildings, mountains, hills, etc.
f) current or anticipated ambient air quality in vicinity of source
g) latest findings relating to effects of ground-level concentrations of the emission on receptors
h) possible hazardous side effects of contaminant in question mixing with contaminants already in ambient air
i) engineering guides which are acceptable to the commissioner

911 H 1-31-68

TABLE 2: Usual Degree of Air Cleaning Required (1) from Processes, and Exhaust and Ventilation Systems for Gases and Liquid Particulate Emissions (Environmental Rating A, B, C and D) and Solid Particulate Emissions (Environmental Rating A and D).

	Emission Rate Potential (lb/hr)									
Environment Rating	Less than 1.0	1 to 10	10 to 20	20 to 100	100 to 500	500 to 1,000	1,000 to 1,500	1,500 to 4,000	4,000 to 10,000	10,000 and Greater
A	See Note (2)	99% OR GREATER								
B		*	90-91%	91-94%	94-96%	96-97%		97-98%	98-99%	99% or Greater
C		*	70-75%	75-85%	85-90%	90-93%		93-95%	95-98%	98% or Greater
D										

* Degree of air cleaning may be specified by the commissioner providing satisfactory dispersion is achieved.

(1) Where multiple emission sources are connected to a common air cleaning device, the degree of air cleaning required will be that which would be required if each individual emission source were considered separately.

(2) For an average Emission Rate Potential less than 1.0 lb/hr, the desired air cleaning efficiency shall be determined by the expected concentration of the air contaminant in the emission stream. Where it is uneconomical to employ air cleaning devices, other methods of control should be considered.

912 H 1-31-68

TABLE 3: Allowable Emissions from Processes, and Exhaust and Ventilation Systems for Solid Particulates (Environmental Rating B & C)

Process Weight* (lb/hr)	Maximum Weight Discharge*** (lb/hr)
100	0.50
500	1.46
1,000	2.30
5,000	6.70
10,000	10.80
25,000	20.00
50,000	31.80
75,000	43.00
100,000**	50.00
250,000**	58.20
500,000**	64.30
750,000**	68.40
1,000,000**	71.10
2,000,000**	78.30
5,000,000**	88.10

* In cases where process weight is not applicable (such as grinding and woodworking) the concentration of solid particulates in the effluent gas stream shall not exceed 0.3 lb/1000 lb of undiluted exhaust gas at actual conditions.

** For process weights in excess of 100,000 lb/hr, the permissible maximum weight discharge may exceed tabular value if the concentration of particulate matter in the effluent gas stream is less than 0.1 lb/1000 of undiluted exhaust gas at actual conditions.

*** To determine intermediate values of maximum weight discharge: for process weights up to 100,000 lb/hr use $E = .024P^{0.665}$; for process weights in excess of 100,000 lb/hr use $E = 39P^{0.082}{}_{-50}$ where E = maximum weight discharge in lb/hr; P = process weight in lb/hr.

913 H 1-31-68

PART 195

Particulate Emissions from Cement and Lightweight Aggregate Industry Pyroprocesses

Section 195.1 Applicability.

(a) This Part shall apply only to those pyroprocesses which were in operation at cement and lightweight aggregate manufacturing plants prior to the effective date of this Part and which, on or prior to such date, had control equipment enabling them to meet at least the emission standards prescribed in table 1 of section 195.3.

(b) This Part shall not apply to those pyroprocesses which, on the effective date of this Part, meet the emission standards of Part 187.

(c) The applicability of this Part shall terminate on January 1, 1981, and this Part shall not, thereafter, be of any force and effect with respect to pyroprocess.

195.2 Definitions.

(a) Pyroprocesses. That part of the cement and lightweight aggregate manufacturing process related to the preheating, calcining, sintering, burning and cooling of clinker.

(b) Process weight. The total weight of all materials introduced into a pyroprocess which may cause any discharge into the atmosphere. Solid fuels used will be considered as part of the process weight but liquid and gaseous fuels, uncombined water and combustion air will not.

195.3 Prohibitions.

(a) No person shall cause, permit, or allow the emission of particulates to the outer air from any pyroprocess which exceeds the limits specified in table 1.

(b) After January 1, 1971, pyroprocesses covered by this Part shall meet the emission standards of Part 187 in accordance with a time schedule as shall be established by the commissioner, except that all pyroprocesses shall meet the emission standards of Part 187 not later than January 1, 1981.

(c) The provisions of this section shall not be construed to permit the emission of air contaminants in quantities which alone or in combination with other sources would contravene the standards applicable under the provisions of Subchapter C of Chapter IV of Title 10 of the Official Compilation of Codes, Rules and Regulations of the State of New York.

195.4 Testing, sampling and records.

(a) When testing for the applicability of and compliance with this Part is deemed necessary by the commissioner, and the commissioner requests such testing, the owner or operator must permit the commissioner to have such testing done. This testing will be at the State's expense except as otherwise provided in subdivision (b) of this section.

TABLE 1: Particulate Emissions from Cement and Lightweight Aggregate Industry Pyroprocesses.

Process Weight (lb/hr)	Maximum Emission Weight (lb/hr)
50,000	94
100,000	134
150,000	164
200,000	190
250,000	212
300,000	233
350,000	252
400,000	268
450,000	284

(b) Sampling holes and pertinent allied facilities as needed to conduct tests required in subdivision (a) of this section shall be requested in writing by the commissioner and shall then be provided at the expense of the owner or operator at such points as the commissioner may request. If sampling holes, in addition to those used for testing dust collection equipment upon initial installation, are required, the cost of providing such additional holes shall be at the State's expense. The owner or operator shall provide, at his expense, a suitable power source and other suitable utilities necessary for the operation of sampling instruments. The commissioner shall consult with the owner or operator with respect to the location of sampling holes.

(c) Operation and maintenance records acceptable to the commissioner shall be kept on file for a period of at least two years by the owner or operator of collection equipment on pyroprocesses. Such records shall be open to inspection by the commissioner and shall include the dates and periods of time during which such collection equipment is inoperative or malfunctioning.

Appendix B

Guidelines for the Preparation of the Environmental Analysis Report for Compliance with 10 NYCRR 187

STATE OF NEW YORK
DEPARTMENT OF HEALTH

GUIDELINES FOR THE PREPARATION OF THE ENVIRONMENTAL ANALYSIS REPORT FOR COMPLIANCE WITH 10 NYCRR 187

The Environmental Analysis Report should contain four sections. Prepare each in triplicate. Cover each report with completed form AIR 111. Consult the field representative of the New York State Department of Health for assistance in preparing the report. A list of references is included on page 3 of these guidelines.

The sections should consist of the following:

Section 1

PLOT PLAN

Prepare a plot plan to scale which includes:

a. north orientation

b. plant property line(s)

c. direction and, if known, velocity of prevailing wind

d. land use. Describe surrounding property and use; e.g., commercial, residential or industrial.

e. location of all existing and proposed emission sources (including those associated with the generation of steam, hot water, heat and electricity). Distinguish between existing and proposed emission points and assign a reference number to each point.

f. horizontal distance and bearing to nearest off-property receptor for each emission point.

g. location of refuse disposal sites. Describe nature of refuse, quantity (tons/yr), disposal method and method of transport to disposal site.

Section 2

EXPLANATION OF PLANT PROCESS

Prepare an explanation of each plant process, including flow diagrams and indicating emission sources by reference numbers assigned on plot plan.

Section 3

INDUSTRIAL EMISSION SOURCE INVENTORY

Prepare form AIR 302A for each emission source identified on plot plan.

Some definitions and calculations which may be helpful are:

Process weight — the total weight of all materials introduced into any specific process which may cause any discharge into the outer air. Liquid fuels, gaseous fuels, uncombined water, combustion air and internally recirculated materials are not be considered in the calculation of process weight.

Emission rate potential — the rate in pounds per hour at which air contaminants would be emitted to the outer air in the absence of air pollution control facilities or other control measures. Two examples of the calculation of emission rate potential for the use of solvents are listed below:

A. Spray Coating. A spray coating operation uses one gallon of paint per hour. The paint is composed of 30% solids and 70% solvents. The solvent is a mixture of toluene, xylene and other aromatics. Most of the solvent mixture is toluene and the specific gravity of 0.87 for toluene is assumed to be applicable to the solvent mixture. It is also assumed that 90% of the solvent is released to the outer air through the spray booth exhaust from the operation.

Use emission rate potential $= Qsg \int_{H_2O}$

where Q $=$ gallons of solvent used in one hour,

sg $=$ specific gravity of solvent

and $\int_{H_2O}$ $=$ density of water (equals 8.3 lb/gal at normal conditions)

therefore, emission rate potential $= 1 \text{ x } 0.7 \text{ x } 0.9 \text{ x } 0.87 \text{ x } 8.3 =$ 4.5 lb/hr

B. Vapor Degreaser. A gas heated vapor degreaser has a vapor condenser and a slot type local exhaust hood. Twenty gallons of perchlorethylene solvent with a density of 13.5 lb/gal is added as make-up each week. The degreaser is operated 30 hours each week. It is assumed that 95% of the make-up solvent is exhausted to the outer air by the degreaser exhaust system.

Use emission rate potential = Q ∫ solvent
where Q = gallons of solvent used in one hour
and $\int_{solvent} = sg_{\ solvent} \times \int H_2O$
therefore, emission rate potential = 20 x 1/30 x 13.5 x 0.95 = 8.6 lb/hr

Section 4

ENVIRONMENTAL RATING PROPOSAL AND PERMISSIBLE EMISSIONS

Propose environmental rating(s) in accordance with Table 1, 10 NYCRR 187. Then calculate permissible emissions using Tables 2 and 3.

For sources emitting gases and liquid particulates and for sources emitting solid particulates with an environmental rating of "A" or "D", use Table 2 to determine the degree of cleaning or treatment required.

For sources emitting solid particulates with an environmental rating of "B" or "C", refer to Table 3 to calculate the permissible emission rate (maximum weight discharge). Two equations are provided. One is to be used if the process weight exceeds 100,000 lb/hr and the other if it does not.

Sample calculation:

A. Process weight does not exceed 100,000 lb/hr

Calculate the maximum weight discharge allowed from a production cupola with an environmental rating of "B" and a process weight of 28,500 lb/hr.

Use $E = 0.024\ P^{0.665}$
where E = maximum weight discharge (lb/hr)
and P = process weight (lb/hr)
$E = 0.024\ (28{,}500)^{0.665}$
$E = 22.2$ lb/hr

B. Process weight exceeds 100,000 lb/hr

Calculate the maximum weight discharge allowed from an asphalt plant with an environmental rating of "B" and a process weight of 325 ton/hr.

Use $E = 39\ P^{0.082} - 50$
$E = 39\ (325 \times 2{,}000)^{0.082} - 50$
$E = 117 - 50$
$E = 67$ lb/hr

AIR 100.2 (6-68)

Linear interpolation should not be used for intermediate values in Table 3.

REFERENCES

1. *Air Pollution*, Stern, A., Vol. 1 and 2, Academic Press 1962.
2. *Air Pollution Field Operations Manual*, 1962, U.S.P.H.S. Publication No. 937.
3. *Air Pollution Handbook*, Magill, P. L., Holden, C. Ackley, C. McGraw Hill.
4. *Chemical Engineer's Handbook*, Perry, R. H., McGraw Hill, 1967.
5. *Chemical Safety Data Sheets*, Manufacturing Chemists Association.
6. *Dangerous Properties of Industrial Materials*, Sax, N. I., Reinhold, (1963).
7. *Foundry Air Pollution Control Manual*, American Foundryman's Society, Second Edition, 1967.
8. *Handbook of Air Pollution*, U. S. Public Health Service.

NEW YORK STATE
DEPARTMENT OF ENVIRONMENTAL CONSERVATION

ENVIRONMENTAL ANALYSIS REPORT–SUMMARY OF SOURCES

For completion by applicant (in triplicate)

Use one copy of this form as a cover sheet for each copy of the Environmental Analysis Report submitted in triplicate.

Report No. ______________ BAQC Assign.

1. Name of firm or owner ______________________________

2. Address of installation ______________________________
Street Number and Name   City, Village or Town   County

3. Person to contact regarding this application ______________________________
Name

4. Proposed Environmental Rating(s) ______________________________
Address

Emission Point No.	Process, Exhaust or Ventilating System	Proposed Env. Rat.	Emission Point No.	Process, Exhaust or Ventilating System	Proposed Env. Rat.

Continue on reverse side for listing of proposed ER's.

5. Date __________ 6. Signature ______________________ 7. Title ______________

For completion by field representative.

I recommend (acceptance) (denial) of the proposed environmental rating(s).

Remarks ______________________________

8. Date __________ 9. Signature ______________________ 10. Title ______________

AIR 111 (2/71)

STATE OF NEW YORK
DEPARTMENT OF ENVIRONMENTAL CONSERVATION
DIVISION OF AIR RESOURCES

PROCESS, EXHAUST AND VENTILATING SYSTEM EMISSIONS

Emission Source
Reference No. ______ Firm Name ________ Report Date ______

Include this completed form or equivalent with Environmental Analysis Report. See AIR 100.2, Guides for Preparation of Environmental Analysis Report.

1. Process, exhaust or ventilating system producing emission (describe)
2. Process weight or emission rate potential, whichever is applicable (show calculation and describe how determined)
3. Gas cleaner or treatment device, describe and specify efficiency (overall and fractional, where applicable)
4. Air contaminant emissions to outer air, list by contaminant name and indicate whether contaminant is (s) solid, (l) liquid, or (g) gas. Describe color and/or odor of visible and/or odorous contaminants.

Contaminant	*Quantity (lb/hr)*	*Contaminant*	*Quantity (lb/hr)*
______	______	______	______
______	______	______	______
______	______	______	______
______	______	______	______
______	______	______	______
______	______	______	______
______	______	______	______
______	______	______	______
______	______	______	______
______	______	______	______

Describe method for determining emissions:

5. Air or gas flow rate
   If cyclic, SCFM/cycle ; hrs/cycle ; cycles/yr
   If continuous, SCFM ; hrs/day ; days/yr

6. Physical characteristics of emission point
   a. gas temperature at point of discarge: F.
   b. inside dimensions of outlet in. x in. or_____in. diameter
   c. height above ground ft.

7. Fuel (complete if fuel used as a process constituent)
   a. Coal (Type) Anthracite_____; Bituminous_____; lbs/hr_____
      %Sulfur by Wgt._____
   b. Oil (Grade) 2_____ 4_____ 5_____ 6_____ GPM_____ %Sulfur by Wgt._____
   c. Gas (Type) MFD_____; Nat._____; _____CFH; _____BTU/CF

8. Is this a new or existing source?____________________

9. If existing, has an environmental rating been certified for this emission source?____________________

10. If yes, give "E" number assigned____________________

AIR 302.1 (9/70)

Appendix C

Commissioner's Orders

STATE OF NEW YORK:
DEPARTMENT OF ENVIRONMENTAL CONSERVATION

In the Matter of Alleged Violations of Part 212 of Title 6 of the Official Compilation of Codes, Rules and Regulations of the State of New York (formerly Part 187 of Title 10 of the Official Compilation of Codes, Rules and Regulations of the State of New York) by	**NOTICE OF HEARING AND COMPLAINT**
Respondent.	**FILE NO.**

NOTICE

PLEASE TAKE NOTICE THAT pursuant to the Environmental Conservation Law and to Article 12-A of the Public Health Law, I shall convene a public hearing at the following time and place:

to consider certain violations you are charged with having committed, as specified in the complaint below.

PLEASE BE ADVISED THAT you may file a written answer to the charge of the violations herein alleged not later than three (3) days before the hearing date; that you may appear at the hearing in person or by representative, with or without counsel; that all witnesses will testify under oath, and a record of the proceeding will be made; that you may produce witnesses and evidence in your own behalf; that you may request issuance of subpoenas to compel attendance of witnesses and production of records relating to the matter under investigation; that you may cross-examine witnesses and examine evidence produced against you.

PLEASE BE FURTHER ADVISED THAT whether or not you appear, the hearing will convene at the stated time and place and, should I find you in violation of Part 212, an order may be issued and entered against you. Attached hereto is a copy of the order I propose to issue should the facts so warrant, which order may be modified either following the hearing or upon your consent.

You may waive your right to a public hearing at any time prior to the hearing and agree to the issuance of the proposed order by fully executing the waiver and consent set forth thereunder.

DATED: Albany, New York
,1972

HENRY L. DIAMOND, Commissioner
New York State Department of
Environmental Conservation

TO:

By ________________________

Alexander B. Grannis
Compliance Counsel

COMPLAINT

1. Respondent owns, maintains and/or exercises control of sources of emissions on premises located in the State of New York, which sources are subject to Part 212 of the air pollution control rules and regulations.

2. Respondent has failed to comply with Part 212 in that the Respondent has either not submitted an environmental analysis report and/or has not regulated and controlled the emissions from said sources of emission as required by said Part and environmental rating(s) assigned pursuant thereto.

STATE OF NEW YORK
DEPARTMENT OF ENVIRONMENTAL CONSERVATION

IN THE MATTER

OF

Compliance with Part 187 of the Air Pollution Control Rules and Regulations by

STIPULATION

ALLEGHENY LUDLUM STEEL CORPORATION

Respondent

It is hereby stipulated and agreed by the parties hereto that there exist valid and sufficient grounds as a matter of law and fact for the issuance of the annexed order of the Commissioner of Environmental Conservation of the State of New York under the Public Health Law and the Environmental Conservation Law, and Respondent consents to its entry, accepts its terms and conditions, and waives its right to a hearing in this proceeding.

DATED:

BY ______________________________

DATED: Albany, New York
1971

____
CHARLES J. LaBELLE, Counsel
New York State Department of
Environmental Conservation

STATE OF NEW YORK
DEPARTMENT OF ENVIRONMENTAL CONSERVATION

IN THE MATTER

OF

Compliance with Part 187 of the Air Pollution Control Rules and Regulations by

ALLEGHENY LUDLUM STEEL CORPORATION

Respondent

ORDER ON CONSENT

Respondent having waived a public hearing in this proceeding and accepted the terms and conditions of this Order by virtue of the Stipulation annexed, I order the following:

I. Respondent shall make such modifications, repairs, or additions to its melt shop fume control system at Watervliet, New York, as are necessary to achieve an air contaminant emission rate therefrom not to exceed the limitations imposed under an environmental rating heretofor assigned pursuant to Part 187 of the New York State Air Pollution Control Rules, nor to result in violation of Part 186 of said Rules, nor to result in contravention of the standards for the quality of the ambient air established under Part 501 of the Rules. Such changes are to be timely made strictly in accordance with the compliance schedule set forth in Appendix A hereto attached.

II. Beginning August 1, 1971, and thereafter on the first day of every third month, Respondent shall file a report of progress made in achieving the goals set forth in Paragraph I above. On request, Respondent shall furnish copies of relevant purchase or construction contracts.

III. Any tests required to be conducted by Respondent to show compliance with Part 187 shall be at Respondent's own expense and performed in a manner acceptable to me, and shall not be deemed to preclude my conducting such other tests as I may think necessary.

IV. Any plans, reports, or other submissions required to be made pursuant hereto shall be filed by Respondent with the Regional Director of Environmental Quality, at his office in Albany, New York.

V. Whenever the Regional Director of Environmental Quality deems it necessary or desirable to inspect the premises of Respondent to verify progress in achieving compliance in connection herewith, he or his representative shall be allowed to go upon said premises at any reasonable hour, and shall be given such assistance by Respondent as is necessary for the proper conduct of such an inspection.

VI. No modification of this order shall be effective except it be in writing executed by me, upon written application to me for the relief sought thereby.

DATED: Albany, New York
1971

HENRY L. DIAMOND
Commissioner of Environmental
Conservation of the State of
New York

TO: R. H. Henke
Vice President
Operations-Planning
Allegheny Ludlum Steel Corporation
c/o Allegheny Ludlum Industries, Inc.
Oliver Building
Pittsburgh, Pennsylvania 15222

APPENDIX A

ALLEGHENY LUDLUM STEEL CORPORATION

Watervliet, New York

Melt shop fume control system

1. According to plans already submitted start construction August 1, 1971
2. Complete construction by January 1, 1972
3. Complete tests by February 1, 1972

STATE OF NEW YORK:
DEPARTMENT OF ENVIRONMENTAL CONSERVATION

In the Matter of the Alleged Violations of Part 212 of Title 6 of the Official Compilation of Codes, Rules and Regulations by the State of New York (formerly Part 187 of Title 10 of the Official Compilation of the Codes, Rules and Regulations of the State of New York) by Respondent.	**ORDER ON CONSENT** **FILE NO.**

WHEREAS:

1. Pursuant to Parts 256, 257 and of Title 6 of the Official Compilation of Codes, Rules and Regulations of the State of New York (formerly Parts 501, 502 and of Title 10 and hereinafter referred to only by Part number), promulgated pursuant to Section 1271 and 1276 of Article 12-A of the Public Health Law, ambient air quality standards were established and assigned to County, New York.

2. Part 212, effective as of February 6, 1968, regulates contaminant emissions from processes, exhaust and ventilation systems throughout the State of New York.

3. Respondent owns, operates and/or maintains control of facili-

ties in the State of New York with emission source(s) subject to Part 212.

4. Part 212 required Respondent to meet certain specified emission rates of all emission sources by January 1, 1971 pursuant to duly assigned environmental ratings.

5. Respondent did not comply with Part 212 by January 1, 1971.

6. Respondent has affirmatively waived its right to a hearing on these matters as provided by law and has consented to the issuing and entering of this Order pursuant to the provisions of Article 12-A of the Public Health Law of the State of New York and has agreed to be bound by the provisions, terms and conditions contained herein.

NOW, having considered this matter and being duly advised, it is ORDERED:

I. THAT, immediately upon service of a conformed copy of this Order upon Respondent, Respondent shall either cease and abate and thereafter keep abated all emissions from its emission sources into the air of the State which cause or contribute to the contravention of the ambient air quality standards heretofore adopted for and assigned to the county wherein such sources are located and, further, so regulate and control all emissions from the aforementioned emission sources so as not to exceed the specific emission limitations imposed under Part 212, or be bound as hereinafter provided.

II. THAT, on or after the date of service of a conformed copy of this Order upon Respondent, any and all emissions from Respondent's emission sources which cause or contribute to the contravention of the aforementioned ambient air quality standards or which exceed the emission limitations imposed under Part 212 shall constitute continuing violations of this Order as well as continuing violations of the Public Health Law and the Environmental Conservation Law of the State of New York and the rules and regulations promulgated thereunder provided, however, that an action for penalties for any such violations pursuant to law shall not be instituted by the Department of Environmental Conservation for so long as Respondent proceeds with and completes its air pollution abatement program in accordance with the provisions, terms and conditions of Schedule A attached hereto and incorporated herein.

III. THAT, upon completion of construction or modification of each facility as herein required, Respondent shall promptly put said facility into operation and shall test said installation at Respondent's expense in a manner approved by the Department and in accordance with Schedule A for the purpose of establishing compliance with Part

212, and immediately after conducting such tests, submit the results thereof to the Department and thereafter regulate the emissions from the source so tested in full conformity with the conditions contained in any certificate to operate issued by the Department and in accordance with all requirements of the Public Health Law and the Environmental Conservation Law of the State of New York and all rules and regulations promulgated pursuant thereto; provided, however, that if test evaluations indicate the need for additional facilities in order to meet the requirements of Part 212 or the aforementioned ambient air quality standards, Respondent shall terminate the use of or so restrict the use of the source of emission involved so as to effect immediate compliance with Part 212 until such time as required additional treatment equipment is installed and operating in accordance with approved plans, specifications and certificates.

IV. THAT, Respondent shall submit bi-monthly statements to the Department on the fifteenth day of each second month commencing in the month after service of a conformed copy of this Order upon Respondent detailing the current status and the action taken by the Respondent to comply with this Order, and said reporting shall continue until such time as the Respondent shall have complied fully with all of the terms and conditions herein stated.

V. THAT, all reports and submissions herein required shall be made to the Director of the Regional Office of the Department having jurisdiction of the area wherein the Respondent's emission sources are located.

VI. THAT, for the purpose of insuring compliance with this Order, duly authorized representatives of the State of New York shall be permitted access to inspect Respondent's premises and the facilities being constructed, owned, operated and/or maintained by the Respondent for the purpose of inspecting said facilities, to make or require such tests as may be deemed necessary for the purpose of determining the status of compliance with the terms of this Order.

VII. THAT, within fifteen (15) days of service of a conformed copy of this Order upon Respondent, as consideration for the issuance of this Order by consent and to insure timely compliance with the provisions, terms and conditions contained herein, Respondent shall post or deposit with the Department a financial undertaking in cash, check or other equivalent negotiable instrument in acceptable form or a surety bond issued by a company licensed to do business in the State of New York in a form acceptable to the Department, in the amount of   Dollars on condition that upon fifteen (15) days written notice to the Respondent, said financial undertaking shall be forfeited to the Commissioner if at any time the Respondent fails to comply with any and all of the provisions of this Order; provided, however, that the Respondent has not requested in writing and been granted prior formal modification of said provisions by the Commissioner of the Department; and provided further, that forfeiture of said amount shall in no way prejudice the right of the Commissioner to institute such other and further action as he may deem necessary in order to insure full compliance with the terms of this Order and the provisions of the Public Health Law and the Environmental Conservation Law of the State of New York and the rules and regulations promulgated thereunder.

Provided further, however, that said financial undertaking shall be returned to the Respondent upon written request to said Department with proof acceptable to the Department to establish that the Respondent has complied fully with the provisions of Schedule A.

VIII. THAT, if because of an act of God, war, strike, riot, catastrophe, or other condition as to which negligence or willful misconduct on the part of Respondent was not the proximate cause, Respondent cannot comply with the compliance schedule set forth on Schedule A, the Respondent shall apply in writing to the Commissioner within a reasonable time after it obtains knowledge of said fact and request an extension or modification of such Schedule.

IX. THAT, no change in this Order shall be made or be effective except as may be specifically set forth by written order of the Commissioner upon written application by the Respondent for the relief sought.

X. THAT the provisions, terms and conditions of this Order shall be deemed to bind Respondent, its officers, directors, agents, servants, employees, successors and assigns and all persons, firms and corporations acting under, or for it.

DATED: Albany, New York

, 1972

HENRY L. DIAMOND, Commissioner
New York State Department of
Environmental Conservation

TO:

SCHEDULE A

FAILURE TO FILE REPORT

Step 1: On or before , submit an approvable environmental analysis report including emission data, pertinent environmental factors and a prepared environmental rating so as to show conformity with Part 212 or proposed corrective measures and schedule for compliance, including specific dates for the following:

A. Submission of approvable final plans and specifications.
B. Start of construction or modification.
C. Completion of construction or modification.
D. Submission of approvable test report to establish compliance with Part 212.

Any abatement program and schedule submitted by the Respondent pursuant to Step 1 and approved by the Department shall be annexed to and deemed a part of this Order and Schedule A to the same extent as if it had been fully set forth herein.

FAILURE TO MEET EMISSION REQUIREMENTS

Step 2: On or before , submit approvable final plans and specifications for the construction or modification of facilities to control emissions as required by Part 212.

Step 3: On or before , start construction or modification of said facilities in accordance with plans and specifications as approved by the Department.

Step 4: On or before , complete construction or modification of the aforesaid facilities in accordance with the aforesaid approved plans and specifications.

Step 5: On or before , submit the test results to the Department as required by paragraph of this Order.

Consent by Respondent

Respondent hereby consents to the issuing and entering of the foregoing Order, waives its right to a hearing herein as provided by law, and agrees to be bound by the provisions, terms and conditions contained therein.

By ______________________________
Title
Date

Corporate
State of)
County of) ss.:

On this day of , 1972, before me personally came to me known, who being by me duly sworn did depose and say that he resides at , that he is the of , the corporation described in and which executed the foregoing instrument; and that he signed his name as authorized by said corporation.

NOTARY PUBLIC

Individual
State of)
County of) ss.:

On this day of , 1972, before me came , to me known and known to me to be the individual described in and who executed the foregoing consent and he duly acknowledged to me that he executed the same.

NOTARY PUBLIC

STATE OF NEW YORK: DEPARTMENT OF HEALTH

In the Matter of Alleged Violations of Parts 175-180 and Part 186 of the New York State Rules to Prevent New Air Pollution by

THE ATLANTIC CEMENT COMPANY, INC.,

Respondent.

NOTICE OF HEARING AND COMPLAINT

TO: THE ATLANTIC CEMENT COMPANY, INC.
Ravena,
New York

PLEASE TAKE NOTICE that pursuant to Article 12-A of the Public Health Law a public hearing will be convened and held on June 24, 1968, at 10:00 A.M., in Room 159 of the New York State Department of Health Building at 84 Holland Avenue in the City and County of Albany, New York, to consider charges that respondent, The Atlantic Cement Company, Inc., by its officers, agents and employees violated the New York State Rules to Prevent New Air Pollution at its cement plant in the Town of Coeymans, County of Albany and the State of New York, as follows:

I. Respondent violated § 179.2 of said Rules by its failure to maintain and operate its air pollution control equipment in a satisfactory manner; such violations having occurred on February 26, 1968, February 27, 1968, February 28, 1968, February 29, 1968, March 14, 1968, and on various other dates and times between January 27, 1967, and the present.

II. Respondent violated § 186.1 of said Rules by permitting or causing certain air contamination sources at said location aforesaid to produce air pollution throughout certain areas of said Town of Coeymans; such violations having occurred on February 26, 1968, February 27, 1968, February 28, 1968, February 29, 1968, March 14, 1968, and on various other dates and times between January 27, 1967, and the present.

TAKE FURTHER NOTICE as follows:

1. A record of the hearing will be made and witnesses will be sworn. The respondent may appear by representative, with or without counsel, and the respondent may produce witnesses and evidence in its behalf, cross-examine witnesses and examine such evidence as may be produced against it.

2. Pursuant to the provisions of Section 1280 of the Public Health Law, the respondent is required to answer the charges set forth above in this Notice of Hearing at the public hearing to be held at the above stated time and place.

3. Pursuant to the provisions of Section 1281 of the Public Health Law, the respondent may file a written answer to the charges set forth in this Notice of Hearing at least three (3) days prior to the hearing.

4. Whether or not the respondent appears at the hearing aforesaid, the Commissioner of Health may issue an Order pursuant to the provisions of Section 1282 of the Public Health Law, or make such determination as he shall deem appropriate under the circumstances, and the respondent will, upon failure or refusal to comply with any such Order, be liable to the penalties specified in Section 1286 of the Public Health Law, in addition to any other remedies or penalties allowed by law.

DATED: Albany, New York
May 27, 1968

HOLLIS S. INGRAHAM, M.D.
Commissioner of Health
of the State of New York

By ______________________________
DONALD A. MacHARG
Commissioner's Designee to
Issue Notice of Hearing
Tel. (518) 474-2955

STATE OF NEW YORK — DEPARTMENT OF HEALTH

In the Matter of Alleged Violations of Parts 175-180 and Part 186 of the New York State Rules to Prevent New Air Pollution by

THE ATLANTIC CEMENT COMPANY, INC.,

Respondent.

STIPULATION

It is hereby stipulated and agreed by and between the attorneys for the respective parties to this proceeding that there exist valid and sufficient grounds as a matter of law and fact for the issuance of the annexed Order of the Commissioner of Health under the Public Health Law and the respondent consents to its entry and accepts its terms and conditions and waives the right to a hearing.

DATED: September 3, 1968

THOMAS F. BURKE
Attorney for Respondent

DONALD A. MacHARG
Counsel
New York State Department of Health

STATE OF NEW YORK — DEPARTMENT OF HEALTH

In the Matter of Alleged Violations of Parts 175-180 and Part 186 of the New York State Rules to Prevent New Air Pollution by

THE ATLANTIC CEMENT COMPANY, INC.

Respondent.

ORDER

A public hearing in the above entitled proceeding having been scheduled to be held on June 24, 1968, at 10:00 A.M., pursuant to due written notice, served in the manner provided by law, before EARL W. MURRAY, Esq., duly designated Hearing Officer and Representative of the Commissioner of Health of the State of New York, and the New York State Department of Health having appeared therein by its Counsel DONALD A. MacHARG, Esq., (William B. Parker, Esq., of Counsel) and the respondent, The Atlantic Cement Company, Inc., having appeared generally therein by George H. Cain, Esq., General Counsel, (Thomas F. Burke, Esq., of Counsel) and the parties hereto having entered into a written Stipulation, a copy of which is attached, providing that there exist valid and sufficient grounds as a matter of law and fact for the issuance of this Order of the Commissioner of Health under the Public Health Law and that the respondent consents to its entry and accepts its terms and conditions and waives the right to a hearing;

NOW, on reading and filing said Notice of Hearing, with proof of service thereof, and said Stipulation, and in accordance with the provisions of the Public Health Law, it is hereby ORDERED THAT:

I.Said Stipulation be and the same hereby is ratified and confirmed.

II. Respondent, the Atlantic Cement Company, Inc., must at all times use and keep in continuous operation the Johnson-Marsh control equipment during the operation of the primary crusher, belt, and related materials handling equipment at its manufacturing plant located in the Town of Coeymans, Albany County, New York; the use of said Johnson-Marsh control equipment must continue during all seasons of the year, all days of the week, and during all hours of the day whenever respondent is operating the facilities above mentioned; in the event that such Johnson-Marsh control equipment remains inoperative, respondent must immediately close down, cease to operate and keep out of operation the primary crusher, belt, and related materials handling equipment above mentioned and may resume the operation of said primary crusher, belt and related materials handling equipment only at such time as said Johnson-Marsh control equipment is put into operation.

III. Respondent must submit reports showing the periods of time during which the Johnson-Marsh control equipment above mentioned and the primary crusher were in operation; such reports must be submitted to the Department of Health of the State of New York commencing on September 1, 1968, and each and every three months thereafter and more frequently and at such times as the respondent is directed to furnish such reports on not less than three (3) days notice by the Department to the respondent; such reports shall indicate in detail the days and hours of the operation of those items by the respondent.

IV. The present Johnson-Marsh control equipment will be closely monitored by the Albany County Health Department, the New York State Health Department and the respondent for a period of not less than six months after the date of this Order to determine whether or not the Johnson-Marsh control equipment is adequate to maintain the quality of the air in accordance with the standards established by the Air Pollution Control Board and in the event that such equipment is found to be incapable of so doing, the respondent must install such other air cleaning devices and equipment as may be necessary to maintain the quality of the air in accordance with such standards within such times as ordered by the Commissioner either by a modification of this Order or the making of a new Order, either of which may be done without further hearings or administrative proceedings against the respondent by the Commissioner of Health.

V. This Order is taking effect immediately upon the service of a copy thereof by registered mail on the respondent.

DATED: Albany, New York
September 4, 1968

HOLLIS S. INGRAHAM, M.D.
Commissioner of Health
of the State of New York

STATE OF NEW YORK:
DEPARTMENT OF ENVIRONMENTAL CONSERVATION

In the matter of alleged violations of a Commissioner's Order and of Part 179, Part 186 and Parts 501 and 504 of the New York State Air Pollution Control Rules by	**NOTICE OF HEARING**
ATLANTIC CEMENT COMPANY, INC.	**COMPLAINT ATTACHED**
Respondent.	

PLEASE TAKE NOTICE that pursuant to the Environmental Conservation Law and Article 12-A of the Public Health Law I will convene a public hearing on Tuesday, 1 December 1970 at 10 a.m. in Room 620 at the offices of the Department at 50 Wolf Road, Albany, New York, to consider charges that you have violated the Order dated 4 September 1968 made by Dr. Hollis S. Ingraham, State Health Commissioner, whose duties referrable to air pollution control have been transferred to me, and further, that you have violated Part 179, Part 186 and Parts 501 and 504 of the State Air Pollution Control Rules, as specified in the complaint attached.

PLEASE BE ADVISED that you may file a written answer to the charges not later than three (3) days before the hearing date; that all witnesses will testify under oath, and a record of the proceeding will be made; that you may produce witnesses and evidence in your own behalf; that you may request issuance of subpoenas to compel attendance of witnesses and production of records relating to the matter under investigation; that you may cross-examine witnesses and examine evidence produced against you.

PLEASE TAKE WARNING that a violation of the Commissioner's Order is punishable by a civil penalty in a sum not exceeding One Thousand Dollars, and an additional sum not exceeding Two Hundred Dollars for each day the violation continues.

PLEASE TAKE FURTHER WARNING that the imposition of civil penalties for violation of the order, rule, or regulation shall not preclude the taking of such other remedial action as may be required.

DATED: Albany, New York
10 November 1970

HENRY L. DIAMOND
Commissioner of Environmental
Conservation of the State of
New York

Inquiries to N.C. Silletti
Telephone No. (518) 457-7060

TO: John E. D. Grunow
President,
Atlantic Cement Co., Inc.
300 Park Avenue
New York City 10022

L. U. Spellman
Vice President
Atlantic Cement Co., Inc.
P.O. Box 30
Stamford, Conn. 06904

STATE OF NEW YORK:

DEPARTMENT OF ENVIRONMENTAL CONSERVATION

In the matter of alleged violations of a Commissioner's Order and of Part 179, Part 186 and Parts 501 and 504 of the New York State Air Pollution Control Rules by

COMPLAINT

ATLANTIC CEMENT COMPANY, INC.

Respondent.

VIOLATION OF COMMISSIONER'S ORDER

The Order of State Health Commissioner Ingraham dated 4 September 1968, in relevant part, directed the following:

"II. Respondent, The Atlantic Cement Company, Inc., must at all times use and keep in continuous operation the Johnson-Marsh control equipment during the operation of the primary crusher, belt, and related materials handling equipment at its manufacturing plant located in the Town of Coeymans, Albany County, New York; the use of said Johnson-Marsh control equipment must continue during all seasons of the year, all days of the week, and during all hours of the day whenever respondent is operating the facilities above mentioned; in the event that such Johnson-Marsh control equipment becomes inoperative for any reason whatsoever, then and in any such event and during and throughout whatever period or periods said Johnson-Marsh control equipment remains inoperative, respondent must immediately close down, cease to operate and keep out of operation the primary crusher, belt, and related materials handling equipment above mentioned and may resume the operation of said primary crusher, belt, and related materials handling equipment only at such time as said Johnson-Marsh control equipment is put into operation."

Notwithstanding the foregoing, Respondent did in fact conduct primary crushing and conveying operations at its said plant without benefit of said Johnson-Marsh control equipment on the following dates:

24 Sept. 69	25 Sept. 69	15 Apr. 70	16 Apr. 70
29 May 70	1 June 70	5 June 70	22 Oct. 70

The right to offer proof of other violations is reserved, subject to five days notice thereof to Respondent or its counsel.

VIOLATION OF PART 179

Respondent, has permitted a fugitive dust condition to continue through improper disposal of contaminants collected from its air cleaning devices (Section 179.3) and has failed to date to provide a satisfactory dust dump facility originally promised for completion by 1 June 1969.

VIOLATION OF PART 186

By frequent shut-down of air-cleaning devices, Respondent has caused its plant to pollute the outdoor atmosphere with cement dust injuring property and interfering with the comfortable enjoyment of life and property at the residences of the following inhabitants of Pantages Mobile Home Park on Route 9W, Selkirk, among others.

Frank Blood
Stanley & Cecilia Stefanik
Janet Martin
Elsabe Friedrich
Rose Marie Albright
Milton & Betty Jean Pitcher
Barry King
Herman King
Judy Murphy
John & Mary Murphy
Miriam Browne
Richard Browne
Ted Pantazis
Karen DeFlippis
Richard & Geraldine Gilbert
Eugene & Dorothy Niemiec
Morris Darling
Yvonne Spinner
Joan Warden
Linda Williams
Teresa Volkov

VIOLATIONS OF PARTS 501 AND 504

Collection of settleable particulates at three receptors in the vicinity of Respondent's plant reveal that Respondent has emitted contaminants in the form of settleable particulates in quantities which alone or in combination with other sources have contravened the air quality standards established for the area, as hereinafter set forth:

LEVEL III

50% to be less than 0.40 mgm/cm^2/mo

84% to be less than 0.60 mgm/cm^2/mo

Receptor 0152-01 Ravena-Coeymans-Selkirk High School	1969	Receptor 0152-03 Ventura property
0.81	Jan.	2.54
1.16	Feb.	4.02
1.09	March	4.81
1.18	April	4.01
0.83	May	4.33
1.98	July	5.08
1.17	Aug.	6.65
2.44	Sept.	discontinued
1.45	Oct.	
——	Nov.	
1.43	Dec.	
	1970	
1.47	Jan.	
2.35	Feb.	
1.81	March	
——	April	
1.43	May	
1.86	June	
1.57	July	
0.83	Aug.	

LEVEL II

50% to be less than 0.30 mgm/cm^2/mo

84% to be less than 0.45 mgm/cm^2/mo

Receptor 0152-02
Peter B. Coeymans
Elementary School

	1969
1.01	Jan.
2.54	Feb.
2.46	March
1.57	April
1.43	May
1.26	July
1.26	Aug.
2.70	Sept.
1.80	Oct.
7.10	Nov.
2.84	Dec.
	1970
1.90	Jan.
1.36	Feb.
2.42	March
1.61	April
1.90	May

NCS/ct
29 Oct 70

STATE OF NEW YORK:
DEPARTMENT OF ENVIRONMENTAL CONSERVATION

In the Matter of alleged violations of a Commissioner's Order and of Part 170, Part 186 and Parts 501 and 504 of the New York State Air Pollution Control Rules by

ATLANTIC CEMENT COMPANY, INC.
Albany County

Respondent.

ORDER ON CONSENT

FILE NO. 60

A Notice of Hearing dated November 10, 1970 with Complaint attached having been duly served upon the Atlantic Cement Company, Inc. (hereinafter "Respondent"), and

Pursuant to said Notice, a public hearing having been convened before Dr. Emanual Bund, a duly designated and deputized Hearing Officer and Representative of the Commissioner of Environmental Conservation, and

Respondent having waived further public hearing and consented to the entering and filing of this Order.

NOW, having considered this matter and being duly advised, it is ORDERED:

I. THAT, Respondent, having already discontinued the use of its old dust dump area for the disposal of dust, shall not again use such area for said disposal.

II. THAT, Respondent, having opened a new dust dump area at the end of the haul road, shall operate such new area so as to comply strictly with the terms and conditions of the attached Certificate to Operate said area.

III. THAT, during such times as Respondent's production system is functioning and feed is entering or contained in the system and the system is capable of emitting particulates to the outer air, Respondent shall use and keep in continuous operation the bag-house collectors and precipitators so as to maximize the efficiency of said devices to collect and remove particulates from the emissions of their respective sources. On kiln start up, the precipitators will be started as soon as possible after feed is introduced into the system, provided, however, that the precipitators shall in all events be started and operating within thirty (30) minutes after feed is so introduced.

IV. THAT, in the event that the aforesaid electrostatic precipitators or more than one section of any bag-house collectors become inoperative in whole or in part for any reason whatsoever, Respondent shall notify the Department of the reason for the reduced collection of particulates from the clinker coolers and/or kilns and the anticipated time duration of such reduced particulate collection and, in addition, Respondent shall reduce the production level of the clinker coolers and/or kilns (volume of its production system) to a level whereby the emissions from said facilities to the outer air do not exceed the particulate emission levels obtained during periods of maximum efficiency under full, normal operating conditions and Respondent shall maintain its production system at such reduced levels of operation until such time as the use of inoperative bag collectors and/or precipitators can be fully resumed at levels of maximum efficiency. In the event the Respondent cannot meet emission levels obtained during periods of maximum collector efficiency under full, normal operating conditions, the kiln or kilns will be shut down until the emission levels can be met.

V. THAT, Respondent shall make such modifications, repairs and/or additions to its facilities at its cement manufacturing plant in Ravena, New York, as are necessary to control and to regulate the emissions therefrom so as to conform, under normal operating conditions, with the environmental ratings assigned to Respondent's emission sources under Part 187 of the air pollution control rules.

Further, Respondent shall so regulate the emissions from said plant so as not to contravene the ambient air quality standards adopted for and assigned to Albany County.

Respondent shall take such steps as may be necessary to ensure the proper control and containment of fugitive dust, so as to prevent such dust from leaving the boundaries of the property of Respondent's plant so as not to contravene applicable air quality standards.

The aforesaid requirements shall be timely met strictly in accordance with the compliance schedule set forth in Appendices A-1 and A-2 attached hereto and incorporated herein.

VI. THAT, the Respondent shall, at its own cost and expense and in a manner acceptable to the Commissioner, test its kiln stack for the purpose of determining compliance with Part 187 of the air pollution control rules. Such tests shall be conducted on a quarterly basis, beginning in May, 1972 and continue until Respondent has complied with Appendix A-1, or until such time as the Commissioner may designate by written directive to Respondent. The Respondent shall give the Department fifteen days notice prior to the date of such stack tests and allow representatives of the Department to observe conduct of the test. The results of such tests shall be submitted to the Department within 15 days of the end of each quarterly period. Nothing herein shall be deemed to preclude the Department from conducting its own tests at said facility.

VII. THAT, on the fifteenth day of each month beginning May 15, 1972, or at such longer intervals that the Commissioner may specify, the Respondent shall submit to the Department such operating reports as may be required by the Department which shall include but not be limited to the following matters for the preceding month:

A. Time and date of kiln shutdown or reduced production and reason therefore.

B. Time and date of kiln start-up or return to full production.

C. Number of control device sections not in good working order.

D. Steps taken to reduce production, and production levels attained, on account of inoperative kiln control device sections and/or clinker cooler bag-house.

VIII. THAT, for the purpose of insuring compliance with this Order, duly authorized representatives of the State of New York shall be permitted access to inspect the facilities being operated, owned, constructed and/or maintained by the Respondent for the purpose of inspecting said facilities, to make or require such tests which may be deemed necessary and for the purpose of determining the status of compliance with the terms of this Order.

IX. THAT, Respondent shall submit all reports and submissions herein required to the Regional Director, Region 4, Department of Environmental Conservation, 50 Wolf Road, Albany, New York 12201, or his representative.

X. THAT, if because of an act of God, war, strike, riot, catastrophe or other condition as to which negligence or willful misconduct on the part of Respondent was not the proximate cause, Respondent cannot meet the compliance schedules set forth in Appendices A-1 and A-2 the Respondent shall apply within a reasonable time after it obtains knowledge of said fact to the Commissioner of the Department and request an extension or modification of such schedules.

XI. THAT, upon written application by the Respondent for the relief sought, this Order may be amended by written order of the Commissioner.

DATED: Albany, New York
May 11, 1972

____

HENRY L. DIAMOND, Commissioner
New York State Department of
Environmental Conservation

TO: Donald M. Halsted, Jr., President
Atlantic Cement Company, Inc.
P.O. Box 30
Stamford, Connecticut 06904

Ainsworth, Sullivan, Tracy and Knauf
Attorneys for Respondent
State Bank Building
75 State Street
Albany, New York 12207

Attn: Thomas F. Tracy, Esq.

ATLANTIC CEMENT COMPANY, INC.

By ____________________________
Title
Date

Appendix A-1

Control Systems for the Kilns

1. By May 1, 1973 — Submit a report indicating status of compliance and decision regarding installation of control equipment or process changes.

If compliance with Part 187 as a result of present actions cannot be demonstrated, either additional control equipment will be installed or the process redesigned to effect compliance with Part 187.

If decision is made to install additional control equipment, Schedule A will apply. If decision is made to design change in process, Schedule B will apply.

Schedule A

2. By September 1, 1973 — Submit application for permit to construct.
3. By December 31, 1973 — Award contracts.
4. By December 31, 1974 — Complete installation of control equipment in accordance with the approved plans.
5. By April 1, 1975 — Complete testing of installation.
6. By May 1, 1975 — Submit test report.

Schedule B

2. By May 1, 1974 — Submit EAR and application for permit to construct.
3. By September 1, 1974 — Award contracts.
4. By December 31, 1975 — Complete construction.
5. By June 30, 1976 — Complete testing.
6. By July 31, 1976 — Submit test report.

Appendix A-2

Ambient Air Study and Concurrent
Preparation of Plans to Meet
Ambient Air Quality Standards

1. March 1, 1972 — Initiate an ambient air quality study with respect to settleable and suspended particulates in a manner acceptable to this Department. This study shall be a continuous on-going study for the purpose of assessing and reporting the ambient air quality in the area.
2. Concurrently, with the study referred to in paragraph 1, all sources of dust, shall be reviewed and a report and plans prepared for the reduction of dust emission from these sources to the point where the ambient air quality standards will be met.

3. March 15, 1973 — At the end of the first year of the ambient air study, the results of this study will be submitted to this Department for review and evaluation. If the data indicate that ambient air quality standards are being violated and will continue to be violated, Atlantic Cement will also submit the aforementioned plans and report.
4. April 1, 1973 — Atlantic Cement will submit satisfactory abatement schedules for all sources covered in the aforementioned report and plans.
5. June 1, 1974 — All work required by the report and plans for compliance with the ambient air standards will be completed.

STATE OF NEW YORK:
DEPARTMENT OF ENVIRONMENTAL CONSERVATION

In the Matter of Alleged Violations of a Commissioner's Order and of Part 170, Part 186 and Parts 501 and 504 of the New York State Air Pollution Control rules by

ATLANTIC CEMENT COMPANY, INC.
Albany County

Respondent.

EXTENSION OF TIME NO. 1

An Order having been entered against Respondent dated May 11, 1972 said Order containing an abatement timetable and Respondent having requested certain modifications of said timetable in a letter dated November 17th, 1972, a copy of which is annexed hereto and Respondent having consented to the making and entry of this Modified Order.

NOW, having considered the request and being duly advised, it is ORDERED:

I. THAT the abatement schedule in Respondent's Order dated May 11, 1972, is hereby modified in accordance with the dates in Schedule A-2 attached hereto and incorporated herein.

II. THAT, with the exception of the modifications reflected herein, said Order remains in full force and effect.

DATED: Albany, New York
December 13, 1972

HENRY L. DIAMOND, Commissioner
New York State Department of
Environmental Conservation

TO: Donald M. Halsted, Jr., President
Atlantic Cement Company, Inc.
P.O. Box 30
Stamford, Connecticut 06904

Ainsworth, Sullivan, Tracy and Knauf
Attorneys for Respondent
State Bank Building
75 State Street
Albany, New York 12207

Attn: Thomas F. Tracy, Esq.

Respondent hereby consents to the issuing and entering of the foregoing Extension of time without further notice and waives its right to a hearing herein and agrees to be bound by the provisions, terms and conditions contained herein.

SCHEDULE A-2

Ambient Air Study and Concurrent Preparation of Plans to meet Ambient Air Quality Standards.

1. Continue the ambient air quality study commenced July 1, 1972 with respect to settleable and suspended particulates in a manner acceptable to this Department. This study shall be a continuous on-going study for the purpose of assessing and reporting the ambient air quality in the area.

2. Concurrently, with the study referred to in Paragraph 1, all sources of dust, shall be reviewed and a report and plans prepared for the reduction of dust emission from these sources to the point where the ambient air quality standards will be met.

3. July 15, 1973 — At the end of the first year of the ambient air

study, the results of this study will be submitted to this Department for review and evaluation. If the data indicate that ambient air quality standards are being violated and will continue to be violated, Atlantic Cement will also submit the aforementioned plans and report.

4. August 1, 1973 — Atlantic Cement will submit satisfactory abatement schedules for all sources covered in the aforementioned report and plans.

5. October 1, 1974 — All work required by the report and plans for compliance with the ambient air standards will be completed.

Appendix D

Tax Relief for Air Pollution Control Facilities

NEW YORK STATE DEPARTMENT OF ENVIRONMENTAL CONSERVATION

Albany, N. Y. 12201

TAX RELIEF FOR AIR POLLUTION CONTROL FACILITIES

The 1966 legislature amended the Public Health Law, the Tax Law and Real Property Tax Law providing tax benefits to encourage construction of air pollution control facilities.

Eligibility

An eligible facility must remove, reduce or render less noxious air contaminants which would otherwise be emitted to the outer air from an air contamination source and must be in compliance with the New York State air pollution control rules. Eligibility is limited to that portion of the facility from a point immediately preceding the removal, reduction or treatment device to the point of discharge. Examples of eligible facilities are: scrubbers, afterburners, centrifugal dust collectors, cloth arrestors and electrostatic precipitators.

Facilities whose primary purpose is the salvage of usable or marketable materials and facilities which rely on dilution, dispersion or assimilation of air contaminants in the ambient air are ineligible. Examples of facilities which are generally excluded are: solvent recovery systems and stacks.

Benefits

1. Tax Law — A deduction shall be allowed for expenditures paid or incurred during the taxable year for construction, reconstruction or improvement of *certified* air pollution control facilities initiated after January 1, 1966 (see Sections 208, 612, 683, 706 and 1083 of the Tax Law).

2. Real Property Tax Law — The change in state law enables legislative bodies of counties, towns and villages to exempt from taxation and special ad valorem levies any increase in value resulting from a certified air pollution control facility constructed or reconstructed after August 1, 1966 (see Section 481, Real Property Law).

Certification

A Certificate of Compliance for Tax Relief for an Air Pollution Control Facility (form AIR 104) is issued for a completed facility for a three-year period and may be renewed by reapplication if the facility is still in operation. A temporary Certificate of Compliance may be issued for a facility under construction, but it shall apply only to those expenditures made in the taxable year for which the certificate is issued.

A person who owns an eligible facility may apply by submitting application form AIR 108 *in triplicate* to the New York State field representative for the air resource management program. Applications may be obtained from the field representatives for the county in which the facility is located. (See form AIR-51 for addresses of field representatives.)

NEW YORK STATE DEPARTMENT OF ENVIRONMENTAL CONSERVATION

APPLICATION
CERTIFICATE OF COMPLIANCE FOR TAX RELIEF
AIR POLLUTION CONTROL FACILITY

See application form AIR-108.1 for filing instructions and form AIR-51 for address of office where application may be filed.

NAME OF APPLICANT	DATE OF APPLICATION	APPLICATION NO. (Leave blank)
ADDRESS (Number & Street)	NAME OF PERSON SIGNING APPLICATION	
City, Town or Village State Zip Code	Title	
APPLICATION FOR ☐ Three-year Certificate ☐ Temporary Certificate ☐ Renewal	IF RENEWAL, INDICATE PREVIOUS CERTIFICATE NO.	

LOCATION OF AIR POLLUTION CONTROL FACILITY

(Number & Street) (City, Town, Village) (County)

AIR POLLUTION CONTROL FACILITY

1. TYPE (Describe)		2. MANUFACTURER AND MODEL NO.	
3. CAPACITY (SCFM)	Cost	4. CERTIFICATE TO OPERATE Date Issued	No.

	MONTH	DAY	YEAR
1. DATE CONSTRUCTION STARTED			
2. DATE CONSTRUCTION COMPLETED			
a. IF NOT COMPLETED, ESTIMATED DATE OF COMPLETION			
3. DATE FACILITY BECAME OPERATIONAL			
4. NEXT REAL PROPERTY TAXABLE STATUS DATE			
5. NEXT CORPORATE INCOME TAX REPORT DUE DATE			

THE SALVAGE OF MARKETABLE OR USABLE MATERIALS IS NOT THE PRIMARY PURPOSE OF THIS AIR POLLUTION CONTROL FACILITY.

Signature (Applicant)

TO BE COMPLETED BY FIELD REPRESENTATIVE

☐ Recommend Approval

☐ Recommend Disapproval (State reasons)

REMARKS:

DATE ______ SIGNED ______
Field Representative

AIR 108.1 (6-72)

New York State Department of Environmental Conservation
Albany, N. Y. 12201

Henry L. Diamond,
Commissioner

Date Issued: Application Number: ☐ Three-year

Expires: Certificate Number: ☐ Temporary
☐ Renewal

CERTIFICATE OF COMPLIANCE FOR TAX RELIEF
AIR POLLUTION CONTROL FACILITY
Issued Pursuant to §§ 19-0307, 19-0309 of the
New York State Environmental Conservation Law

Owner/Operator: Location of Facility:

Facility Description:

This is to certify that the owner/operator has completed the construction or reconstruction of an air pollution control facility at the above location, and that this facility is operating in compliance with the appropriate provisions of the State Environmental Conservation Law, State Public Health Law and rules, permits, certificates or orders issued pursuant thereto.

Conditions:

1. This certificate is subject to revocation if the facility is not operated in compliance with the State Environmental Conservation Law, State Public Health Law, and rules, permits, certificates or orders issued pursuant thereto.

2. To continue eligibility for tax relief the holder of this certificate is required to submit to the field representative a triennial operating report with a renewal application (form AIR 108) in triplicate not later than sixty days before this certificate expires.

AIR 104 (3/72)

DEDUCTIONS FROM INCOME UNDER NEW YORK STATE TAX LAW

Article 9-A Franchise Tax on Business Corporations
Section 208 Definitions

9. The term "entire net income" means total net income from all sources, which shall be presumably the same as the entire taxable income which the taxpayer is required to report to the United States treasury department. . . .

(g) At the election of the taxpayer, a deduction shall be allowed for expenditures paid or incurred during the taxable year for the construction, reconstruction, erection or improvement of industrial waste treatment facilities and air pollution control facilities.

(1) (A) The term "industrial waste treatment facilities" shall mean facilities for the treatment, neutralization or stabilization of industrial waste (as the term "industrial waste" is defined in section twelve hundred two of the public health law) from a point immediately preceding the point of such treatment, neutralization or stabilization to the point of disposal, including the necessary pumping and transmitting facilities, but excluding such facilities installed for the primary purpose of salvaging materials which are usable in the manufacturing process or are marketable.

(B) The term "air pollution control facilities" shall mean facilities which remove, reduce, or render less noxious air contaminants emitted from an air contamination source (as the terms "air contaminant" and "air contamination source" are defined in section twelve hundred sixty-seven of the public health law) from a point immediately preceding the point of such removal, reduction or rendering to the point of discharge of air, meeting emission standards as established by the air pollution control board, but excluding such facilities installed for the primary purpose of salvaging materials which are usable in the manufacturing process or are marketable and excluding those facilities which rely for their efficacy on dilution, dispersion or assimilation of air contaminants in the ambient air after emission.

(2) However, such deduction shall be allowed only

(A) with respect to tangible property which is depreciable, pursuant to section one hundred sixty-seven of the internal revenue code,[4] having a situs in this state and used in the taxpayer's trade or business, the construction, reconstruction, erection or improvement of which, in the case of industrial waste treatment facilities, is initiated on or after January first, nineteen hundred sixty-five, and only for expenditures paid or incurred prior to January first, nineteen hundred seventy-two, or which, in the case of air pollution control facilities, is initiated on or after January first, nineteen hundred sixty-six, and

(B) on condition that such facilities have been certified by the state commissioner of health or his designated representative, pursuant to the public health law, as complying with applicable provisions of the public health law, the state sanitary code and regulations, permits or orders issued pursuant thereto, and

(C) on condition that entire net income for the taxable year and all succeeding taxable years be computed without any deductions for such expenditures or for depreciation of the same property other than the deductions allowed by this paragraph (g), except to the extent that the basis of the property may be attributable to factors other than such expenditures, or in case a deduction is allowable pursuant to this paragraph for only a part of such expenditures, on condition that any deduction allowed for federal income tax purposes for such expenditures or for depreciation of the same property be proportionately reduced in computing entire net income for the taxable year and all succeeding taxable years, and

(D) where the election provided for in paragraph (d) of subdivision three of section two hundred ten of this chapter has not been exercised in respect to the same property.

(3) (A) If expenditures in respect to an industrial waste treatment facility or an air pollution control facility have been deducted as provided herein and if within ten years from the end of the taxable year in which such deduction was allowed such property or any part thereof is used for the primary purpose of salvaging materials which are usable in the manufacturing process or are marketable, the taxpayer shall report such change of use in its report for the first taxable year during which it occurs, and the tax commission may recompute the tax for the year or years for which such deduction was allowed and any carryback or carryover year, and may assess any additional tax resulting from such recomputation within the time fixed by paragraph nine of subsection (c) of section ten hundred eighty-three.

(B) If a deduction is allowed as herein provided for expenditures paid or incurred during any taxable year on the basis of a temporary certificate of compliance issued pursuant to the public health law and if the taxpayer fails to obtain a permanent certificate of compliance upon completion of the facilities with respect to which such temporary certificate was issued, the taxpayer shall report such failure in its report for the taxable year during which such facilities are completed, and the tax commission may recompute the tax for the year or years for which such deduction was allowed and any carryback or carryover year, and may assess any additional tax resulting from such recomputation within the time fixed by paragraph nine of subsection (c) of section ten hundred eighty-three.

(4) In any taxable year when property is sold or otherwise disposed of, with respect to which a deduction has been allowed pursuant to this paragraph, such deduction shall be disregarded in computing gain or loss, and the gain or loss on the sale or other disposition of such property shall be the gain or loss entering into the computation of entire taxable income which the taxpayer is required to report to the United States treasury department for such taxable year.

Article 23
Section 706 Unincorporated business deductions
(Under paragraph (9) of this section the above provisions of Article 9-A, Section 208, paragraph 9 are made applicable to unincorporated businesses.)

EXEMPTIONS FROM LOCAL REAL PROPERTY TAXES UNDER NEW YORK STATE REAL PROPERTY TAX LAW

Article 4 Exemptions

Section 481. Tax exemption for air pollution control facilities

1. Air pollution control facilities which were constructed or reconstructed in order to comply with the provisions of the public health law and codes, rules, regulations, permits or orders issued pursuant thereto shall be exempt from taxation and special ad valorem levies to the extent of any increase in value thereof by reason of such construction or reconstruction.

2. Such air pollution control facilities shall not be entitled to any exemption from taxation unless such facilities have been certified by the commissioner of health or his designated representative, pursuant to section twelve hundred seventy-seven-a of the public health law, as complying with applicable provisions of the public health law and codes, rules, regulations, permits or orders issued pursuant thereto.

3. Such exemptions shall be applicable only to air pollution control facilities which were constructed or reconstructed subsequent to the effective date of this act.

4. Such exemption from taxation shall be granted only upon an

application by the owner of such facility on a form prescribed by the state board. The applicant shall furnish such information as such board shall require. The original of such application shall be filed with the assessor of the city, town, village or county having the power to assess property for taxation on or before the appropriate taxable status date of such city, town, village or county. A copy of such application shall be filed simultaneously with the state board.

5. If the assessor is satisfied that the applicant is entitled to an exemption pursuant to this section, he shall approve the application and such air pollution control facilities shall forthwith be exempt from taxation and special ad valorem levies as herein provided.

6. The assessed value of any exemption granted pursuant to the authority granted by this section shall be entered by the assessor on the portion of the assessment roll provided for property exempt from taxation.

7. The provisions of this section shall be applicable only to the assessment rolls of a county, city, town or village which has adopted a local law or a school district which has adopted a resolution as provided in this section.

8. A county, city, town or village acting through its local legislative body is hereby authorized and empowered to adopt and amend local laws providing for an exemption from taxation to the extent provided by this section of air pollution control facilities located within such county, city, town or village as follows: where such local law is adopted by a county, such exemption shall apply to taxes and special ad valorem levies imposed by or on behalf of the county for county or part county purposes; in the case of a city, to taxes imposed for city purposes, in the case of a town, to taxes and special ad valorem levies imposed for town or part town purposes; and, in the case of a village, to taxes imposed for village purposes. In the case of a city school district where taxes imposed for city school district purposes are not levied by such city school district, the local law adopted by the city shall apply to taxes imposed for city school district purposes.

9. A school district which levies school taxes through its governing body is hereby authorized and empowered to adopt and amend resolutions authorizing an exemption from taxation for school purposes to the extent provided by this section of air pollution control facilities located within such school district, provided, however, that

a local law providing for such exemption from taxation for school purposes is adopted by each city or town wholly or partly within such school district wherein such facilities are located.

10. The term "air pollution control facilities" shall mean facilities which remove, reduce, or render less noxious air contaminants emitted from air contamination sources (as the terms "air contaminant" and "air contamination source" are defined in section twelve hundred sixty-seven of the public health law) from a point immediately preceding the point of such removal, reduction, or rendering to the point of discharge of air, meeting emission standards as established by the air pollution control board, but excluding such facilities installed for the primary purpose of salvaging materials which are usable in the manufacturing process or are marketable and excluding those facilities which rely for their efficacy on dilution, dispersion or assimilation of air contaminants in the ambient air after emission. Added L.1966, c. 902, § 40, eff. Aug. 1, 1966.

NOTICE

A copy of ths application must be attached to the federal income tax return of the applicant for the taxable year in which falls the first month of the 60 month amortization period elected, along with a copy of the certification. If that return has been filed when this application is completed or when the certification is received then the copy of this application or the certification or both should be sent to the District Director, or the Director of the Internal Revenue Service Center, with whom the return referred to in the preceding sentence was filed. These documents should *not* be sent to the national office of the Internal Revenue Service or to the Department of the Treasury.

ENVIRONMENTAL PROTECTION AGENCY
Region II Office
26 Federal Plaza
New York, N. Y. 10007

Gentlemen:

In response to your request, I am enclosing the forms you will need to apply for both State and Federal certification of pollution control facilities eligible for rapid amortization under Section 169 of the Internal Revenue Code of 1954, as amended.

Certification by the U. S. Environmental Protection Agency will be in accordance with EPA regulations published at 36 Federal Register 9509 (May 26, 1971), and with regulations of the Treasury Department published at 36 Federal Register 9010 (May 18, 1971). In addition, EPA published interpretive guidelines for its Regional Administrators at 36 Federal Register 19132 (September 29, 1971). You may wish to refer to the foregoing sources before completing the enclosed application.

Requests for additional copies of the forms and any questions you may have concerning their completion can be directed to:

Mrs. Dorothy Burke
Acting RTA Coordinator
Legal Section, Enforcement Division
U. S. Environmental Protection Agency
26 Federal Plaza
New York, New York 10007
(Area Code 212-264-9884)

Your interest and cooperation is very much appreciated.

Sincerely yours,
Gerald M. Hansler, P. E.
Regional Administrator

Enclosures:
EPA Form 3300-1 — Application for Certification of Pollution Control Facility (5 pages)
EPA Form 3300-1A — Instructions for Completing and Filing EPA Form 3300-1
EPA Form 3300-2 — Notice of State Certification
EPA Form 3300-3 — Notice of Federal Certification

Form Approved
OMB No. 158-R0013

ENVIRONMENTAL PROTECTION AGENCY
INSTRUCTIONS FOR COMPLETING AND FILING EPA FORM 3300-1,
APPLICATION FOR CERTIFICATION OF POLLUTION CONTROL FACILITY
(Pursuant to Part 602 of Title 18 of the Code of Federal Regulations)

GENERAL

1. Applicants are advised that separate regulations pertaining to accelerated depreciation under Section 169 of the Internal Revenue Code have been published by EPA as Part 602, Chapter I, Title 18, Code of Federal Regulations (Volume 36, *Federal Register,* p. 9509, May 26, 1971) and by the Treasury Department as Section 1.169 of the Income Tax Regulations, Part 1, subchapter A, Chapter I, Title 26, Code of Federal Regulations (Volume 36, *Federal Register,* p. 9010 May 18, 1971). These instructions do not include all the information contained in the statute and regulations, nor do they in any way modify the statute and regulations, to which applicants are encouraged to refer.

2. Applicants seeking certifications of facilities used for pollution control and eligible for rapid amortization as authorized by section 169 of the Internal Revenue Code shall complete one application (original and 3 copies) for each facility for which certification is sought. When necessary, attach additional sheets of paper to furnish required information, referring to the relevant section and item number on each such additional sheet. If any of the information requested on the application form is inapplicable to the facility for which certification is being sought, so indicate by writing the word "inapplicable" in the space provided after each item. In accordance with section 602.3 of the EPA regulations, an application for certification may pertain to several identical control facilities installed at the same plant, and information submitted to support certification of a control facility may be incorporated by reference in a subsequent application pertaining to an identical facility.

3. Applicants shall submit the original of the completed application (with attachments such as drawings, flow sheets, charts or other explanatory material) to the Regional Administrator for the region in which the control facility is located. Copies 1 and 2 of the completed application shall be submitted (with attachments) to the appropriate State Water or Air Pollution Control Agency of the State in which the control facility is located. Copy 3 is for the applicant's files.

4. The responsible State Water or Air Pollution Control Agency may complete the attached State Certification Form, or may use such other form containing substantially the same information, as it may deem appropriate. The completed State Certification, together with Copy 1 of the application and associated documents, should be forwarded by the State Agency to the appropriate EPA Regional Administrator, and a copy of the State Certification furnished the applicant. Copy 2 of the application may be retained by the State Agency for its records.

5. In accordance with section 602.4 of the EPA regulations, the Regional Administrator will notify the applicant and the State Water or Air Pollution Control Agency that Federal certification will be issued if the control facility is completed and operated in accordance with the application. Such a notice of intent to certify shall be issued only after receipt from the State certifying authority of a

statement that the facility, if constructed, reconstructed, acquired, erected, installed and operated in accordance with the application, will be in conformity with the State program or requirements for abatement or control of water or air pollution. The Notice of Federal Certification, however, will be issued only if it is determined that the facility has been completed and is operating in accordance with the application, and only after receipt of a completed State Certification. When the application indicates that the facility to which it relates is not yet in operation, such application may be amended by a letter addressed to the Regional Administrator specifying the date on which the facility was placed in operation.

6. Certification of a control facility by an official of the Environmental Protection Agency does not of itself entitle an applicant to rapid amortization pursuant to Section 169 of the Internal Revenue Code. Such entitlement shall be determined by the Commissioner of Internal Revenue in accordance with applicable provisions of the Internal Revenue Code and rules and regulations issued thereunder.

SPECIFIC

SECTION A—IDENTITY AND LOCATION OF POLLUTION CONTROL FACILITY

Items 1 thru 6—Self-explanatory.

SECTION B—DESCRIPTION OF POLLUTION CONTROL FACILITY

Item 1—Include in the description of the control facility a reference to the types of effuents or emissions controlled by the facility, and attach a process flow diagram, if available.

Item 2—In most cases, the date the facility was placed in operation will be easily ascertainable. As is more fully set forth in section 1.169-2(b)(2)(iv) of the Income Tax Regulations, however, a taxpayer's depreciation practices may affect the determination of when a facility is deemed to be placed in operation.

Item 3—Section 169 does not permit rapid amortization of a building unless it is exclusively devoted to the abatement of pollution. A building which performs no function other than housing or sheltering a pollution control facility is itself considered to be exclusively devoted to the abatement of pollution. The term "building" is explained in section 1.169-2(b)(2)(i) of the Income Tax Regulations, which provides, in part, that the term "building" does *not* include "an enclosure which is so closely combined with the machinery or equipment which it supports, houses, or serves that it must be replaced, retired, or abandoned contemporaneously with such machinery or equipment, and which is depreciated over the life of such machinery or equipment."

SECTION C—DESCRIPTION OF COMMERCIAL PROCESS OR ACTIVITY

Item 1—Describe briefly in a narrative manner the general nature of the operation conducted at the location of the control facility.

Item 2—If known, provide the Standard Industrial Classification (SIC) Code number for the activity in connection with which the control facility is used.

Item 3—Self-explanatory.

Item 4—Section 169 permits rapid amortization only of facilities used in connection with a plant or other property in operation prior to January 1, 1969. When a facility serves more than one plant or other property, therefore, it may be necessary to determine the portion of the cost of the facility which is attributable to its use in connection with plants or properties in use prior to January 1, 1969. In many cases, a proper allocation will be based on the effluent output capacities of the plants or properties served, in comparison to the treatment capacity of the facility to which the application relates. Exceptions to the foregoing may be justified if adequately explained in Part (b) of this Item; for example, the effluent capacities of the plants or properties served may differ substantially from the amounts of effluents actually produced and treated over a period of time.

Item 5—Section 169 does not permit certification of a facility to the extent it performs a function other than the control of pollution. When the facility to which the application relates performs such an additional function, it will be necessary to identify that portion of its cost which is allocable only to pollution control. The need to make such an allocation should seldom arise if the facility to which the application relates is defined with as much particularity as circumstances permit. If such need is unavoidable, the proper manner of making the allocation may vary, depending on the type of equipment involved. If, for example, the facility serves a production function when it is not being used for abatement purposes, then a proper allocation would be based on the percentage of on-stream time devoted to each of its several functions. If those features of the facility which result in the abatement of pollution are inseparable from its production-related features, then it may be appropriate to make the necessary allocation by reference to the cost of a similar facility which lacks the pollution abatement features.

SECTION D—WASTEWATER CHARACTERISTICS (Water Pollution Control Facilities only)

Item 1—Self-explanatory.

Item 2—Self-explanatory.

Item 3—Provide actual measured or design rates of the wastes (including heat) in wastewater stream as discharged without the pollution control facility and with the pollution control facility. (Such data can be suitably illustrated on a process flow diagram with material balances of the process wastewater stream from input through outflow; or, in cases where actual data are not available, the design capacity or rates as given in an engineering report, catalogue, etc., may be used and such material appended to the application.)

Items 4, 5, 6, 7 and 8—Self-explanatory.

Item 9—If the degree of treatment performed by the facility is required by state or local law or regulation, describe the applicable standard, giving statutory references, if known.

SECTION E—EMISSION CHARACTERISTICS (Air Pollution Control Facilities only)

Item 1—Self-explanatory.

Item 2—On lines designated (a) through (d), list the common name or chemical description of each pollutant the emission of which is to be controlled by the facility. All particulate emissions may be described in the aggregate as "particulates," unless an applicable State or Federal air quality standard is in effect for a specific type of particulate (e.g., asbestos), in which case such specifc type of particulate should be listed separately.

Item 3—Self-explanatory.

Item 4—Provide the indicated information for each type of gaseous emission listed in response to Item E-2, using for each the line prefixed by the letter corresponding to the line of Item E-2 on which it is listed.

Items 5 thru 7—Self-explanatory.

Item 8—If the degree of treatment performed by the facility is required by state or local law or regulation, describe the applicable standard, giving statutory references, if known.

SECTION F—COST INFORMATION

NOTE: APPLICANTS MAY, IF THEY WISH, FURNISH THE INFORMATION REQUIRED BY SECTION F ON A SEPARATE PIECE OF PAPER, WHICH NEED BE ATTACHED ONLY TO THE ORIGINAL OF THIS FORM SUBMITTED TO THE REGIONAL ADMINISTRATOR OF EPA. EPA WILL CONSIDER ANY INFORMATION SO FURNISHED AS "CONFIDENTIAL" WITHIN THE MEANING OF SECTION 552(b) OF TITLE 5, UNITED STATES CODE, AND WILL DIVULGE SUCH INFORMATION ONLY TO OFFICIALS AND AGENCIES OF THE UNITED STATES GOVERNMENT.

Item 1—Identify all by-products and materials recovered in the course of operation of the facility to which the application relates, including heat (if it is disposed of other than by dissipation to the atmosphere), whether or not such by-products and materials are recycled, and describe the methods used to dispose of each such by-product or material. Applicants need not impute revenues from recovered by-products or materials used or reused by them in their own operations.

Item 2—In part (a), provide the expected annual dollar amount of revenues from any sales of by-products or materials identified in response to Item F-1. In part (b), provide the expected annual dollar amount of any other revenues derived from the facility (e.g., rentals, service charges to persons other than the applicant).

Item 3—Provide estimates, if no prior history is available.

FORM APPROVED
OMB NO. 158-R0013

ENVIRONMENTAL PROTECTION AGENCY

APPLICATION FOR CERTIFICATION OF POLLUTION CONTROL FACILITY
(Pursuant to Section 169 of the Internal Revenue Code of 1954, as amended)

TO: REGIONAL ADMINISTRATOR *(Region, Street, City, State, Zip Code)*:	THRU: APPROPRIATE STATE WATER OR AIR POLLUTION CONTROL AGENCY *(Name of State Agency, Street, City, State, Zip Code)*:

Application is hereby made for certification of the pollution control facility described herein. The following information is submitted in accordance with provisions of Part 602 of Title 18 of the Code of Federal Regulations (Volume 36, Federal Register, page 9509, May 26, 1971) and to the best of my knowledge and belief is true and correct.

APPLICANT	DATE
SIGNATURE	STREET ADDRESS, CITY, STATE, ZIP CODE
TITLE	

NOTE: READ ACCOMPANYING INSTRUCTIONS CAREFULLY PRIOR TO COMPLETING FORM.

EPA Form 3300-1 (9-71) (Page 1)

FORM APPROVED
OMB NO. 158-R0013

SECTION A – IDENTITY AND LOCATION OF CONTROL FACILITY

1. FULL BUSINESS NAME OF APPLICANT

2. TYPE OF OWNERSHIP
☐ INDIVIDUAL ☐ OTHER *(Describe):*
☐ PARTNERSHIP
☐ CORPORATION

3. PERSON TO CONTACT REGARDING THIS APPLICATION *(Name and Title)* | TELEPHONE

ADDRESS *(Street, City, State, Zip Code)*

4. PERSON AUTHORIZED TO RECEIVE CERTIFICATION *(Name and Title)*

ADDRESS *(Street, City, State, Zip Code)*

5. BUSINESS NAME OF PLANT *(If different from Item 1) (Street, City, State, Zip Code)*

6. APPLICANT'S EMPLOYER IDENTIFICATION NO.

SECTION B – DESCRIPTION OF CONTROL FACILITY

1. DESCRIBE THE FACILITY FOR WHICH CERTIFICATION IS SOUGHT. INCLUDE TYPE OF EQUIPMENT, MANUFACTURER AND MODEL NUMBER. SUBMIT DESIGN CRITERIA, ENGINEERING REPORT AND/OR PERFORMANCE SPECIFICATIONS WHICH DESCRIBE FUNCTION AND OPERATION OF FACILITY:

2. IS FACILITY IN OPERATION?
☐ YES ☐ NO

A. IF "YES" DATE FACILITY WAS PLACED IN OPERATION

B. IF "NO" DATE FACILITY IS EXPECTED TO BE PLACED IN OPERATION

3. IF FACILITY CONSISTS OF A BUILDING, IS IT EXCLUSIVELY FOR CONTROL OF POLLUTION?
☐ YES ☐ NO

SECTION C – DESCRIPTION OF COMMERCIAL PROCESS OR ACTIVITY

1. DESCRIBE PROCESS OR ACTIVITY IN CONNECTION WITH WHICH FACILITY IS OR WILL BE USED.

2. STANDARD INDUSTRIAL CLASSIFICATION (SIC) CODE NUMBER

3. DATE THAT EACH PLANT OR OTHER PROPERTY IN CONNECTION WITH WHICH FACILITY IS OR WILL BE USED, COMMENCED OPERATION

PLANT OR PROPERTY	DATE
A.	
B.	
C.	

EPA Form 3300-1 (9-71) (Page 2)

FORM APPROVED
OMB NO. 158-R1003

SECTION C – DESCRIPTION OF COMMERCIAL PROCESS OR ACTIVITY

4A. IF FACILITY IS OR WILL BE USED IN CONNECTION WITH MORE THAN ONE PLANT OR PROPERTY, AND IF ONE OR MORE OF THE PLANTS OR PROPERTIES IN CONNECTION WITH WHICH THE FACILITY IS OR WILL BE USED WAS NOT IN OPERATION PRIOR TO JANUARY 1, 1969, STATE THE PERCENTAGE OF THE COST OF FACILITY WHICH IS ALLOCABLE TO THE PLANT(S) OR PROPERTY(IES) IN OPERATION PRIOR TO THAT DATE. ________%

4B. DESCRIBE THE REASONING AND FURNISH THE DATA USED TO ARRIVE AT THE PERCENTAGE GIVEN IN RESPONSE TO ITEM 4(A).

5A. IF FACILITY PERFORMS A FUNCTION OR FUNCTIONS IN ADDITION TO THE ABATEMENT OF POLLUTION, STATE THE PERCENTAGE OF THE COST OF FACILITY ALLOCABLE TO THE ABATEMENT OF POLLUTION. ________%

5B. DESCRIBE THE REASONING AND FURNISH THE DATA USED TO ARRIVE AT THE PERCENTAGE GIVEN IN RESPONSE TO ITEM 5(A).

SECTION D – WASTEWATER CHARACTERISTICS (To be completed only in connection with facilities for the control of water pollution)

DESCRIBE THE EFFECT OF POLLUTION CONTROL FACILITY IN TERMS OF QUANTITY AND QUALITY OF EFFLUENT OR WASTEWATER DISCHARGED AND OF WASTES OR BY-PRODUCTS REMOVED, ALTERED OR DISPOSED OF. IF FEASIBLE, ATTACH PROCESS FLOW OR SCHEMATIC DIAGRAM WITH MATERIAL BALANCES OF THE WASTE OR WASTEWATER STREAM OR DISCHARGE. REPORT EITHER ON ACTUAL BASIS OR, IF FACILITY IS NOT YET IN OPERATION, ON DESIGN BASIS (Use Standard Units – pounds/gallon, grams/liter, ppm, etc.)

1. HOURS PLANT OR PROPERTY IS IN OPERATION:
a. Per Month: Min. ____ Max. ____ Avg. ____
b. Per Year: Min. ____ Max. ____ Avg. ____

2. WASTEWATER DISCHARGE IN · (A) GALLONS PER MINUTE, (B) MILLIONS OF GALLONS PER MONTH.	WITHOUT POLLUTION CONTROL FACILITY			WITH POLLUTION CONTROL FACILITY		
	a. Min. ____	Max. ____	Avg. ____	Min. ____	Max. ____	Avg. ____
	b. Min. ____	Max. ____	Avg. ____	Min. ____	Max. ____	Avg. ____

3. POLLUTANTS OR WASTE PRODUCTS						
3. a ____	Min. ____	Max. ____	Avg. ____	Min. ____	Max. ____	Avg. ____
3. b ____	Min. ____	Max. ____	Avg. ____	Min. ____	Max. ____	Avg. ____
3. c ____	Min. ____	Max. ____	Avg. ____	Min. ____	Max. ____	Avg. ____
3. d ____	Min. ____	Max. ____	Avg. ____	Min. ____	Max. ____	Avg. ____
3. e ____	Min. ____	Max. ____	Avg. ____	Min. ____	Max. ____	Avg. ____
3. f ____	Min. ____	Max. ____	Avg. ____	Min. ____	Max. ____	Avg. ____
3. g ____	Min. ____	Max. ____	Avg. ____	Min. ____	Max. ____	Avg. ____
3. h ____	Min. ____	Max. ____	Avg. ____	Min. ____	Max. ____	Avg. ____
3. i ____	Min. ____	Max. ____	Avg. ____	Min. ____	Max. ____	Avg. ____
3. j ____	Min. ____	Max. ____	Avg. ____	Min. ____	Max. ____	Avg. ____

EPA Form 3300-1 (9-71) (Page 3)

FORM APPROVED
OMB NO. 158-R1003

4. DESCRIBE METHOD (GRAB OR COMPOSITE) AND FREQUENCY OF SAMPLING AND METHODS USED TO DETERMINE QUANTITIES OF POLLUTANTS.

5. IS FACILITY A PRETREATMENT FACILITY TO PREPARE WASTEWATER FOR RECEIPT BY ANOTHER FACILITY, PUBLIC OR PRIVATE, FOR FURTHER TREATMENT? IF "YES", SKIP ITEMS 6, 7 AND 8 AND IDENTIFY RECEIVING FACILITY. ☐ YES ☐ NO

6. IDENTIFY THE BODY OR STREAM OF WATER INTO WHICH WASTEWATER FROM THE PLANT OR PROPERTY, IN CONNECTION WITH WHICH THE FACILITY IS USED, IS OR WILL BE DISCHARGED.

7. DESCRIBE LOCATION OF DISCHARGE OR OUTFALL WITH RESPECT TO RECEIVING WATERS.

8. IS THE RECEIVING BODY OR STREAM OF WATER A NAVIGABLE WATERWAY OF THE UNITED STATES OR A TRIBUTARY THEREOF?
☐ YES ☐ NO IF "NO," PROCEED TO ITEM 9.

A. IF "YES" HAS A U.S. ARMY CORPS OF ENGINEERS DISCHARGE PERMIT BEEN APPLIED FOR? ☐ YES ☐ NO IF "NO," EXPLAIN, THEN PROCEED TO ITEM 9.

B. IF ANSWER TO ITEM 8A IS "YES" HAS A U.S. ARMY CORPS OF ENGINEERS DISCHARGE PERMIT BEEN ISSUED? ☐ YES ☐ NO
(1) IF "YES," ATTACH COPY OR PROVIDE PERMIT NUMBER__________ OMIT ITEM 9.
(2) IF "NO," EXPLAIN, GIVING DATES OF ANY OFFICIAL ACTION WITH RESPECT TO APPLICATION.

9. IF ITEM 8B HAS NOT BEEN ANSWERED "YES," IDENTIFY APPLICABLE STATE AND LOCAL WATER POLLUTION CONTROL REQUIREMENTS AND STANDARDS.

SECTION E – EMISSION CHARACTERISTICS (To be completed only in connection with facilities for the control of air pollution)

DESCRIBE THE EFFECT OF POLLUTION CONTROL FACILITY IN TERMS OF QUANTITY AND QUALITY OF EMISSION AND OF WASTES OR BY-PRODUCTS REMOVED, ALTERED OR DISPOSED OF. IF FEASIBLE, ATTACH PROCESS FLOW OR SCHEMATIC DIAGRAM WITH MATERIAL BALANCES OF POLLUTANTS IN THE EMISSION STREAM. REPORT EITHER ON ACTUAL BASIS, OR, IF FACILITY IS NOT YET IN OPERATION, ON DESIGN BASIS.

1. HOURS PLANT OR PROPERTY IS IN OPERATION: a. Per Month: Min. ___ Max. ___ Avg. ___
b. Per Year: Min. ___ Max. ___ Avg. ___

2. POLLUTANTS TO BE CONTROLLED *(Specify each)*	a.	
	b.	
	c.	
	d.	
3. VOLUMETRIC FLOW RATE OF EMISSION *(actual cubic feet/minute)*	WITHOUT POLLUTION CONTROL FACILITY	WITH POLLUTION CONTROL FACILITY
	Min. ___ Max. ___ Avg. ___ at ___ °F	Min. ___ Max. ___ Avg. ___ at ___ °F
4. CONCENTRATION *(in volume % of gaseous components)*	a. Min. ___ Max. ___ Avg. ___ at ___ °F	Min. ___ Max. ___ Avg. ___ at ___ °F
	b. Min. ___ Max. ___ Avg. ___ at ___ °F	Min. ___ Max. ___ Avg. ___ at ___ °F
	c. Min. ___ Max. ___ Avg. ___ at ___ °F	Min. ___ Max. ___ Avg. ___ at ___ °F
	d. Min. ___ Max. ___ Avg. ___ at ___ °F	Min. ___ Max. ___ Avg. ___ at ___ °F
5. CONCENTRATION *(grains/cubic feet of all particulate matter)*	Min. ___ Max. ___ Avg. ___ at ___ °F	Min. ___ Max. ___ Avg. ___ at ___ °F
6. CONCENTRATION *(grains/cubic feet of any specific particulate listed in E-2 above)*	Min. ___ Max. ___ Avg. ___ at ___ °F	Min. ___ Max. ___ Avg. ___ at ___ °F

EPA Form 3300-1 (9-71) (Page 4)

FORM APPROVED
OMB NO. 158-R0013

7. DESCRIBE METHODS OF DETERMINING RATES, CONCENTRATION AND CHARACTERISTICS OF EMISSIONS.

8. IDENTIFY APPLICABLE STATE AND LOCAL AIR POLLUTION CONTROL REQUIREMENTS AND STANDARDS.

SECTION F – COST INFORMATION (See Note to instructions for this section)

1. IS THERE ANY BY-PRODUCT OR MATERIAL WHICH, WITHOUT THE CONTROL FACILITY, WOULD BE LOST AND WHICH IS RECOVERED THROUGH THE USE OF THE FACILITY? ☐ YES ☐ NO

A. IF YES, IDENTIFY

B. INDICATE THE DISPOSITION OF EACH TYPE OF RECOVERED MATERIAL, INCLUDING IF APPLICABLE, THE SALE OR SIMILAR DISPOSITION OF RECLAIMED OR RECOVERED MATERIAL TO INDUSTRIAL WASTE RECOVERY FIRMS OR OTHERS.

2. ANNUAL COST RECOVERY	A. MATERIAL RECOVERED AND SOLD	$
	B. OTHER	$
	C. TOTAL	$
3. TOTAL AVERAGE ANNUAL MAINTENANCE AND OPERATING COSTS *(Not applicable if no cost recovery is reported in Item 2)*		$

EPA Form 3300-1 (9-71) (Page 5)

FORM APPROVED
OMB NO. 158-R0013

ENVIRONMENTAL PROTECTION AGENCY **NOTICE OF STATE CERTIFICATION** **(Pursuant to Section 169 of the Internal Revenue Code of 1954, as amended)**	STATE WATER OR AIR POLLUTION CONTROL AGENCY OR AUTHORITY

It is hereby certified that the control facility described in the attached application is in conformity with State and local programs and requirements for the control of ☐ water pollution ☐ air pollution, as required by section 169 of the Internal Revenue Code of 1954, as amended, and regulations issued thereunder. According to the applicant, this control facility ☐ was placed ☐ will be placed in operation on , 19

In the case of control facility not yet in operation, this notice is certification only that the control facility, if constructed and operated in accordance with the application, will be in conformity with State and local programs or requirements for abatement or control of water or air pollution.

1. NAME OF APPLICANT	2. PERSON AUTHORIZED TO RECEIVE CERTIFICATION
ADDRESS *(Street, City, State, Zip Code)*	TITLE ADDRESS *(Street, City, State, Zip Code)*

3. DESCRIPTION OF CONTROL FACILITY

4. LOCATION OF CONTROL FACILITY *(Street, City, State, Zip Code)*	5. RECEIVING BODY OR STREAM OF WATER, IF ANY

6. USE OF THE CONTROL FACILITY CERTIFIED HEREBY IS IN CONFORMITY WITH THE FOLLOWING APPLICABLE STATE PLAN OR REQUIREMENTS FOR THE CONTROL OF ☐ WATER POLLUTION ☐ AIR POLLUTION.

ISSUED THIS ____ DAY OF ______________________ 19____	SIGNED *(Official of State Agency)*
STATE CERTIFICATION NUMBER	TITLE

EPA Form 3300-2 (9-71)

FORM APPROVED
OMB NO. 158-R0013

ENVIRONMENTAL PROTECTION AGENCY

NOTICE OF FEDERAL CERTIFICATION

(Pursuant to Section 169 of the Internal Revenue Code of 1954, as amended)

PLEASE TAKE NOTICE that pursuant to section 169 of the Internal Revenue Code of 1954, as amended, and Part 602 of Title 18 of the Code of Federal Regulations, the control facility identified herein

☐ Is certified

☐ Will, if constructed, reconstructed, acquired, erected, installed and operated in accordance with the accompanying application, be certified

as being in compliance with the applicable regulations of Federal agencies and the general policies of the United States for cooperation with the States in the prevention and abatement of ☐ water pollution ☐ air pollution under the Federal Water Pollution Control Act, as amended (33 U.S.C. 1151 et seq.) or the Clean Air Act, as amended (42 U.S.C. 1857 et seq.). This certification is based on facts furnished by the applicant, and is valid for purposes of section 169 only to the extent that such facts are complete and accurate.

1. NAME OF APPLICANT	ADDRESS *(Street, City, State, Zip Code)*
2. EMPLOYER IDENTIFICATION NUMBER	

3. PERSON AUTHORIZED TO RECEIVE CERTIFICATION:

NAME	ADDRESS *(Street, City, State, Zip Code)*
TITLE	

4. DESCRIPTION OF CONTROL FACILITY

5. LOCATION OF CONTROL FACILITY *(Street, City, State, Zip Code)*

6. EFFLUENT DISCHARGED TO

7. THE CONTROL FACILITY IDENTIFIED HEREIN ☐ DOES ☐ DOES NOT GENERATE PROFITS THROUGH THE RECOVERY AND SALES OF WASTES, OR OTHERWISE.

8. THE CONTROL FACILITY IDENTIFIED HEREIN ☐ IS ☐ IS NOT A BUILDING THE ONLY FUNCTION OF WHICH IS THE ABATEMENT OR CONTROL OF POLLUTION, AS DETERMINED IN ACCORDANCE WITH SECTION 1.169-2 (2) (i) OF THE INCOME TAX REGULATIONS.

9.
☐ A. THE CONTROL FACILITY IDENTIFIED HEREIN IS USED ONLY IN CONNECTION WITH PLANTS OR PROPERTIES THAT WERE IN SERVICE ON OR BEFORE DECEMBER 31, 1968.

☐ B. _____% OF THE AMORTIZABLE BASIS OF THE FACILITY IS ALLOCABLE TO ITS USE IN CONNECTION WITH PLANTS OR PROPERTIES THAT WERE IN SERVICE ON OR BEFORE DECEMBER 31, 1968.

10.
☐ A. THE CONTROL FACILITY PERFORMS NO FUNCTION IN ADDITION TO THE ABATEMENT OR CONTROL OF POLLUTION.

☐ B. _____% OF THE AMORTIZABLE BASIS OF THE CONTROL FACILITY IS ALLOCABLE TO THE ABATEMENT OR CONTROL OF POLLUTION.

ISSUED THIS _____ DAY OF ___________________, 19_____	SIGNATURE
STATE CERTIFICATION NUMBER	TITLE

EPA Form 3300-3 (9-71)

Appendix E

Boomer et al. v. Atlantic Cement

55 Misc., 2d Series 1023

287 New York Supplement, 2d Series 112

Oscar H. BOOMER and June C. Boomer, Plaintiffs, v. The ATLANTIC CEMENT COMPANY, Inc., Defendant.

Theodore J. RICHARD and Miriam W. Richard, Plaintiffs, v. The ATLANTIC CEMENT COMPANY, Inc., Defendant.

Avie KINLEY, Martha Kinley and Mary L. Kinley, Plaintiffs, v. The ATLANTIC CEMENT COMPANY, Inc., Defendant.

Kenneth R. LIVENGOOD and Delores M. Livengood, Plaintiffs, v. The ATLANTIC CEMENT COMPANY, Inc., Defendant.

Floyd W. MILLIOUS and Barbara A. Millious, Plaintiffs, v. The ATLANTIC CEMENT COMPANY, Inc. Defendant.

Joseph L. VENTURA and Carrie Ventura, Plaintiffs, v. The ATLANTIC CEMENT COMPANY, Inc., Defendant.

James W. McCALL, Plaintiff, v. The ATLANTIC CEMENT COMPANY, Inc., Defendant.

Charles J. MEILAK and Angelina Meilak, Plaintiffs, v. The ATLANTIC CEMENT COMPANY, Inc., Defendant.

Supreme Court, Albany County.

Aug. 14, 1967

R. WALDRON HERZBERG, Justice.*

Plaintiffs in this action seek an injunction against defendant cement company (Atlantic) to restrain it from emitting dust and raw materials and conducting excessive blasting in operating its plant in such a manner as to constitute a nuisance upon plaintiffs' lands. In addition damages to the time of trial are sought.

Atlantic commenced the production of Portland Cement at its plant in the Town of Coeymans in the County of Albany on or about September 1, 1962. Prior to that date defendant expended more than $40,000,000 in the erection of one of the largest and most modern cement plants in the world. The company installed at great expense the most efficient devices available to prevent the discharge of dust and polluted air into the atmosphere.

(1) Although the evidence in this case establishes that Atlantic took every available and possible precaution to protect the plaintiffs from dust, nevertheless, I find that the plaintiffs have sustained the burden of proof that Atlantic in the operation of its cement plant between September 1, 1962 and June 1, 1967 (a period of 57 months) created a nuisance insofar as the lands of the plaintiffs are concerned. The discharge of large quantities of dust upon each of the properties and excessive vibration from blasting deprived each party of the reasonable use of his property and thereby prevented his enjoyment of life and liberty therein.

(2) I have given careful consideration to the plea of plaintiffs that an injunction should issue in this action. Although the Supreme Court has the power to grant and enforce an injunction, equity forbids its employment in this instance. The defendant's immense investment in the Hudson River Valley, its contribution to the Capital District's economy and its immediate help to the education of children in the Town of Coeymans through the payment of substantial sums in school and property taxes leads me to the conclusion that I should adhere to the often quoted words of Judge Collin in McCann v. Chasm Power Co., 211 N.Y. 301, at page 305, 105 N.E. 416, at page 417: " 'It is not safe to attempt to lay down any hard and fast rule for the guidance of courts of equity in determining when an injunction shall

---

* Surrogate of Columbia County and Acting Justice of the Supreme Court. 287 N.Y.S.2d—8.

issue.' (Quoting from Judge Werner's opinion in Whalen v. Union Bag & Paper Co., 208 N.Y. 1, 4, 101 N.E. 805.) The ownership of property will be protected unless there are other considerations which forbid, as inequitable, the remedy of the prohibitive or mandatory injunction. A court of equity can never be justified in making an inequitable decree. If the protection of a legal right even would do a plaintiff but comparatively little good and would produce great public or private hardship, equity will withhold its discreet and beneficent hand and remit the plantiff to his legal rights and remedies." After reviewing all the evidence in this action, I find that an injunction "would produce great public . . . hardship".

(3) In awarding damages to the time of trial I am bound by precedent to grant only the loss of rental value or loss of usable value sustained. After considering the testimony of the experts called by the parties and the other evidence in this case, I find that the loss of usable value per month of each party is as follows:

Oscar H. Boomer and June C. Boomer	$ 50.00
Theodore J. Richard and Miriam W. Richard	125.00
Avie Kinley, Martha Kinley and Mary L. Kinley	150.00
Kenneth R. Livengood and Delores M. Livengood	40.00
Floyd W. Millious and Barbara A. Millious	40.00
Joseph L. Ventura and Carrie Ventura	40.00
James W. McCall	40.00
Charles J. Meilak and Angelina Meilak	50.00
Total	$535.00

In addition the plaintiffs Oscar H. Boomer and June C. Boomer are entitled to judgment against Atlantic pursuant to a stipulation made during the trial in the amount of $14,370 for damages to automobiles stored on their premises.

Since the trial of this action extended for several weeks and in order to effect a final determination, I find that the reasonable market value of each property as of September 1, 1962 (the date of the commencement of operations by Atlantic), the reasonable market value as of June 1, 1967 (the time of trial) and the permanent loss to each plaintiff, are as follows:

	Reasonable Market Value 9/1/1962	Reasonable Market Value 6/1/1967	Permanent Damage
Oscar H. Boomer and June C. Boomer	25,000.	12,500.	12,500.
Theodore J. Richard and Miriam W. Richard			
Real Property	30,000.	12,000.	18,000.
Business	40,000.	16,000.	24,000.
Avie Kinley, Martha Kinley and Mary L. Kinley	140,000.	70,000.	70,000.
Kenneth R. Livengood and Delores M. Livengood	18,000.	7,000.	11,000.
Floyd W. Millious and Barbara A. Millious	20,000.	8,000.	12,000.
Joseph L. Ventura and Carrie Ventura	25,000.	12,500.	12,500.
James W. McCall	22,000.	11,000.	11,000.
Charles J. Meilak and Angelina Meilak	26,000.	12,000.	14,000.
		Total	$185,000.

In the event any plaintiff or plaintiffs and the defendant agree in writing to accept the permanent damages found herein within thirty days after the rendering of this decision with the provision that no subsequent action shall be brought by either the plantiff or plaintiffs or any successor in title against this defendant or any successor to it, judgment for said amount with costs may be entered in said action.

This decision in no way makes any finding in respect to the conduct of Atlantic in the operation of its plant between September 1, 1962 and June 1, 1967, except insofar as the plaintiffs herein are concerned. Further, I make no findings in respect to the operation by Atlantic of its plant subsequent to June 1, 1967.

All motions reserved upon the trial are denied.

Judgments for the plaintiffs as hereinbefore set forth with costs.

294 New York Supplement, 2d Series 452

30 A.D.2d 480

Oscar H. BOOMER et al., Appellants, v. ATLANTIC CEMENT CO., Inc., Respondent. (And 5 Other Actions.)

Supreme Court, Appellate Division, Third Department.

Nov. 4, 1968

AULISI, Justice.

These are appeals from judgments of the Supreme Court in favor of the plaintiffs, entered September 26, 1967 in Albany County, upon a decision of the court at a Trial Term.

Involved in this appeal are eight separate actions commenced by residents of the Town of Coeymans whose homes and businesses are in the immediate vicinity of defendant's main cement plant and quarry located in the Town of Coeymans, Albany County, adjacent to U.S. Route 9-W. The relief sought in those actions was an injunction restraining defendant from emitting dust and other raw materials and conducting excessive blasting operations in such a manner as to create a nuisance and the recovery of damages sustained as a result of the nuisance so created.

Despite its conclusion that the defendant in the operation of its plant had, in fact, created a nuisance with respect to plaintiffs' properties, the trial court refused to issue an injunction. In reaching its decision on the propriety of granting the injunctive relief sought, the court carefully considered, weighed and evaluated the respective equities, relative hardship and interests of the parties to this dispute and the public at large. Reexamining the record, we note the zoning of the area, the large number of persons employed by the defendant, its extensive business operations and substantial investment in plant and equipment, its use of the most modern and efficient devices to prevent offensive emissions and discharges, and its payment of substantial sums of real property and school taxes. After giving due consideration to all of these relevant factors, the trial court struck the balance in defendant's favor and we find no reason to disturb that determination.

The trial court did award damages based upon the loss of usable value sustained. Plaintiffs' contention to the contrary notwithstanding, we find no ground for interfering with either the court's determination of the proper measure of damages or its application of same to the facts of this case.

The judgments should be affirmed, without costs.

Judgments affirmed, without costs.

HERLIHY, J. P., and REYNOLDS, STALEY and GABRIELLI, JJ., concur.

---

309 New York Supplement, 2d Series 312

26 N.Y.2d 219

Oscar H. BOOMER et al., Appellants, v. ATLANTIC CEMENT COMPANY, Inc., Respondent. (And Five Other Actions.)

Charles J. MEILAK et al., Appellants, v. ATLANTIC CEMENT COMPANY, Inc., Respondent.

Court of Appeals of New York.

March 4, 1970

BERGAN, Judge.

Defendant operates a large cement plant near Albany. These are actions for injunction and damages by neighboring land owners alleging injury to property from dirt, smoke and vibration emanating from the plant. A nuisance has been found after trial, temporary damages have been allowed; but an injunction has been denied.

The public concern with air pollution arising from many sources in industry and in transportation is currently accorded ever wider recognition accompanied by a growing sense of responsibility in State and Federal Governments to control it. Cement plants are obvious sources of air pollution in the neighborhoods where they operate.

But there is now before the court private litigation in which individual property owners have sought specific relief from a single plant operation. The threshold question raised by the division of view on this appeal is whether the court should resolve the litigation between the parties now before it as equitably as seems possible; or whether, seeking promotion of the general public welfare, it should channel private litigation into broad public objectives.

A court performs its essential function when it decides the rights of parties before it. Its decision of private controversies may sometimes greatly affect public issues. Large questions of law are often resolved by the manner in which private litigation is decided. But this is normally an incident to the court's main function to settle controversy. It is a rare exercise of judicial power to use a decision in private litigation as a purposeful mechanism to achieve direct public objectives greatly beyond the rights and interests before the court.

Effective control of air pollution is a problem presently far from solution even with the full public and financial powers of government. In large measure adequate technical procedures are yet to be developed and some that appear possible may be economically impracticable.

It seems apparent that the amelioration of air pollution will depend on technical research in great depth; on a carefully balanced consideration of the economic impact of close regulation; and of the actual effect on public health. It is likely to require massive public expenditure and to demand more than any local community can accomplish and to depend on regional and interstate controls.

(1) A court should not try to do this on its own as a by-product of private litigation and it seems manifest that the judicial establishment is neither equipped in the limited nature of any judgment it can pronounce nor prepared to lay down and implement an effective policy for the elimination of air pollution. This is an area beyond the circumference of one private lawsuit. It is a direct responsibility for government and should not thus be undertaken as an incident to solving a dispute between property owners and a single cement plant—one of many—in the Hudson River valley.

The cement making operations of defendant have been found by the court at Special Term to have damaged the nearby properties of plaintiffs in these two actions. That court, as it has been noted, accordingly found defendant maintained a nuisance and this has been affirmed at the Appellate Division. The total damage to plaintiffs' properties is, however, relatively small in comparison with the value of defendant's operation and with the consequences of the injunction which plaintiffs seek.

The ground for the denial of injunction, notwithstanding the finding both that there is a nuisance and that plaintiffs have been damaged substantially, is the large disparity in economic consequences of the nuisance and of the injunction. This theory cannot, however, be sustained without overruling a doctrine which has been consistently reaffirmed in several leading cases in this court and which has never been disavowed here, namely that where a nuisance has been found and where there has been any substantial damage shown by the party complaining an injunction will be granted.

(2) The rule in New York has been that such a nuisance will be enjoined although marked disparity be shown in economic consequence between the effect of the injunction and the effect of the nuisance.

The problem of disparity in economic consequence was sharply in focus in Whalen v. Union Bag & Paper Co., 208 N.Y. 1, 101 N.E. 805. A pulp mill entailing an investment of more than a million dollars polluted a stream in which plaintiff, who owned a farm, was "a lower riparian owner." The economic loss to plaintiff from this pollution was small. This court, reversing the Appellate Division, reinstated the injunction granted by the Special Term against the argument of the mill owner that in view of "the slight advantage to plaintiff and the great loss that will be inflicted on defendant" an injunction should not be granted (p. 2, 101 N.E. p. 805). "Such a balancing of injuries cannot be justified by the circumstances of this case," Judge Werner noted (p.4, 101 N.E. p. 805). He continued: "Although the damage to the plaintiff might be slight as compared with the defendant's expense of abating the condition, that is not a good reason for refusing an injunction" (p. 5, 101 N.E. p. 806).

Thus the unconditional injunction granted at Special Term was reinstated. The rule laid down in that case, then, is that whenever the damage resulting from a nuisance is found not "unsubstantial", viz., $100 a year, injunction would follow. This states a rule that had been followed in this court with marked consistency.

There are cases when injunction has been denied. McCann v. Chasm Power Co., 211 N.Y. 301, 105 N.E. 416 is one of them. There, however, the damage shown by plaintiffs was not only unsubstantial, it was nonexistent. Plaintiffs owned a rocky bank of the stream in which defendant had raised the level of the water. This had no economic or other adverse consequence to plaintiffs, and thus injunctive relief was denied. Similar is the basis for denial of injunction in Forstmann v. Joray Holding Co., 244 N.Y. 22, 154 N.E. 652 where no benefit to plaintiffs could be seen from the injunction sought (p. 32, 154 N.E. 655). Thus if, within Whalen v. Union Bag & Paper Co., supra which authoritatively states the rule in New York, the damage to plaintiffs in these present cases from defendant's cement plant is "not unsubstantial," an injunction should follow.

Although the court at Special Term and the Appellate Division held that injunction should be denied, it was found that plaintiffs had been damaged in various specific amounts up to the time of the trial and damages to the respective plaintiffs were awarded for those amounts. The effect of this was, injunction having been denied, plaintiffs could maintain successive actions at law for damages thereafter as further damage was incurred.

The court at Special Term also found the amount of permanent damage attributable to each plaintiff, for the guidance of the parties in the event both sides stipulated to the payment and acceptance of such permanent damage as a settlement of all the controversies among the parties. The total of permanent damages to all plaintiffs thus found was $185,000. The basis of adjustment has not resulted in any stipulation by the parties.

This result at Special Term and at the Appellate Division is a departure from a rule that has become settled; but to follow the rule literally in these cases would be to close down the plant at once. This court is fully agreed to avoid that immediately drastic remedy; the difference in view is how best to avoid it.*

(3) One alternative is to grant the injunction but postpone its effect to a specified future date to give opportunity for technical advances to permit defendant to eliminate the nuisance; another is to grant the injunction conditioned on the payment of permanent damages to plaintiffs which would compensate them for the total economic loss to their property present and future caused by defendant's operations. For reasons which will be developed the court chooses the latter alternative.

If the injunction were to be granted unless within a short period—e.g., 18 months—the nuisance be abated by improved methods, there would be no assurance that any significant technical improvement would occur.

The parties could settle this private litigation at any time if defendant paid enough money and the imminent threat of closing the plant would build up the pressure on defendant. If there were no improved techniques found, there would inevitably be applications to

* Respondent's investment in the plant is in excess of $45,000,000. There are over 300 people employed there.

the court at Special Term for extensions of time to perform on showing of good faith efforts to find such techniques.

Moreover, techniques to eliminate dust and other annoying by-products of cement making are unlikely to be developed by any research the defendant can undertake within any short period, but will depend on the total resources of the cement industry nationwide and throughout the world. The problem is universal wherever cement is made.

For obvious reasons the rate of the research is beyond control of defendant. If at the end of 18 months the whole industry has not found a technical solution a court would be hard put to close down this one cement plant if due regard be given to equitable principles.

On the other hand, to grant the injunction unless defendant pays plaintiffs such permanent damages as may be fixed by the court seems to do justice between the contending parties. All of the attributions of economic loss to the properties on which plaintiffs' complaints are based will have been redressed.

(4) The nuisance complained of by these plaintiffs may have other public or private consequences, but these particular parties are the only ones who have sought remedies and the judgment proposed will fully redress them. The limitation of relief granted is a limitation only within the four corners of these actions and does not foreclose public health or other public agencies from seeking proper relief in a proper court.

It seems reasonable to think that the risk of being required to pay permanent damages to injured property owners by cement plant owners would itself be a reasonable effective spur to research for improved techniques to minimize nuisance.

The power of the court to condition on equitable grounds the continuance of an injunction on the payment of permanent damages seems undoubted.

(5) The damage base here suggested is consistent with the general rule in those nuisance cases where damages are allowed. "Where a nuisance is of such a permanent and unabatable character that a single recovery can be had, including the whole damage past and future resulting therefrom, there can be but one recovery" (66 C.J.S. Nuisances § 140, p. 947). It has been said that permanent damages are allowed where the loss recoverable would obviously be small as compared with the cost of removal of the nuisance.

The present cases and the remedy here proposed are in a number of other respects rather similar to Northern Indiana Public Service Co. v. W. J. & M. S. Vesey, 210 Ind. 338 N.E. 620 decided by the Supreme Court of Indiana. The gases, odors, ammonia and smoke from the Northern Indiana company's gas plant damaged the nearby Vesey greenhouse operation. An injunction and damages were sought, but an injunction was denied and the relief granted was limited to permanent damages "present, past, and future" (p. 371, 200 N.E. 620).

Denial of injunction was grounded on a public interest in the operation of the gas plant and on the court's conclusion "that less injury would be occasioned by requiring the appellant [Public Service] to pay the appellee [Vesey] all damages suffered by it . . . than by enjoining the operation of the gas plant; and that the maintenance and operation of the gas plant should not be enjoined" (p. 349, 200 N.E. p. 625).

The Indiana Supreme Court opinion continued: "When the trial court refused injunctive relief to the appellee upon the ground of public interest in the continuance of the gas plant, it properly retained jurisdiction of the case and awarded full compensation to the appellee. This is upon the general equitable principle that equity will give full relief in one action and prevent a multiplicity of suits" (pp. 353-354, 200 N.E. p. 627).

It was held that in this type of continuing and recurrent nuisance permanent damages were appropriate. See, also, City of Amarillo v. Ware, 120 Tex. 456, 40 S.W.2d 57 where recurring overflows from a system of storm sewers were treated as the kind of nuisance for which permanent depreciation of value of affected property would be recoverable.

There is some parallel to the conditioning of an injunction on the payment of permanent damages in the noted "elevated railway cases." Decisions in these cases were based on the finding that the railways created a nuisance as to adjacent property owners, but in lieu of enjoining their operation, the court allowed permanent damages.

Judge Finch, reviewing these cases in Ferguson v. Village of Hamburg, 272 N.Y. 234, 239-240, 5 N.E.2d 801, 803, said: "The courts decided that the plaintiffs had a valuable right which was being impaired, but did not grant an absolute injunction or require the railway companies to resort to separate condemnation proceedings. Instead they held that a court of equity could ascertain the damages and grant an injunction which was not to be effective unless the defendant failed to pay the amount fixed as damages for the past and permanent injury inflicted."

Thus it seems fair to both sides to grant permanent damages to plaintiffs which will terminate this private litigation. The theory of damage is the "servitude on land" of plaintiffs imposed by defendant's nuisance. (See United States v. Causby, 328 U.S. 256, 261, 262, 267, 66 S.Ct. 1062, 90 L.Ed. 1206, where the term "servitude" addressed to land was used by Justice Douglas relating to the effect of airplane noise on property near an airport).

(6) The judgment, by allowance of permanent damages imposing a servitude on land, which is the basis of the actions, would preclude future recovery by plaintiffs or their grantees.

This should be placed beyond debate by a provision of the judgment that the payment by defendant and the acceptance by plaintiffs of permanent damages found by the court shall be in compensation for a servitude on the land.

Although the Trial Term has found permanent damages as a possible basis of settlement of the litigation, on remission the court should be entirely free to re-examine this subject. It may again find the permanent damage already found; or make new findings.

The orders should be reversed, without costs, and the cases remitted to Supreme Court, Albany County to grant an injunction which shall be vacated upon payment by defendant of such amounts of permanent damage to the respective plaintiffs as shall for this purpose be determined by the court.

JASEN, Judge (dissenting).

I agree with the majority that a reversal is required here, but I do not subscribe to the newly enunciated doctrine of assessment of permanent damages, in lieu of an injunction, where substantial property rights have been impaired by the creation of a nuisance.

It has long been the rule in this State, as the majority acknowledges, that a nuisance which results in substantial continuing damage to neighbors must be enjoined. To now change the rule to permit the cement company to continue polluting the air indefinitely upon the payment of permanent damages is, in my opinion, compounding the magnitude of a very serious problem in our State and Nation today.

In recognition of this problem, the Legislature of this State has enacted the Air Pollution Control Act (Public Health Law, Consol. Laws, c. 45, §§ 1264 to 1299-m) declaring that it is the State policy to require the use of all available and reasonable methods to prevent and control air pollution (Public Health Law § 1265).

The harmful nature and widespread occurrence of air pollution have been extensively documented. Congressional hearings have revealed that air pollution causes substantial property damage, as well as being a contributing factor to a rising incidence of lung cancer, emphysema, bronchitis and asthma.

The specific problem faced here is known as particulate contamination because of the fine dust particles emanating from defendant's cement plant. The particular type of nuisance is not new, having appeared in many cases for at least the past 60 years. It is interesting to note that cement production has recently been identified as a significant source of particulate contamination in the Hudson Valley. This type of pollution, wherein very small particles escape and stay in the atmosphere, has been denominated as the type of air pollution which produces the greatest hazard to human health. We have thus a nuisance which not only is damaging to the plaintiffs, but also is decidedly harmful to the general public.

I see grave dangers in overruling our long-established rule of granting an injunction where a nuisance results in substantial continuing damage. In permitting the injunction to become inoperative upon the payment of permanent damages, the majority is, in effect, licensing a continuing wrong. It is the same as saying to the cement company, you may continue to do harm to your neighbors so long as you pay a fee for it. Furthermore, once such permanent damages are assessed and paid, the incentive to alleviate the wrong would be eliminated, thereby continuing air pollution of an area without abatement.

It is true that some courts have sanctioned the remedy here proposed by the majority in a number of cases, but none of the authorities relied upon by the majority are analogous to the situation before us. In those cases, the courts, in denying an injunction and awarding money damages, grounded their decision on a showing that the use to which the property was intended to be put was primarily for the public benefit. Here, on the other hand, it is clearly established that the cement company is creating a continuing air pollution nuisance primarily for its own private interest with no public benefit.

This kind of inverse condemnation may not be invoked by a private person or corporation for private gain or advantage. Inverse condemnation should only be permitted when the public is primarily served in the taking or impairment of property. The promotion of the interests of the polluting cement company has, in my opinion, no public use or benefit.

Nor is it constitutionally permissible to impose servitude on land, without consent of the owner, by payment of permanent damages where the continuing impairment of the land is for a private use. This is made clear by the State Constitution (art. I, § 7, subd. [a]) which provides that "[p]rivate property shall not be taken for public use without just compensation" (emphasis added). It is, of course, significant that the section makes no mention of taking for a private use.

In sum, then, by constitutional mandate as well as by judicial pronouncement, the permanent impairment of private property for private purposes is not authorized in the absence of clearly demonstrated public benefit and use.

I would enjoin the defendant cement company from continuing the discharge of dust particles upon its neighbors' properties unless, within 18 months, the cement company abated this nuisance.

It is not my intention to cause the removal of the cement plant from the Albany area, but to recognize the urgency of the problem stemming from this stationary source of air pollution, and to allow the company a specified period of time to develop a means to alleviate this nuisance.

I am aware that the trial court found that the most modern dust control devices available have been installed in defendant's plant, but, I submit, this does not mean that better and more effective dust control devices could not be developed within the time allowed to abate the pollution.

Moreover, I believe it is incumbent upon the defendant to develop such devices, since the cement company, at the time the plant commenced production (1962), was well aware of the plaintiffs' presence in the area, as well as the probable consequences of its contemplated operation. Yet, it still chose to build and operate the plant at this site.

In a day when there is a growing concern for clean air, highly developed industry should not expect acquiescence by the courts, but should, instead, plan its operations to eliminate contamination of our air and damage to its neighbors.

Accordingly, the orders of the Appellate Division, insofar as they denied the injunction, should be reversed, and the actions remitted to Supreme Court, Albany County to grant an injunction to take effect 18 months hence, unless the nuisance is abated by improved techniques prior to said date.

FULD, C. J., and BURKE and SCILEPPI, JJ., concur with BERGAN, J.

JASEN, J., dissents in part and votes to reverse in a separate opinion.

BREITEL and GIBSON, JJ., taking no part.

In each action: Order reversed, without costs, and the case remitted to Supreme Court, Albany County, for further proceedings in accordance with the opinion herein.

Appendix F

The State of New York v. United States Steel Corporation

At a Special Term, Part I, of the Supreme Court of the State of New York, held in and for the County of Albany at the Albany County Courthouse in the City of Albany, on the 21 day of April, 1972.

PRESENT: HONORABLE EDWARD S. CONWAY
Justice.

STATE OF NEW YORK
SUPREME COURT — COUNTY OF ALBANY

THE STATE OF NEW YORK,

Plaintiff,

— against —

UNITED STATES STEEL CORPORATION,

Defendant.

JUDGMENT

Index No. 3256-72

This action having been duty instituted by the service of a summons and a complaint, verified on November 11, 1971, for injunctive relief against defendant with respect to the manner of its operations of certain premises situated at 628 South Saratoga Street, Cohoes, New York;

Said summons and verified complaint having been personally served on defendant on November 15, 1971, by delivery of a true copy thereof to Andrew J. LaBarge, Plant Manager and Managing Agent of defendant;

Defendant's answer, verified on December 14, 1971, which contains denials of certain material allegations of the complaint and asserts an affirmative defense, having been duly served on or about December 16, 1971, by its attorneys, DeGraff, Foy, Conway and Holt-Harris;

Plaintiff having duly served, on January 20, 1972, a notice of motion for summary judgment dated January 20, 1972, with supporting affidavits, said motion having been returnable at a Special Term, Part I, of this Court on January 28, 1972, and having thereafter been adjourned by consent several times and defendant's time to submit answering affidavits having been extended by consent;

Defendant having duly served on February 9, 1972, an answering affidavit with respect to said motion; and

The parties hereto having agreed that this judgment is consented to by defendant for settlement purposes only and does not in any manner constitute an admission that it has violated any law, statute, rule or regulation;

NOW, upon the consents of Louis J. Lefkowitz, Attorney General of the State of New York, attorney for plaintiff, and DeGraff, Foy, Conway and Holt-Harris, attorneys for defendant, it is hereby

ORDERED, ADJUDGED AND DECREED, that the defendant shall, on or before the dates hereinafter set forth, complete the following repairs, installations, and changes in operating procedures at its lightweight aggregate plant, related facilities and shale quarry at 628 South Saratoga Street, Cohoes, New York:

a. Repair the raw storage silo roof and install a bagged vent for such silo by April 22, 1972;

b. Install a roof and bagged vent on the large finished product silo by May 27, 1972;

c. Install a belt cleaning device and collection hopper on the belt feeding the screens at the finished product silos by April 22, 1972.

d. Partially enclose the truck loading area by April 22, 1972, in accordance with the understanding reached with representatives of the Albany County Department of Health;

e. Install a triple telescoping spout at the rail car loading area by April 22, 1972;

f. Install screw feeders at the ball mill and remove from service the existing blower by June 1, 1972;

g. Adopt procedures, by May 1, 1972, to minimize airborne dust from the stock piles by adequately dampening the working faces of same;

h. Submit to the New York State Environmental Conservation Department, through the Albany County Department of Health, by April 22, 1972, stack test reports on the cooler stack showing whether there is compliance with Part 187 of the New York Air Pollution Control Rules;

and it is further

ORDERED, ADJUDGED AND DECREED, that if the acts required in the first decretal paragraph above do not result in compliance with the requirements of Part 186 or Part 187 of the New York State Air Pollution Control Rules, or the above-described cooler stack test reports do not show compliance with said Part 187, plaintiff's attorney shall notify defendant, in writing, of any deficiency or deficiencies. Defendant shall thereafter submit to the New York State Department of Environmental Conservation, through the Albany County Department of Health, and expeditiously carry out, a new or modified program and schedule, which program and schedule will result in compliance with said Parts 186 and 187, said new or modified program to be submitted within ninety days after receipt of such notice if a capital improvement is involved, otherwise within thirty days. Any abatement program and schedule submitted by the defendant and approved by the New York State Department of Environmental Conservation pursuant to this paragraph shall be deemed a part of this judgment to the same extent as if it had been fully set forth herein; and it is further

ORDERED, ADJUDGED AND DECREED, that defendant shall, by April 22, 1972, submit to the New York State Department of Environmental Conservation, through the Albany County Department of Health, plans and specifications for an air contaminants' control system at the primary crusher and kiln at said plant which will result in compliance with Part 187 of the New York State Air Pollution Control Rules, together with an application for a construction permit, this system to include, but not be limited to:

a. Enclosure of the area around the south end of the primary crusher, below the truck hopper and pan feeder;
b. Dump hopper sprays which will have automatic controls; and
c. The suspension of crushing operations when the hopper water sprays are not in operation;

and it is further

ORDERED, ADJUDGED AND DECREED, that defendant shall, by April 28, 1972, commence the installation of said air contaminants' control system at the primary crusher and kiln in accordance with said plans and specifications and a construction permit, and thereafter expeditiously proceed with said installation; and it is further

ORDERED, ADJUDGED AND DECREED, that by July 7, 1972, defendant shall complete the installation of said contaminants' control system at the kiln and crusher in accordance with said plans and specifications and construction permit and place same in operation; and it is further

ORDERED, ADJUDGED AND DECREED, that after a period for evaluation of the contaminants' control system for the primary crusher and kiln, which will end on October 7, 1972, this system shall be operated in such a manner that emissions from the primary crusher and kiln will meet the requirements of Part 187 of the New York State Air Pollution Control Rules, and it is further

ORDERED, ADJUDGED AND DECREED, that whenever because of accident, malfunction or otherwise, the contaminants' control system for either the primary crusher or kiln ceases to function, defendant shall cease operations of both the crusher and kiln and not recommence these operations until the control system does function, except that if a portion of said control system which affects only one of these sources, ceases to function, defendant may continue to operate the other. Also, whenever because of accident, malfunction or otherwise, said contaminants' control system for the primary crusher and kiln ceases to function, defendant shall notify either the Albany County Health Department or the Regional Office of the New York State Environmental Conservation Department. In the event such failure to function occurs during the normal working hours of these departments, defendant shall give the required notice within one hour. Should said failure to function occur during non-working hours of these departments, defendant shall give the required notice within one hour after the next opening of business of said departments; and it is further

ORDERED, ADJUDGED AND DECREED, that defendant shall conduct the following inspection and maintenance program at said plant, related facilities and quarry, which will be instituted within ten days after the entry of this judgment unless otherwise indicated herein:

a. Monthly inspection of the quarry drill dust collector;

b. Oiling of the quarry roads and plant roads as needed, depending upon weather conditions;

c. Visual check, each operating shift, of the manometer readings, electric eye, sprays, fans and duct at the primary crusher, commencing October 7, 1972;

d. Visual check, each operating shift, of the vent pipe and bag at the raw storage silo, commencing upon the completion of item "a" of the first decretal paragraph of this judgment;

e. Visual check, each operating shift, of the vent pipes and bags at the finished product storage silos, commencing upon completion of item "b" of the first decretal paragraph of this judgment;

f. Visual check of the cooler stack, each operating shift;

g. Visual check, each operating shift, of the chute and sprays at the clinker conveyor;

h. Visual check, each operating shift, of the vent pipe at the truck loading area;

i. Internal inspection of each scrubber quarterly, commencing with the quarter beginning October 1, 1972;

and it is further

ORDERED, ADJUDGED AND DECREED, that any deficiencies noted in the above inspections and checks shall be corrected expeditiously by defendant and a record of said inspections and checks and of any deficiencies found during same shall be maintained by defendant at the plant and be available for inspection by authorized representatives of the Albany County Department of Health and the New York State Department of Environmental Conservation during regular business hours; and it is further

ORDERED, ADJUDGED AND DECREED, that if at any time blasting at the quarry produces any noise, concussion or vibration of such a degree or nature as to create a public nuisance, upon written notice from the plaintiff's attorney to defendant, defendant shall either: (a) immediately cease all blasting operations at the quarry and not thereafter recommence same until it has taken the necessary measures to prevent noise, concussion or vibration of such degree or nature; or (b) if it disputes the existence of such public nuisance, immediately apply to this Court for an order to show cause requesting a determination by this Court as to whether a public nuisance has been created. In the same proceeding (under "b", above), in addition to any other rights it has under this judgment or otherwise, plaintiff may request a temporary restraining order and a preliminary injunction by the Court pending the Court's final determination and a permanent injunction, if the Court determines that a public nuisance has been created; and it is further

ORDERED, ADJUDGED AND DECREED, that irrespective of any other decretal provision herein, if at any time emissions produced by operations of the plant or related facilities create a public nuisance, upon written notice from plaintiff's attorney to defendant, defendant shall either: (a) immediately eliminate the emissions causing said public nuisance, or suspend operations at the plant and related facilities and not recommence same until these operations are carried on without causing a public nuisance; or (b) if it disputes the existence of a public nuisance, immediately apply to this Court for an order to show cause, requesting a determination as to whether a public nuisance has been created. In the same proceeding (under "b", above), in addition to any other rights it has under this judgment or otherwise, plaintiff may request a temporary restraining order and a preliminary injunction by the Court pending the Court's final determination and a permanent injunction, if the Court determines that a public nuisance has been created; and it is further

ORDERED, ADJUDGED AND DECREED, that to determine whether or not there is compliance with the terms and conditions of this judgment, authorized representatives of the Albany County Department of Health and the New York State Environmental Conservation Department are authorized and permitted, at any time, to enter upon the premises on which the plant, related facilities and quarry are situated and to inspect such premises, plant, related facilities and quarry, provided that, immediately upon entering the premises, such representatives shall notify plant personnel of their presence; and it is further

ORDERED, ADJUDGED AND DECREED, that if at any time plaintiff shall deem that there has been a failure by defendant to comply with any of the terms or conditions of this judgment, in addition to any other rights provided by law, plaintiff's attorney may apply to this Court for a temporary restraining order, or upon due notice to defendant, as directed by the Court in an order to show cause, for an order enforcing the terms and conditions of this judgment by contempt proceedings or otherwise; provided, however, that no such application shall be made unless prior written notice is given by plaintiff's attorney to defendant as to the terms and conditions of this judgment which it has failed to comply with and unless the defendant shall have failed either to immediately correct the violations or immediately shut down the facility or facilities causing the violations; and it is further

ORDERED, ADJUDGED AND DECREED, that if a facility or facilities are shut down in accordance with the decretal paragraph immediately above, such facility or facilities shall not again be placed in operation, except for testing, until operations are conducted in accordance with the terms and conditions of this judgment; and it is further

ORDERED, ADJUDGED AND DECREED, that if because of an act of God, war, strike, riot, catastrophe, failure or delay of supplier where there is no reasonable opportunity for substitution, or other conditions beyond its control, including conflicting or supervening statutes, rules or regulations, or other laws, regulating said plant, related facilities or quarry; defendant determines that it cannot meet the aforesaid air pollution abatement program and schedule; or, if after completion of said abatement program, the defendant for any of the reasons specified above in this decretal paragraph is unable to meet any repair or remedial schedule or to continue operations; it may, on five days' written notice to plaintiff's attorney, apply to this Court for an extension or modification of such program and schedule; and it is further

ORDERED, ADJUDGED AND DECREED, that this Court shall retain continuing jurisdiction of the parties in this action and, in addition to any other rights granted herein, plaintiff may apply for a temporary restraining order, and either party may, upon due notice to the other, at any time, apply to this Court for such other or further relief as may be appropriate and proper in the premises; and it is further

ORDERED, ADJUDGED AND DECREED, that this judgment shall be entered without the assessment of costs to either party as against the other.

E.S.C.

Signed at Albany, New York, this 21 day of April 1972.

ENTER:

/s/ Edward S. Conway

JUSTICE OF THE SUPREME COURT

We hereby consent to entry of the above judgment.

Signed at Albany, New York, on the 21 day of April, 1972.

LOUIS J. LEFKOWITZ
Attorney General of the State of New York
Attorney for Plaintiff

By:

/s/ Stanley Fishman

STANLEY FISHMAN
Assistant Attorney General in Charge
Water and Air Resources Bureau

Signed at Albany, New York, on the 20 day of April, 1972

DeGRAFF, FOY, CONWAY AND HOLT-HARRIS, ESQS.
Attorneys for Defendant

By:

/s/ W. F. Conway

INDEX